LANDSCRIPT 5

Material Culture

LAN

RIP

D S C

T 5

JANE HUTTON (ED.)

MATERIAL CULTURE

ASSEMBLING AND DISASSEMBLING LANDSCAPES

Material as Method

Jane Hutton

In the text that follows, Nancy Takahashi and Garth Anderson trace the material flows between Thomas Jefferson's famed Academical Village at the University of Virginia and its little known "mountain" backdrop. The backdrop is, not surprisingly, more than that. It provides the essential material resources of wood, stone, and water for the construction and evolution of the university; later, it absorbs the university's contaminated refuse, risks, and controversies into its wooded slopes. The authors chronicle two centuries of material exchange between the designed landscape, where significant attention is concentrated and meaning is constructed, and the material source landscape, obscured from view yet intrinsic to the former. While the Academical Village, a model of societal and pedagogical ideals, is iconic for its symbolic gravitas, Takahashi and Anderson's material account offers alternative ways of seeing this well-trodden landscape. By tracing the reciprocal movement of materials between these two parcels of land, much is illuminated: the transformation of bedrock and forest into construction materials; the enslaved and contracted persons who shaped them; the ambiguous boundary between valued resource and dump; and the conflicts between what a designer wants a landscape to mean and the real conditions of its making.

Within just acres of land, this case encapsulates material relations of designed landscapes at large.

Sites are bounded by property lines, yet their material relationships—from the transport of construction commodities to water cycles—extend to untold limits. And while criticism tends to focus on the discrete form, performance, and meaning of specific projects, the people and processes associated with their construction and demolition are often overlooked. Designed landscapes are models of human-nature relationships, and at the same time they *are* human-nature relationships, simultaneously representing and co-producing the world. These relationships are typically beyond design's scope, yet are constitutive of landscape's *material culture*—its entanglement of materials, effects, and affects. This issue of *Landscript* proposes these relationships as pressing subjects of inquiry for landscape criticism and design.

If postmodernism saw the separation of meaning from material in favor of semiotic readings and social constructions of the world, today we see movements to "re-materialize" scholarship (often through engagements with science and technology studies) from cultural geography to feminist theory to political science, and in the formalization of material culture as a concentration within anthropology and archaeology.—[1] Material culture approaches, often narrowly understood as the study of human artifacts and their cultural meanings, in contrast, offer significantly more.—[2] They can open stubborn apertures for how landscapes are analyzed and understood: to see beyond the site boundary towards the hidden constellation of material (and political) relations that constitute it; to examine a project beyond meaning and probe instead its myriad effects in the world and the affects it engenders in different people; to move beyond anthropocentric, social-construction-of-nature paradigms and begin to understand how the non-human world pushes back.

One could argue that the discipline of landscape architecture, whose concerns inherently engage human and non-human worlds, never succeeded in fully dematerializing, despite its best intentions. It is nearly impossible to

1 See, for example, Peter Jackson, "Rematerializing Social and Cultural Geography," *Social & Cultural Geography* 1, no. 1 (September 1, 2000): 9–14; Sarah Whatmore, "Materialist Returns: Practicing Cultural Geography in and for a More-Than-Human World." *Cultural geographies*, 2006, 13: 600–609; and Diana Coole, ed. *New Materialisms: Ontology, Agency, and Politics*, (Durham NC; London: Duke University Press, 2010).

2 See Dan Hicks and Mary C. Beaudry, eds., *The Oxford Handbook of Material Culture Studies*, (Oxford: Oxford University Press, 2010).

sever the idea of landscape from land's staunch materiality; the heft of the ground is too great, the decay of plants too pungent to disregard. And while designed objects are assumed to be entirely cultural products, designed landscapes, in contrast, are never seen as entirely cultural.—[3] Postmodern landscape architects resisted this association head on, swapping mass-produced plastic plants and rocks for authentic ones, shedding the weight of nature's authority and instead insisting on nature as a socially constructed phenomenon.—[4]

More recently however, landscape theory and practice has re-engaged with material concerns shifting away from symbolic representation and towards the sites and conditions of post-Fordism. Focusing on logistics facilities, dredging operations, and military sites as subjects for practice and inquiry, they foreground the material flows, processes, and contingencies of late capitalism. At the same time, contemporary landscape thinkers have embraced and appropriated concepts from the ecological sciences, designing in consort with non-human forces. Engaging both the ecological and capital flows of landscape production, contemporary landscape research and practice has just begun to explore how material analysis might impact the discipline. At the same time, this work has remained largely human-centric, often instrumentalizing non-human entities as services or strategies. And even though the focus is on humans, few authors have focused on the uneven social dimensions behind landscape production.

The contributors to this volume explore these very potentials, offering generative methods and models for landscape architecture. Their texts swarm around and between three themes. The first focuses on specific material trajectories as authors trace materials through the sites of landscape production to unearth their myriad effects. The second focuses on human labor and participation in constructing and imagining future landscapes, including the risks, experiences, and affects associated

3 Chandra Mukerji, "The Landscape Garden as Material Culture: Lessons From France," in Dan Hicks and Mary C. Beaudry, eds., *The Oxford Handbook of Material Culture Studies*, (Oxford: Oxford University Press, 2010), 551.

4 This work empowered landscape architects as autonomous culture-makers (not as stewards or servants of the land), and unsettled fixed notions of a benevolent nature.

with doing so. And the third theme examines material-human interactions, and the implications for reconsidering how we work with, live with, and understand matter itself.—5

5 I have examined similar themes in: Jane Hutton, "Reciprocal Landscapes: Material Portraits in New York City and Elsewhere." *JoLA—Journal of Landscape Architecture* 8, no. 1 (May 1, 2013): 40–47, and in a forthcoming manuscript titled, "Reciprocal Landscapes: Cases in Material Movements," to be published by Routledge in 2018.

Material Trajectories

Today, we view landscape architecture projects as dynamic and ever changing unto themselves. But to also consider a project's assembly and disassembly is to acknowledge a longer scale of temporality, its infinite mutability, and its physical connections to the world. By expanding the conception of a landscape to include the materials, beings, and efforts that conspire to form and un-form it, we explode the notion of a fixed landscape and see instead a cacophonous network of material relations. The texts in this first theme expand on contemporary interests in charting material flows. They elaborate on how these flows—not neutral vectors on a map—reveal instead the broader mechanisms of globalized capitalism, the so-called externalities of material extraction, and the mutable boundaries between what we understand as "production" and "consumption."

Just as Takahashi and Anderson traced materials between two sites to chart an alternative history of the University of Virginia campus, Jennifer Foster and Heidy Schopf look at material accumulations on the Leslie Street Spit in Toronto to render a different narrative of urban ecological transformation of the past 150 years. The Leslie Street Spit—an uncanny landscape of demolition materials—registers the migration of minerals from Ontario aggregate and clay pits, through brick and processing facilities, through different building typologies, and their eventual demolition and subsumption into the Spit's naturalistic landform. Sifting through this material repository, Foster and Schopf articulate how cycles of construction and destruction have solidified social difference whether through colonial land grabs or urban renewal.

As Alessandra Ponte and Stephan Kowal point out in

"Making the North," examining even a single case of material production (in their text, steel-making in northern Quebec) can enable an understanding of the global distribution and dynamics of matter. Disparate landscapes are intricately linked: the speed and depth of Quebec mines reflect the rapid vertical growth of Asian cities, for example. Ponte and Kowal chronicle how the exploitation of the Labrador Trough—a formidable 1,600-km iron ore deposit—not only supplied urbanizing centers with structural materials, but also urbanized a region, laying out a complex network of infrastructure, new towns, and troubling ecological and human consequences. Here, the authors shed light on the layers of "externalities" which are, in fact, intrinsic to material practice.

While material production is often assumed to take place in ex-urban areas and material consumption is aligned with the city, Sonja Dümpelmann's text complicates this assumption. Chronicling the changing status of street trees in Chicago during the twentieth century, Dümpelmann marks changes in the way that the urban street tree canopy was conceived, managed, and ultimately utilized. As Chicago formalized and standardized its canopy into an "urban forest" through developments in arboriculture and management, the trees shifted from aesthetic transplants from nature into productive crops and as fuel to address the late twentieth-century oil crisis. Dümpelmann's case demonstrates how mutable the perception and use of materials can be—particularly when they are alive.

Labor and Affect

Intrinsic to the flow of construction materials are the people who extract, assemble, interact with, maintain, and (in so doing) experience them. Contemporary emphasis on material agency has the potential to erase, trivialize, or make equivalent people's differentiated roles and experiences in construction. Probing the uneven social realities of landscape making does more than simply acknowledge what would otherwise be invisible; it can fundamentally change *how* we see. Contributors in this second theme demonstrate how the inclusion of social history—of economic decline, of incarceration, of enslavement—offers transformative rewritings of old landscape narratives, but also new approaches to conceiving and designing.

Jane Wolff's illustrated text, "Saint Louis, Brick City," exemplifies this. Wolff chronicles the imbricated social, political, and physical history of Saint Louis through bricks—"artifacts of geology, economics, technology, craft, politics, law, and custom." The humble brick is a vehicle through which to conjure disparate but entwined aspects of the city's social history: the arrival of southern and European brick makers and layers, the cumulative physical efforts of untold workers, the racist legislation that segregated and then evacuated the brick city, and the insights that brick recyclers offer the city as it is built anew. Wolff reinforces the notion that a material history is, in fact, a social history.

The people who build and maintain landscapes are rarely seen. Despite the fact that they are required to produce a desired condition, their presence might contradict or conflict with the idealized landscape. In her text "Picturing Modernity," Jana Cephas examines how, in contrast, primarily black chain gang workers were forced to build roads in early twentieth-century Georgia (USA) such that their labor *was* made visible. The system of chain-gang labor, the cruel successor of slavery, reinforced "old South" associations of black bodies with landscape toil, entrenching racist ideologies. At the same time, the work served the state's modernization agenda, in the name of building a "new South." Cephas's text raises the inherent contradictions between the image of progress and the regressive practices that often enable its making.

In Sara Zewde's "Transatlantic Memory," the excavated remnants of the Valongo Wharf in Rio de Janeiro serve as a physical landmark of the millions of Africans who entered the Americas through its slave port. The wharf also serves as a focal point for acknowledging how four centuries of enslaved people transformed the city, country, and continent through forced labor and everyday practices of culture and resistance. In a proposal to memorialize the district around Valongo Wharf, Zewde and her team develop a multi-site living memorial that engages Afro-Brazilian botanical culture and ongoing spatial practices. Rather than a singular monument with a singular “meaning,” the project is a constellation of sites that respond to material and immaterial memory. Zewde reinforces the idea that material culture is as much about matter as it is about the invisible and ephemeral daily practices, affects, and memories integral to it.

Cornelia Escher and Kim Förster’s text describes the social processes and material factors involved in the making of Görlitzer Park in Berlin, a postmodern park known for its highly symbolic agenda to harmonize disparate communities. Looking beyond the park’s official plan, Escher and Förster chronicle the ways in which Berlin’s alternative scene, radical planners, and politicized residents—in response to their context of industrial ruins, emergent vegetation, and cultural relics—created discourse, design strategies, and ways of living that prefigured the ultimate design. Their case highlights how design ideas are powerfully shaped by sociopolitical conditions and material experience.

Making With

If the first two themes focused on material flows and the humans working with them, the final theme looks more specifically at how humans conceive of, work with, and are contiguous with materials. Any close study of the ceaseless transformation of matter—as it moves through water, earth, species, and the atmosphere—quickly challenges the idea that humans and materials are distinct or that heroic humans shape an inert material world on their own. Material investigations reveal our profound continuities with and dependencies on all that is more-than-human. The texts which close this book ask how interactions with matter (whether situated, fluid, or anticipated) shape ideas, and conversely, how those ideas might spawn new ways of, as Donna Haraway terms it, sympoiesis, or *making with*.—6

6 Donna J. Haraway, "Sympoiesis: Symbiogenesis and the Lively Arts of Staying with the Trouble," in *Staying with the Trouble: Making Kin in the Chthulucene* (Duke University Press: Durham, 2016), 58.

In "Matter Displaced, Organized, Flattened," for example, Martin Hogue takes the starting point of most design projects—site analysis—as an opportunity for intensive and generative material interaction. Hogue argues that, in contrast to passively acquired site data, experimental fieldwork can allow the site to reveal itself in unpredictable and meaningful ways. By applying open-ended creativity, typically reserved for the design phase, to a site, designers might recognize and connect with—as New Materialist thinkers might put it—its material vibrancy. Drawing from speculative fieldwork practices, Hogue describes how different methods of working with site matter provoke new ways of understanding, and therefore of designing with, sites.

In her text, "Feminist Hydro-Logics," Katie Lloyd Thomas reflects on the inhabitants of the oceanic moon in Joan Slonczewski's 1986 science-fiction novel, *A Door into Ocean*. Surrounded by water and living on rafts of entwined organisms, they have no conception of private property or domination over others, and shape their existence through symbiotic practices with other species. As co-designers and participatory engineers of their fluid, boundless environment, they exemplify the concept of sympoiesis. As such, the interwoven aqueous and alternate social world depicted in *A Door* resonates with the ambitions of contemporary designers interested in co-producing living systems. Through her reading of *A Door*, Lloyd Thomas offers these contemporary practices a valuable provocation: in order for material innovation to be truly transformative, it must be aligned with social and economic transformation.

As Lloyd Thomas pulls from the oceanic world of *A Door* to consider models of co-existence and design, Adam

Bobbette approaches an active volcano. "We all Live in the Wrong Place" looks at the shared behaviors and activities of Mount Merapi (central Java, Indonesia), the people who live nearby, the scientists studying it, and the volcano's human medium. In this context, where the threat of eruption is perpetual and massive, Bobbette describes the ways in which people see and interact with the volcano in order to know it and live with it—all eschewing simple culture-nature boundaries. If designers, too, are perpetually working to form a relationship with changing land, the volcano and its residents present a useful model of what that relationship could be—one ultimately based in intimacy.

A volcano's imminent eruption is an apt metaphor for this moment in time, which geographer Sarah Whatmore describes as environmentally, politically, and technologically "molten."—[7] It is no coincidence that the scholarly return to *the material* corresponds with unprecedented planetary change. These massive changes (from climate-driven global migration to species extinction) reflect capitalism's prowess, as Jason Moore writes, at organizing the matter of nature—[8] and its supporting ideology of human separation from nature. As the authors in this volume demonstrate, material culture offers us tools to unlearn this separation and experiment with issues of imminent material concern. First, examining material flows can help us to visualize the connectivity between distant sites, challenging our commodified and fragmented understanding of material exploitation; second, including human labor in landscape narratives can unearth the inherent contradictions of construction, ideally prompting more politically active scholarship and design; and third, learning how to "make with," rather than simply exploit other species and materials, might unsettle anthropocentric limitations and transform the means of design. Because material culture probes *how* landscape is made and unmade, it is not merely a topic to describe the discipline, but a tool to transform it.

7 Whatmore, "Materialist Returns," 605.

8 Jason Moore, "Capitalism Is a Way of Organizing Nature," https://jasonwmoore.wordpress.com/2014/03/22/capitalism-as-a-way-of-organizing-nature/, (accessed July 25, 2017).

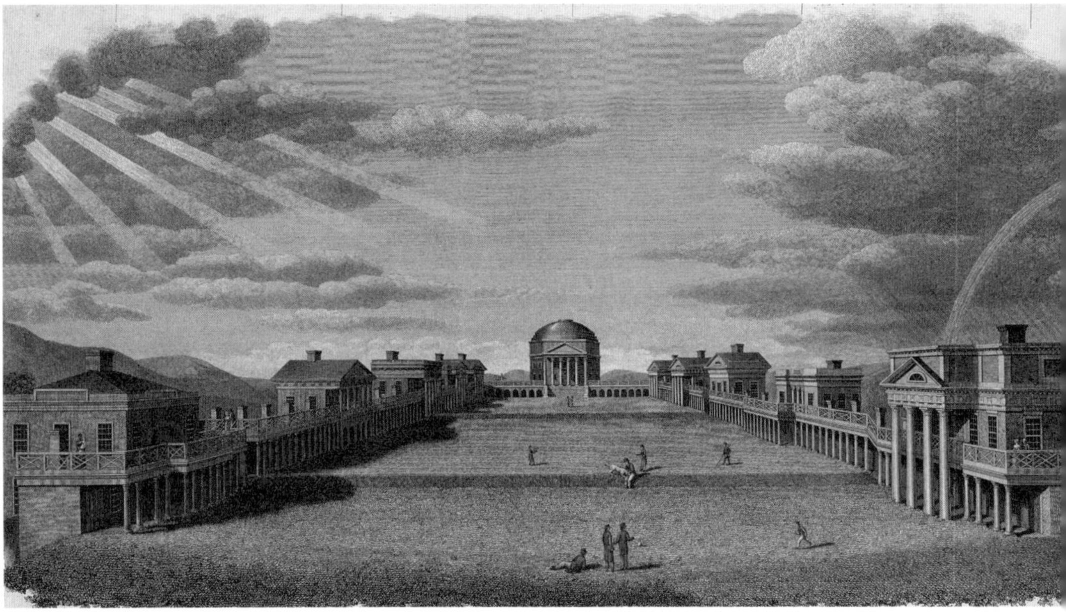

Detail of Academical Village. B. Tanner, engraver, Boye's Map of Virginia, 1827.

Downhill/Uphill: Material Flows Between a Mountain and an Academical Village

Nancy Takahashi and Garth Anderson

Two Parcels

Thomas Jefferson's Academical Village at the University of Virginia in Charlottesville has long been celebrated as a visionary model of an integrated classroom and residential community of students and faculty. The Village's lawn is the central organizing figure of the 43.75-acre parcel purchased in 1817 by the governing Board of Visitors (BoV) of Central College, soon-to-be named the University of Virginia (UVA). To the north is the Rotunda, modeled on Rome's Pantheon, which originally housed the library and classrooms. "The Lawn" is a series of terraces stepping down and southward to an open view of the Southwest Mountains.—1 Flanking both sides of the Lawn are rows of student rooms, punctuated by ten larger "Pavilions," which housed the ten original faculty and families, and also served as classrooms on the ground floor. Behind each Pavilion sat a serpentine-walled garden originally intended as a private utility yard for the resident faculty families, where they could work and raise food. Conjoined residential quarters, teaching spaces, and productive gardens, all surrounding a public open green, created a model of a self-sufficient community of students and teachers living and learning together—a vision Jefferson famously coined "Academical Village."

1 The Lawn's open view was closed off by new buildings designed by the architecture firm McKim, Mead, and White in 1898.

Less known is that the original land purchase for the college actually included two land tracts—Parcels 1A and 1B. Parcel 1A was a cleared, farmed parcel on which Jefferson's Academical Village was built. Parcel 1B, a discrete parcel roughly a quarter mile to the west, was a 153-acre wooded hill tract, labeled simply as "Mountains" on the land survey that Jefferson drew in 1817. On June 23, 1817, the sale of these two noncontiguous parcels was executed for a price of $1,421 and the lands passed into the hands of the college's Board of Visitors and its Rector, Thomas Jefferson.

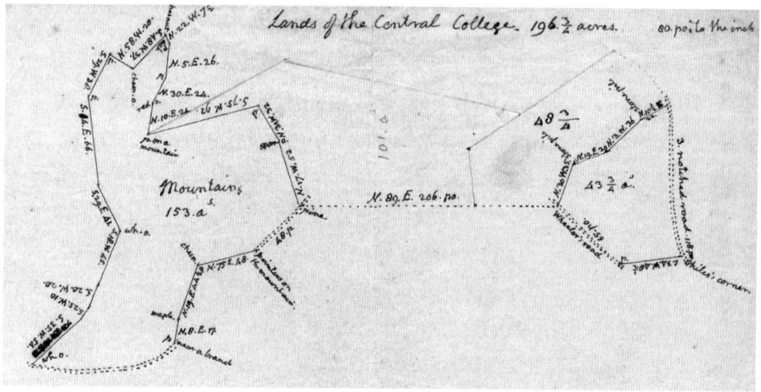

Lands of the Central College 196.3/4 acres, Thomas Jefferson surveyor, 1817.

Acknowledgement of the second "other" parcel has been evidenced over time in artist renderings that have been created of the university since its inception. The illustrations typically foreground the Academical Village, with the wooded mountain residing quietly behind. The mountain, rising roughly 290 feet above the uppermost terrace of the Lawn, is portrayed as a topographic counterpart to the domed Rotunda, its rural wooded aspect in contrast to the village below.

While the university's spatial and mythic memory is imprinted with the mountain backdrop, little has been written about this other land tract. Two hundred years after the founding, the once discrete tract Parcel 1B is now fully integrated into the fabric of the university grounds by roads and twentieth-century buildings, which occupy the lower slopes of the once isolated mountain. The higher elevations, however, have evaded the pressures of university expansion and exist as the quiet forested domain of a handful of research faculty and recreationists. At first glance, the mountain appears untouched. Yet, a walk up the hill and a look into the history of artifacts and buildings on Parcel 1B reveal a significant and fascinating history of occupation.

This chapter discusses the unrecognized contributions that Parcel 1B has played throughout the university's history from its founding to current times. The long-standing relationship between the two tracts tells a story of material dependency based on the ever-changing needs of a growing teaching and research institution. Over time, pure and life-sustaining materials—along with covert and lethal ones—flowed back and forth uniting the two pieces of land in the life story of UVA. History reflects periods of neglect, if not abuse, toward Parcel 1B; but in the twenty-first century, the wooded mountain tract reasserts its material value to the institution. Jefferson's insight in purchasing the mountain tract for its resource wealth has proved critical to the success of UVA, although history illustrates how changeable the material flows would be over time—in ways that even Jefferson never could have anticipated.

The Mountain: Material Resources on Parcel 1B

The mountain emerged 300 million years ago during the Alleghany Orogeny, when mountain ridges were raised, folded, and eroded under the heat and pressure of colliding African and North American continental plates. The resulting compressed and sheared belts of rock formed into the anticlines and synclines of the Blue Ridge Mountain Range, running northeast to southwest from New York to Georgia. Rising to a peak elevation of 865 feet above sea level, Mountain Parcel 1B is a small rise in the linear formation of rocky outcrops in the western Virginia

Piedmont. An underlying 1200-foot-thick geologic bedrock named Rockfish Conglomerate gives Parcel 1B its topographic stature. Initially composed of loosely bound small and large quartz sand and pebbles, the substrate metamorphosed into a resistant, dense homogenous rock that emerged at the ground surface.—[2] Over time, long internal fractures developed, creating avenues for the movement and storage of ground water.

2 Wilbur A. Nelson, *Geology and Mineral Resources of Albemarle County* (Charlottesville: Virginia Division Of Mineral Resources, 1962), 19.

Atop this rocky foundation lies a thin, highly porous mantle of residual soils formed by the *in situ* weathering of the bedrock and accumulated plant detritus held in place by plant roots. A shallow eight to twelve inches at higher elevations, the mantle thickens to depths of two to three feet in the lower valleys due to the effects of gravity and erosion. This thin, nutrient-poor, but highly porous soil layer supports only the most shallow-rooted forest community. Dominating the canopy tree mix of hickory and oak is the chestnut oak (*Quercus prinus*), a native species of the eastern Appalachian region. Common to dry, infertile, rocky ridgetops, the chestnut oak grows up to sixty to seventy feet using its wide spreading lateral roots to cling to the rocky substrate. Associated species are tulip poplar, black gum, dogwood, blueberry, and mountain laurel. The soil mattress combined with fractured gaps in the underlying Rockfish Conglomerate creates a surprisingly sponge-like environment for storing and releasing water. Across the mountain in wetter seasons, water surfaces from springs located at low valley points and at the base of rock outcrops where low topography meets the ground water table.

In contrast to the resource-rich mountain parcel, Parcel 1A was a fallow field whose forests had been cleared by its former owners. It is situated atop an extensive and resistant coarsely grained igneous intrusion known as an amphibolite dike. This 830-foot-wide amphibolite dike cuts across bedrock of metagraywacke stone—a hard sandstone with a low capacity for holding groundwater.—[3] On this site, the only nearby water would have been from

3 Wilbur A. Nelson, *Geology and Mineral Resources of Albemarle County*, 37.

small springs to the south, shallow dug wells, and rain from roofs stored in subterranean cisterns.

Connecting Parcels 1A and 1B

In short time, Jefferson was forced to tackle a problem created by the college's purchase of two noncontiguous parcels: the university straddled two sites and therefore lacked control of the land and flow of mountain waters between. Recognizing the imperative to secure the land and its water rights before it became impossible, he appealed to the BoV. He was successful, and by June 1825, the connecting 132-acre parcel was secured, representing full legal control and access to the creek waters running off of Parcel 1B.

Shortly after, an east-west road paralleling the creek to the south connected the two original parcels. This road, later named McCormick Road, would become the chief armature for all future buildings developed after the Academical Village. Jefferson's insight in purchasing the mountain and later securing water and road rights between the two parcels would dictate the course of the university's development for the next 150 years.

Material Resources Flowing Downhill

Flowing Downhill: Wood and Stone

A well-known 1906 lithograph suggests the university's early dependency on the resources of Parcel 1B. From a birds-eye view, the mountain rises in the upper right corner in the distance. New buildings depicted west of the Academical Village foretell the campus's future westward expansion toward Parcel 1B. The artist depicts the top of the mountain as wooded, but the lower east and north slopes below are denuded, evidence that the chestnut oak forests had been largely cleared by this time. Wood would

University of Virginia, W. T. Littig and Co., 1906.

likely have been in heavy demand to fuel the university's kitchens, domestic fireplaces, and the brick kilns of the time. The Proctor's records suggest that enslaved laborers and independent contractors cut wood.—4

4 Papers of the Proctor of the University of Virginia, RG-5/3/1.111. Box 19, Bills & Accounts July – December 1827. Albert and Shirley Small Special Collections Library, University of Virginia.

Rock quarries found on Parcel 1B speak to another material dependency on the mountain. The first stone extracted on Parcel 1B came from a small quarry sited at the eastern base of the mountain next to the headwaters of Meadow Creek. While the Rockfish Conglomerate proved unsuitable for architectural components like column capitals and bases, it was used extensively in the original structures for steps and sills, and building walls in the landscape.—5

5 Frank Edgar Grizzard, Jr., "Documentary History of the Construction of the Buildings at the University of Virginia, 1817–1828" Chapter 3, Irish Stonecutter; (PhD Diss., University of Virginia, 1996), http://xtf.lib.virginia.edu/xtf/view?docId=grizzard/uvaGenText/tei/grizzard.xml;brand=default (accessed July 12, 2017).

Flowing Downhill: Piped Water

Builders of the new university thoroughly surveyed the water emanating from Parcel 1B. A first system was immediately constructed to transport water through hollowed wood logs from a reservoir vessel on the mountain. From the beginning however, sourcing potable water proved problematic. In 1856, the university commissioned the design services of the prominent civil engineer Charles Ellet to deal with its chronic water problems. Ellet's plan called for replacing the original, failing wood pipes with cast iron pipe laid from the mountain spring to the base of the Rotunda. Ellet's proposal included an in-ground, excavated reservoir whose greater size would retain water during surplus periods and release it during periods of scarcity. At that time, the engineering of upland reservoirs was a new and controversial concept, raising concerns about the stagnation of open bodies of water. For over a century, the reservoir was maintained and was a popular leisure destination, but in 2007 the dam was breached to meet new regulations for safety and monitoring.

Miss Estelle Burthe, stepdaughter of Prof. Mallet, and her dog (swimming) at the Old Reservoir in 1893.

In 1888, the building of a larger off-site reservoir effectively terminated the university's dependency on Parcel 1B as the source of its water. However, Parcel 1B's role in providing water would continue. The university leased a 3.5-acre site on the upper eastern slope of Parcel 1B to the city, where they built and operated a new water treatment facility. When it opened in 1923, the Observatory Water Treatment Plant, with its state-of-the-art system of sand filtering beds and open-air water storage basins, began providing safe water for the university and the city. Over the decades, the mountain plant has seen expansions and upgrades, and today treats approximately 450 million gallons of water annually to service the university population of roughly 36,000.—6

6 Facilities Management, "Operations Annual Report," (Charlottesville: Universty of Virginia, 2015), Appendix G.

Flowing Downhill: Creek Waters

While the story of sourcing potable water from the mountain spring through reservoirs and pipes is well recorded, the story of the rest of the spring water that flowed downhill in a small creek is little known. The creek joined another smaller tributary east of the mountain and ponded on the western edge of Parcel 1A, roughly sixty feet below the Academical Village. First referred to as the University Pond, and later taking on the unexplained moniker of Nameless Field, this was a wetlands meadow whose clay soils were derived from deeply weathered bedrock. These creek waters would engender three transformative chapters in the history of the university.

First, University Pond would be the first area for expansion after the Academical Village. The gardens behind the Pavilion residences had proven too small for raising food and livestock, and so the forests west of Parcel 1A were cleared to make way for new garden plots and grazing areas. Logically and equitably devised, the grazing lots were parsed out to give livestock access to the banks of the creek flowing from Parcel 1B.

The second chapter of the University Pond site describes the transformation of the watery wetlands to a recreational space, in order to meet the demands of a growing university community. By the late nineteenth century, the process of formalizing the creek waters on Nameless Field was well underway. Plans from the mid eighteen-fifties indicate how the low dams had been constructed to create discrete ponds, whose water would be harvested for ice. Photo images from the late nineteenth century also indicate that the seasonally frozen ponds were popular for skating, enriching the social life of the university community.

Students skating, circa 1895.

In 1929, the wetland ponds at Nameless Field underwent a final formalization when they were turned into a large oval reflecting pond, part of a new magnificent and imposing gymnasium built as a memorial to fallen student soldiers from World War I. The pond, which was noted by the Architectural Commission as giving the structure "a charming reflection and an approach of unusual beauty," existed through the early nineteen-fifties until maintenance of its waters became problematic and it was filled in.—7

Third, Nameless Field, with its ample water resources from Meadow Creek, inspired a legacy of teaching gardens at UVA. Less than three months before he died in 1826, Rector Thomas Jefferson pushed for plans to create a botanical garden as an integral instructional component of his university.—8 Jefferson was explicit in his design for a six-acre garden featuring useful plants

7 Board of Visitors minutes, November 29, 1921, (Charlottesville: University of Virginia), http://xtf.lib.virginia.edu/xtf/view?docId=2006_09/uvaGenText/tei/bov_19211129.xml (accessed July 12, 2017).

8 Lily Fox-Bruguiere, "'To be pursued at all spare times': Thomas Jefferson's botanical garden at the University of Virginia," *Studies in the History of Gardens & Designed Landscapes* 32 (2012): 302–11.

for the new country along Meadow Creek. Numerous attempts to carry out his plan surfaced but failed, until nearly two centuries later when a teaching garden was finally realized on this site. In 2004, university and city residents were once again connected to water and plants in a notable civic park, known as Dell Pond Park, designed by the firm Nelson Byrd Woltz. Meadow Creek resurfaced as a designed storm water management landscape of constructed meanders, planted floodplains, and a pond. With the addition of native plants along the creek, interpreted for students and passers-by, the Dell Pond Park stands as the closest fruition of Jefferson's plan for a didactic teaching garden on university grounds—made possible, in great part, by water flowing from Parcel 1B.

Material Resources Flowing Uphill

Throughout the nineteenth century, the material dependency of Parcel 1A on Parcel 1B was clear. The downhill displacement of water, stone, and lumber from the mountain built and sustained a university. Later, flowing creek waters from Parcel 1B down to Nameless Field influenced university expansion, inspired teaching gardens, and enabled forms of recreation. By the turn of the century, however, the material relationship would change radically. The university no longer relied on Parcel 1B for its water; and the firing up of the first coal-powered heating plant at the south end of the Lawn in 1898 meant that university classrooms and residences would be heated by steam, reducing the need for timber from Parcel 1B.

A 1962 promotional brochure put out by the local Chamber of Commerce hinted at the new relationship between the two parcels.—[9] Touting the assets of living and doing business in the region, the opening pages highlight Charlottesville as "A University Center" and feature the expected image of the Rotunda on the left. Opposite it on the right page is an image of a less familiar

9 Charlottesville and Albemarle Industrial Commission, *Charlottesville and Albemarle County Virginia: View from Monticello* (Charlottesville, 1962).

building—the Nuclear Experimental Reactor, a new engineering research lab that had opened three years earlier on Parcel 1B. With its "associated laboratories and hot cell [that] provide extremely valuable facilities for nuclear radiation research and tests ... [and] handle over a million dollars a year of research for the government and private industry," the facility on Parcel 1B was proof that UVA was in the modern age. Perhaps influenced by the departments of astronomy and forestry, which had been established earlier on the mountain, the experimental reactor would be the second of three high energy modern science facilities that would make their way onto Parcel 1B in the mid twentieth century.

With the ever-expanding needs of a growing community, Parcel 1B also became the de facto location for waste and construction material dumps, maintenance facilities, radioactive and toxic material handling facilities, military projectile and missile testing sites, and medical waste dumping sites; many of which ended up degrading the very creek that Jefferson had so deliberately procured for its pure waters. Topographically and geographically remote, the wooded mountain became the domain where material operations could be carried out invisibly and "... secret work could be carried out without disturbance to others."—10

10 John W. Stewart, "History of the UVA Physics Department" (Charlottesville, privately published), 4. Albert and Shirley Small Special Collections Library, University of Virginia.

Flowing Uphill: Uranium-235 and Noise

Facing an arms race with Nazi Germany during the Second World War, UVA joined the ranks of classified military research institutions comprising the top-secret Manhattan Project. Led by renowned physicist and UVA Professor Dr. Jesse Beams, a distinguished research team of chemists and physicists from UVA, Oak Ridge Institute of Nuclear Studies in Tennessee, and the Naval Research Council assembled on the grounds of UVA to develop a high-speed centrifuge for uranium isotope separation to power the first nuclear bombs. Operating in the

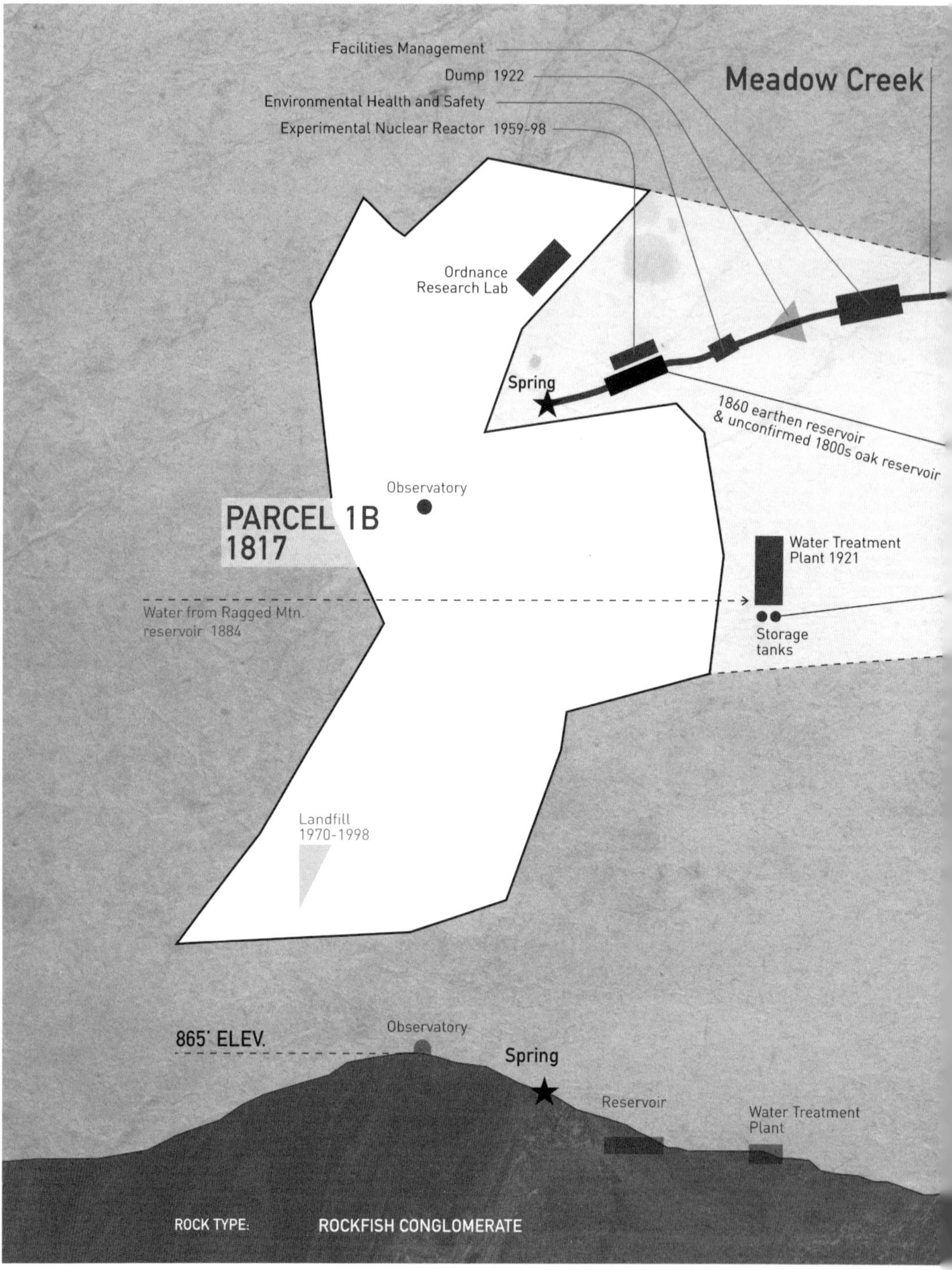

Map and timeline of down- and uphill material flows.

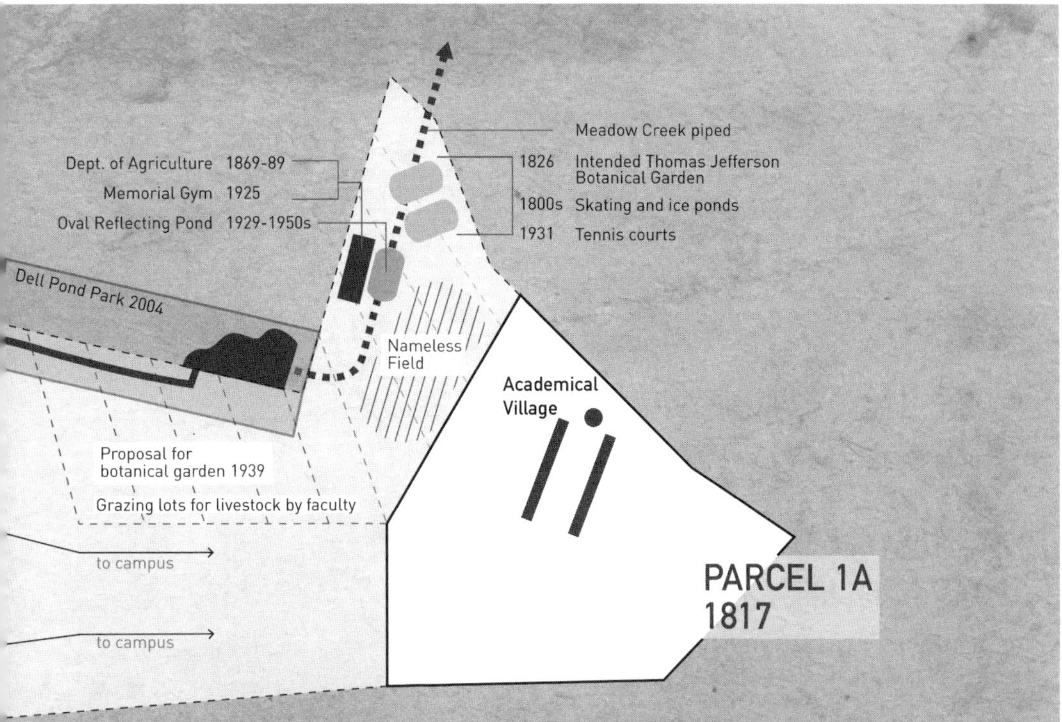

DOWNHILL / UPHILL EVENTS

Rock quarrying	**1817—1924**
Water collection	**1817-present**
Droughts	**1830,1852, 1872**
McCormick Observatory	**1885**
Evidence of deforestation	**1900**
University dump	**1922**
Ordnance Research Lab	**1948**
Experimental Nuclear Reactor	**1959—98**
University Landfill	**1970**
Dell Pond Park	**2004**

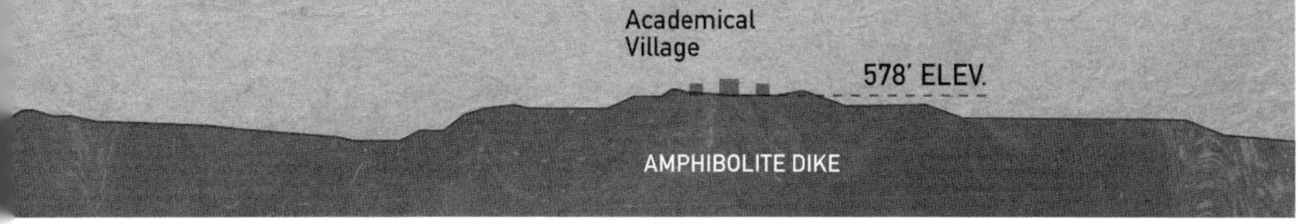

shrouded seclusion of the basement of Rouss Hall—one of the McKim, Mead, and White buildings constructed just south of the Academical Village—the secretive and dangerous nature of Beam's lab required that the buildings be patrolled by armed guards around the clock and surrounded by a barbed wire fence. However, the high level of noise, vibration, secrecy, and dangers of wartime engineering proved incompatible with campus life and by 1946 plans were underway to relocate a new Ordnance Research Laboratory (ORL) away from the campus center to Parcel 1B.

Security fence at Ordnance Research Laboratory, ultracentrifuge tower at the right.

The new facility required challenging construction and site work. For security, a wide swath of forest had to be cleared and high barbed wire enclosed the precinct. Because the large and powerful high-speed centrifuges could shatter and send out radioactively contaminated, metal shrapnel if the mechanism broke down, the centrifuges had to operate below ground in deep pits for safety. Drilling the two pits—one thirty feet and the other fifty feet—through the dense Rockfish Conglomerate rock of Parcel 1B proved slow-going. Once completed, massive centrifuges, shipped by truck from the Oak Ridge Institute in Tennessee, were carefully lowered into the pits by crane through hinged doors on the roof of the tall centrifuge structure. Deliveries occurred at night to minimize public attention. Beam's work would continue at ORL until 1986, when funding was discontinued in favor of other isotope separation technologies and due to a declining demand for enriched uranium.

Flowing Uphill: More Uranium

With the end of the Second World War, nuclear engineering could turn its attention from a military focus to the promise of atomic power to effect positive change—to heat American homes, light its cities, perhaps even cure cancer. In 1958, under the urging of the Dean of Engineering, UVA joined seventy-five universities across the country and created its own nuclear engineering program, producing hundreds of nuclear scientists up until 1998.

To house the program, a state-of-the-art, one-megawatt nuclear reactor was erected on Parcel 1B in June 1960. Central to the facility was its swimming pool reactor—a 70,000-gallon water reservoir into which samples were lowered for irradiation. The pool's massive seven-foot-thick concrete walls shielded researchers from harmful radiation emitted by ten to twenty aluminum fuel "plates" containing "bomb-grade" or 93 percent enriched 235-isotope uranium. With the precedent of Beam's Ordnance Research Lab on Parcel 1B, the mountain became the site for a second science facility utilizing uranium. The decision was made to place the reactor facility near ORL and directly on the north bank of the university's original water reservoir from the eighteen-sixties. Nestled into the slope, the bedrock was seen as a protective barrier against potential radiation.

It is ironic that the reactor facility was built next to the body of water that was constructed to safeguard clean water one hundred years earlier. The site plan for the reactor annotates the former reservoir as a "Waste Pond."

Construction photo of the Experimental Nuclear Reactor, note the reactor sitting above the original reservoir in the bottom left of the image, 1958.

The former reservoir provided a holding area for routine dilution of effluent and nonsoluble matter, as well as for controlled release of radioactive waters during repairs.—11 In 1968, leaks in the walls of the concrete pool forced the facility's closure, and the pool had to be drained entirely. Concerned about the history of leakage, in 1997 the university installed three groundwater-monitoring wells between the pond and the reactor, however no evidence of leakage was found.

11 Records of the University of Virginia nuclear reactor facility, (manuscript, Charlottesville, University of Virginia, circa 1959–2005).

Following the catastrophic meltdown at Three Mile Island Power Station in Pennsylvania in 1979 and the Chernobyl Power Plant accident in 1986, the country's appetite for nuclear applications declined. Student applications to nuclear engineering programs dropped and many programs around the country were discontinued. At UVA, costs to upgrade the aging facility and mounting hostility from the community led to the decision to close the program in 1998. A five-year decommissioning and cleanup process followed. Nonsoluble particulate sediment, which had built up at the bottom end of the reservoir, was removed. Core samples, taken throughout the reactor pool and every ten meters outside the building, determined that no remediation was required. The core of the reactor was sent to the Department of Energy.

Flowing Uphill: Trash

A decision by the university's BoV in the early twentieth century sealed Parcel 1B's fate as the de facto destination for the institution's trash. In the early decades of the new institution, garbage and human waste were disposed of in drains and small dumping sites on the outskirts of the Academical Village. As the university community expanded and trash volume grew, a centralized dumping and burning area was established on the southern terminus of the Lawn below Cabell Hall. In 1922, residents in the increasingly gentrifying neighborhood to the south—apparently suffering from the noxious smoke—made a "prayerful" petition to the BoV to relocate the "injurious" dump. The BoV conceded and relocated the dump to the eastern base of Parcel 1B. The chosen site was along the banks of the mountain creek in the quarry that had been the original source of stone for the Academical Village.—12

In time, this relocated dump along Meadow Creek would expand into what is now the base of operations for the university's Facilities Management, which oversees the maintenance of the UVA buildings and grounds. The university's increasing volume of waste would continue to move uphill, now to a landfill built in the nineteen-thirties on the south slope of Parcel 1B. In time, this landfill would expand to cover over five acres, replacing the 1922 dump. The landfill was the university's dumping site for large-scale rubbish and building demolition rubble until the nineteen-eighties, when more stringent EPA regulations took effect. The landfill remains in use today as a staging area where fallen trees and leaf matter collected

12 Board of Visitors minutes, April 26, 1922, 214, http://xtf.lib.virginia.edu/xtf/view?docId=2006_09/uvaGenText/tei/bov_19220426.xml (accessed July 12, 2017).

on campus are piled and composted for use on the UVA grounds. It is yet another ironic reversal of material flow; Jefferson's Mountain, once the source of timber flowing downhill to build and sustain the university, is now the repository for tree debris and leaf litter carried uphill.

Another signal of Parcel 1B's status as the university's waste repository was the decision in 1985 to place the Special Materials Handling Facility and Environmental Health and Safety Building on the mountain. While such a facility reflects new and positive protocols for the safe handling of toxic and chemical waste produced in research labs and facilities, a questionable decision was made to locate this facility on top of Meadow Creek, whose waters were diverted into a twenty-four-inch diameter pipe running around the building perimeter. Similar to the siting of the dumps, landfills, and the Nuclear Reactor Facility, the siting of this facility marked yet another ironic chapter in the life of the Academical Village, which founder Jefferson had proclaimed a century earlier to be, "furnished with good water, and nothing in its vicinity could threaten the health of the students."—13

13 Thomas Jefferson, Joseph C. Cabell, and Nathaniel Francis Cabell, "Early History of the University of Virginia: As Contained In the Letters of Thomas Jefferson and Joseph C. Cabell," Hitherto Unpublished; with an Appendix, Consisting of Mr. Jefferson's Bill for a Complete System of Education and Other Illustrative Documents; and an Introduction, Comprising a Brief Historical Sketch of the University, and a Biographical Notice of Joseph C. Cabell. (Richmond: J. W. Randolph, 1856), 400.

UVA's Center for Applied Biomechanics gathering for cremains dispersal ceremony at the Observatory on Parcel 1B Mountain.

The use of cadavers goes back to the early history of the university when dissection was conducted in the Anatomical Theater designed by Jefferson just west of the Academical Village. Throughout the nineteenth century, dissected cadavers were processed into skeletons for educational use. Today, cadavers continue to be essential teaching elements in Schools of Medicine. Additionally, military and automobile safety industry researchers in the School of Engineering and the Center for Applied Biomechanics depend on human cadavers to measure the impact of force on bones and tissue in the science of improving protective devices.

In 1919, Virginia established the State Anatomical Program under the Office of the Chief Medical Examiner for the procurement and treatment of human bodies for research and teaching. The policy that stipulated: "[t]he disposition of the body is arranged by the school and the remains are either buried or cremated and cremains scattered in a respectful manner."—[14] Revelations surfaced that the UVA Medical Center carried out a practice from 1970 to 1980 of dumping "relatively small quantities of hospital-generated waste" on a one-acre site on Parcel 1B, including human remains.—[15] This illegal and unethical practice—perhaps explained by periods when there were incinerator problems—was halted in the nineteen-eighties when neighbors complained, and the site was put on an EPA list as a solid waste contaminated site. In response, the university undertook its own voluntary EPA review in 1998 to evaluate the environmental impact of human waste burial on groundwater. Test pits unearthed human body parts along with medical waste, petri dishes, and embalmed body parts of pigs and dogs. Groundwater monitoring revealed higher than desired levels of contamination, but within the acceptable concentrations, thus the ground was not capped or removed.

14 "State Anatomical Program," http://www.vdh.virginia.gov/stateanatomicalprogram/ (accessed December 29, 2015).

15 The Environmental Company, Source Characterization Investigation of Two Former Waste Disposal Sites at Observatory Hill, University of Virginia (Charlottesville: The Environmental Company, 2001), Section 1-1.

Partly in response to revelations of egregious and illegal body disposal on the hill, concerned administrators from the Medical Center set out in 1989 to create appropriate protocols that would respectfully acknowledge the body donors. As a result, at several points now during the year, students and faculty communities from UVA's Applied Biomechanics and the Medical School gather on Parcel 1B for commemoration services. Following a brief service of readings, responsive litanies, and a moment of silence, the researchers who have benefited from the donors disperse and cast the cremains across the forest floor. University hospital Chaplain Dick Haines, who presided for years over the cremains ceremony and helped devise the ritual practice, wrote powerfully about his experience:

> All those who participate in such services are also challenged to remember that they are the beneficiaries of the life, work, and donation of others. The use of Observatory Mountain as the final and permanent resting place for all cremains is the final demonstration of the University's commitment to respecting donors.—[16]

16 Richard Haines, in discussion with the authors, May 2014.

Parcel 1B Re-evaluated

If the nineteenth century saw the downhill movement of materials from Parcel 1B in service of the Academical Village, the early to mid twentieth century saw the reverse uphill displacement of lethal and waste materials of the modern age. Throughout, the material dependency weighed heavily on Parcel 1B as the supplier, the repository, and the refuge. However, in the twenty-first century—due to concerns for the planet's threatened future—attitudes toward Parcel 1B and its material forest resources have shifted yet again.

In 2009, UVA's BoV adopted a resolution to reduce the institution's greenhouse gas emissions to 25 percent below 2009 levels by the year 2025. Along with energy reduction programs and plans to move from carbon-based to renewable energy sources, UVA has sought to improve the institution's carbon budget through carbon sequestration in its unbuilt and forested landholdings. Calculating that an acre of woodland sequesters 3.3 metric tons of carbon per year, the mountain—with its still near entirely intact hardwood forest cover—gets a new valuation as a zero-cost contributor to carbon reduction.—[17] The mountain forest also hits other important environmental targets in sustainability planning regarding recharging, purifying, and reducing the impact of upstream water.—[18]

The BoV's sustainability actions also harken back to Jefferson's original idea of instructing through the landscape by calling for the creation of new teaching goals "using our Grounds as a living lab for sustainability."—[19] Several departments already use the mountain for hands-on experiential instruction, including Professor Hank Shugart of Environmental Sciences. In conjunction with the Office of the University Architect, he has worked with students in his Forest Management courses to record the vegetation of roughly 120 thirty-meter plots covering roughly 10 percent of the forest. Shugart researches the future potential of forests and believes that denser, healthier forests can be engineered to match precolonial forest conditions through a program of selective plant removals that reduce root and light competition and strategic replanting to increase biodiversity.

Once the neglectful consumer, the modern university institution finds itself increasingly assuming the role of mountain protector, reliant on Parcel 1B for its educational, resource, and ecological benefits.

17 Julia Monteith and Jeff Sitler, "Natural Systems Planning," (Office of the Architect, University of Virginia, 2013), http://officearchitect.virginia.edu/pdfs/MPC02042013.pdf (accessed December 30, 2015).

18 Andropogon Associates, *Strategic Plan for Water Resources Management*, (Philadelphia: Andropogon Associates, 1999), 60.

19 Facilities Management, "University of Virginia Sustainability Annual Report 2014–15" (Charlottesville: University of Virginia, 2015), 5.

Summary

Parcel 1B's relevance to UVA's story and mission to research and teach has not been sufficiently recognized. What began in 1826 as a one-way flow of utilitarian materials from a nearby mountain down to a village had a profound influence on the course of the campus's development. The temporal and dynamic downhill and uphill flow of materials between Parcels 1A and 1B laid the foundation for the system of roads, gardens, and buildings, which we today know as the UVA campus. It is a rich story of material flows over generations, starting with Jefferson and his unexpected, but ultimately sage, dual land purchase. In time, a cast of enslaved and free laborers, teaching and research scientists, and students would influence material flows on and off Parcel 1B. It has been a history of benign neglect, which will be rectified as current and future generations step forward as stewards championing the hill.

The case of UVA illustrates how shifts in material culture can cause societies to confront past abuses and attitudes toward lands. A prime example is New York City's Fresh Kills Landfill, which was filled with city garbage from 1948 to 2001, closed and then briefly reopened to receive the building and site remains of the World Trade Center, and finally converted into a public park. The case also raises questions about the scale of material flows—whether food, construction materials, or energy—and how these currently shape the landscape. Communities formerly dependent on food sources from afar are once again farming locally on sites that, until recently, were marginalized, neglected, even trashed. Viewing sites through the lens of material culture, designers need to acknowledge the often invisible, yet significant histories of material and land resources, and anticipate their possible and unknown future callings.

Dumping at the Leslie Street Spit between 1980 and 1998.

Mineral Migration: Extracting, Recomposing, Demolishing, and Recolonizing Toronto's Landscape

Jennifer Foster and Heidy Schopf

The Leslie Street Spit is a five-kilometer-long archive of urban demolition. Amid verdant meadows, thickets of trees, and vibrant shorelines, the material detritus of building destruction is laid bare. Open water, only fifty-five years ago devoid of terrain, has now been transformed into Toronto's construction waste yard. Mineral base materials that form the Split—limestone, clay, and sand—embody the city's evolution from a colonial backwater, to emerging metropolis, to a megacity preoccupied with the processes and emblems of modernity and late capitalism. As the city has developed over the past 150 years, these minerals have shifted across the landscape and mutated between natural and built forms. Moving from the countryside moraines and escarpment surrounding Toronto to the buildings and infrastructure that support the city, and now comprising a unique landmass jutting from the downtown into Lake Ontario, these minerals are witness to striking urban evolution.

The minerals that now form the Leslie Street Spit were extracted from aggregate sites within and at the periphery of the city. These minerals were processed into usable building materials: primarily brick in the nineteenth and early twentieth centuries, and thereafter mainly concrete. Once processed, the materials were used to construct buildings and infrastructure in the city. Over time, these built elements of the city were demolished and deposited at the Leslie Street Spit. How can we understand spontaneous and unplanned hybrid landscapes like the Leslie Street Spit? Composed of mutable urban materials that have transfigured numerous times, what do they tell us about the interface between nature and built form? And how is the fluidity of their morphology, their ability to transform according to evolving urban preoccupations, tied to questions of equity and justice? This chapter responds to these questions by considering the biophysical attributes of the Spit as refractions of socioeconomic dynamics, and tracks the mobile history of the Leslie Street Spit's minerals to help develop an understanding of the political ecology of Toronto. In contrast to widespread contemporary fascination with urban decay as "ruin porn" and the celebration of verdant colonization of structural remains, the aim here is to summon a deeper understanding of the sociocultural politics that move materials across the landscape in the name of creative destruction. This is a perspective that also illuminates how urban planning decisions that appear ecologically beneficial may also mask social injustices through territorial dispossession.

Ecological and Aesthetic Experience of the Leslie Street Spit

The Leslie Street Spit is remarkably untamed for a modern urban waterfront in the throes of a development boom. There is a tendency to fetishize spaces like this: where nature so effusively cloaks urban ruins, where built matter is both durable and vulnerable in the face of invasive ecological processes. The flourishing ecologies of the Leslie Street Spit give new meaning to crushed buildings and new function to the minerals absorbed by plants and animals, and this five-kilometer-long display of these transformations is fascinating. The Spit serves as a prominent spectacle of urban nature. It is adorned with conservation designations that protect it from land use development and is widely cherished as a jewel of the city. But it is also a repository of urban ecological contaminants and particular histories that are less celebrated, and these stories—including the events that led to material displacement onto the Spit—are buried and obscured by fascination with greenness. For matters of urban sustainability and civic integrity, there is great value in seeking aesthetic relationships with spaces like these, which are appreciative of urban nature, but also honest about ecological histories and the lives and experiences of communities that have been displaced.

The vegetation and wildlife at the Leslie Street Spit are mostly volunteers. They are the result of species invasion and natural succession that was unanticipated by postwar, urban decision-makers and planners. Seeds transported by migratory birds traveling across Lake Ontario, as well as by wind and other vectors, have gradually built a substantial base of biomass now occupied by thousands of species of flora and fauna. From season to season, things change dramatically. No matter the season, the ecological associations at the Spit are always vibrant, and evolve differently each year. The regular pace of succession is both disturbed and amplified by the site's status as an active dump (with a weekly influx of newly discarded materials reconfiguring the landscape contours) and *terra nova,* where the temporal scale of ecological succession

The endikement of the Leslie Street Spit jutting out of the headlands, 1980–1998.

is compressed. Since ecological succession has been so rapid on the Spit, it is impossible to foresee which species will gain a foothold from year to year, which species may decline, and the ecological patterns and functions of their coalescence. Shifts in migratory bird populations and their effects on vegetation are particularly noteworthy. Over the past decade, the local population of double-crested cormorants has exploded, inspiring concern about the species' ability to outcompete and displace other valued bird species.—[1] While the Spit's diverse bird population prompted its designation as a provincial Environmentally Sensitive Area in 1982, the expanding cormorant population is now edging out the other species. At the same time, the rapid colonization of the Spit by cormorants has diminished the city's ability to fulfill its goal of doubling the city's forest cover to 34 percent by 2050.—[2] Yet, many celebrate cormorant population growth as a victory against human persecution and the ravaging effects of the synthetic insecticide DDT, which almost decimated the species up to the nineteen-nineties.

If visitors only glance from the headlands across the surface of the Spit, they may simply apprehend the abundant vegetation and aesthetically fuse the Spit with other conventional nature reserves of the region. But this perception is disrupted within 200 meters, as the edges of the narrow central spine (or as it is termed here, the endikement) come into focus.

Broken telephone poles, smashed sidewalks, shattered tiles, demolished culverts, and pieces of lavatories are all easily identified along the exposed edges of the Spit. The Spit's verges are steep, short bluffs where constant wave friction from Lake Ontario ensures this landmass's underpinning remains visible in perpetuity. As the visitor progresses along the next five kilometers into Lake Ontario and away from the city, the foundation becomes increasingly visible and the synthesis with plant and animal life becomes ever more curious.

1 Jennifer Foster and Gail Fraser, "Predators, prey and the dynamics of change at the Leslie Street Spit," in *Urban Explorations: Environmental Histories of the Toronto Region*, ed. L. Anders Sandberg, Stephen Bocking, Colin Coates, and Ken Cruikshank. (Hamilton: L.R. Wilson Institute for Canadian Studies, 2013).

2 City of Toronto, Change is in the Air: Climate Change, Clean Air and Sustainable Energy Action Plan: Moving From Framework to Action, Phase 1, 2007.

The Spit is imagined today as an urban wildlife refuge, a space where nature thrives amid the wreckage of the city. It is beloved by legions of Torontonians, and has been fiercely protected by citizen groups to ensure that it remains free of development.—[3] It is both an active dump and a nature preserve, divided by a straight narrow paved path along the central endikement of waste. The endikement was conceived as a narrow barrier that could protect an anticipated shipping industry, which never materialized. Along the eastern side of the endikement, dozens of heavy dump trucks navigate and build up piles of rubble every weekday. They leave scraps of brick, concrete, porcelain, and rebar among the diffuse assortment of construction debris.

3 Jennifer Foster and Anders Sandberg, "Friends or foe? Invasive species and public space in Toronto, Canada," *Geographical Review* 94, no. 2 (2004): 178–98.

All of this material is classified as "clean fill." Yet, the three retention ponds that lace the eastern side of the endikement are regularly filled with dredgeate from the harbor—material that cannot be dumped into the open water due to toxicity regulations of the *Great Lakes Water Quality Agreement* between Canada and the United States (U.S.). One of the retention ponds has been filled to capacity and is now configured as a wetland and shore habitat. The other side of the endikement is a municipal park, with public access only on weekends. Attracting migrating neotropical songbirds and ducks, owls in the winter, and tens of thousands of nesting waterbirds in the spring and summer, this is a favorite birding destination. Mammals like foxes, beavers, minks, snakes, rabbits, and voles inhabit the Spit, along with hundreds of thousands of insects, amphibians, reptiles, and fish. With a great deal of patience or luck, visitors might glimpse the resident pair of coyotes and their pups. What inspired protective measures at the Spit, however, is that it hosts 6 percent of the worldwide breeding population of Ring-billed gull (*Larus delawarensis*), as well as colonies of Herring gull (*Larus argentatus*), Common tern (*Sterna hirundo*), Black-crowned night-heron (*Nycticorax nycticorax*, as much as 30 percent of Canada's population), and Double crested cormorant

4 Toronto and Region Conservation (TRCA) 2000 Tommy Thompson Park Public Urban Wilderness Habitat Creation and Enhancement Projects, 1995–2000.

(*Phalacrocorax auritus*).—[4] In addition to the western side being designated as an Environmentally Sensitive Area, the entire Spit is recognized by BirdLife International as an Important Bird and Biodiversity Area.

How did the Spit evolve such a radiant ecological status? Lake filling only began in 1959, so it is a nascent landscape feature by geological standards. What prompted its construction, beyond the desire to dump loads of construction waste? Employing a critical urban ecologies lens may help us understand how the Spit is merely the most recent way station for the resident minerals, and how the passageway of these materials relates the story of Toronto's political evolution from precolonial to advanced capitalism. In the case of the Spit, this is useful for examining four distinct junctures in the story of material migration to the Spit, which in turn give rise to a number of critical questions about urban mutability, equity, and justice.

Critical Urban Ecologies

A critical urban ecologies perspective is developed here to elucidate the underlying forces that have shaped the Leslie Street Spit. In this instance, key insights are gleaned from the fields of political ecology, critical urban theory, and environmental aesthetics.

Political ecology is an analytical perspective that can help us to understand ecology as politics using other means. The field is broadly concerned with substantive ecological themes relating to science, knowledge, power, discourse, states, markets, and political and social movements.—[5] According to political ecology, ecological outcomes are not absolute or mediated by the laws of nature alone; rather, when diverse interests negotiate the progression of ecological settings, a wide range of possible outcomes emerge.—[6] This is to say that ecological trajectories are not inevitable, but the biophysical expression of complex sociopolitical undercurrents.—[7] Paul H. Gobster probes some of the dynamics of how urban nature is politically and

5 R. Peet, P. Robbins and M.J. Watts, "Global nature," in *Global* Political Ecology, ed. R. Peet, P. Robbins, and M.J. Watts (London: Routledge, 2011).

6 See, Peet and Watts 2000; Philip Stott and Sian Sullivan, ed., *Political Ecology Science, Myth and Power* (Oxford: Oxford University Press, 2000); Paul Robbins, *Political Ecology* (Oxford: Blackwell, 2004).

7 R.B. Hull and D. Robertson, "The language of nature matters: We need a more public ecology," in *Restoring Nature: Perspectives from the Social Sciences and Humanities*, ed. P.H. Gobster and R.B. Hull (Washington: Island Press, 2000), 97–118.

aesthetically constructed when he asks, "To what extent are people's visions of nature compatible with one another? What elements will most likely be points of conflict?... Whose nature will prevail? Or can different visions coexist in time and space?"—[8]

8 Paul H. Gobster, "Visions of nature: Conflict and compatibility in urban park restoration," *Landscape and Urban Planning* 56, no. 1/2 (2001): 35–51.

Two perspectives within critical urban theory enhance an understanding of how ecosystems may be politically charged in rapidly evolving urban environments: creative destruction and the "Right to the City." Urban nature may be understood as a historical product of capitalism,—[9] but also as an effect of cultural social dynamics that involves aesthetic, social, discursive, and relational processes.—[10] The perspective popularly known as Right to the City, initially proposed by Henri Lefebvre (1968), has evolved into a contemporary movement that "asserts that everyone, particularly the disenfranchised, not only has a right to the city, but as inhabitants, have a right to shape it, design it, and operationalize an urban human rights agenda."—[11] This perspective is central to a critical urban ecologies interpretation, since it centers the ability to shape and form ecological systems as a matter of equity. Urban ecological systems are coproduced by human and natural agencies, and intensive human settlement is an essential aspect of the evolution of interactions between species.

9 Neil Smith, *Uneven Development* (London: Blackwell, 1984); D. Harvey, *The Limits to Capital* (Chicago: University of Chicago Press, 1987).

10 M. Gandy, "Urban nature and the ecological imaginary," in *In the Nature of Cities: Urban Political Ecology and the Politics of Urban Metabolism*, ed. N. Heynen, M. Kaika, and E. Swyngedouw (London: Routledge, 2006); P. Robbins and J. Sharp, "Turfgrass Subjects: The political economy of urban monoculture," in *In the Nature of Cities: Urban Political Ecology and the Politics of Urban Metabolism*, ed. N. Heynen, M. Kaika and E. Swyngedouw (London: Routledge, 2006).

11 Right to the City (RTTC), "Mission and history," http://righttothecity.org/about/mission-history/, (accessed November 9, 2015).

It is the hybridity of urban ecologies—the mingling of natural and artificial, spontaneous and planned, visible and invisible—that makes them interesting and always novel. Overt decision-making about the form and function of urban ecological systems is typically something determined by experts who maintain epistemological power—for example, scientists or engineers—or who are acting strictly in the name of capital accumulation, often in consort. Decisions about urban form and function often advance a cycle of spatial redefinition, where existing space is "renewed" to more productively advance economic ideals. This cycle of creative destruction is described by David Harvey as a critical process that harms those who are already marginalized.—[12] This perspective is germane to

12 D. Harvey, "The right to the city," *The New Left Review* 53 (2008): 23–40, 33.

a critical urban ecological interpretation, because it helps illuminate some of the main trajectories that compel change in cities. As neoliberal market strategies usher new development, entire neighborhoods are typically transformed, impacting both human lives and ecological systems. People and materials relocate as a result of creative destruction, at times propelling environmental injustice. To date, most of the discussions about creative destruction have focused on the built dimensions of cities, but the ecological dimensions are also profound.—[13]

13 Heidy Schopf and Jennifer Foster, "Buried Localities: Archaeological exploration of a Toronto dump and wilderness refuge," *Local Environment* 19, no.10 (2014): 1086–1109.

The field of environmental aesthetics is useful in developing an understanding of how the Leslie Street Spit has grown and changed over time in relation to human experiences of landscapes. The field provides rich insight into how people's sense of beauty and desirability shape the physical and emotional qualities that form urban space. The emotional affect of these aesthetic encounters helps mold ideals and values about what is desirable, and this works across temporal scales. As people convene with the Spit, they instinctively form stories about the past based in part on shared accounts, but also largely on the visual cues of the surroundings; these are powerful stories that help bring conceptual order to unfamiliar settings. What happened here? Where did these materials come from? Why did they move? These types of questions are often uppermost in people's minds, and the responses to them are aesthetically mediated by both visual and sensory signals and the emotional affect of the landscape. Equally important in terms of political ecology is how emotional affect informs conceptions of the future and what is ecologically possible.

Paths of Mineral Movement

Before arriving at the Leslie Street Spit, the sandstone, limestone, and clay that form its foundation were part of built structures within the city of Toronto. The widespread use of brick is one of Ontario's most distinctive landscape characteristics.—[14] Easily accessible surface clays

14 Thomas E. McIlwraith, *Looking for Old Ontario: Two Centuries of Landscape Change* (Toronto: University of Toronto Press, 1997), 88; Ontario Bureau of Mines, *Ontario Department of Mines Annual Report* Vol. 12 (Toronto: The Bureau, 1903), 28.

belonging to Toronto's Don and Scarborough beds provided the building materials for much of the early construction of the city. The exposure of the mineral resources like clay and gravel of southern Ontario can be largely attributed to the construction of the railways in the latter half of

Photo of a brickyard located on the west side of Greenwood Avenue, looking north, 1917.

the nineteenth century. As Thomas McIlwraith explains, "Heavy subsurface clay and bedrock shales became exposed, available for burning into bricks. Railway builders cut through the undulating land seeking level alignments after 1850 and uncovered vast deposits of glacial gravels."—[15]

When wood buildings were outlawed in Toronto after repeated fires and the Great Fire of 1904, brick became the main construction material used in Toronto.—[16] Many historically significant buildings were constructed of brick sourced in the city, including the Canadian National Exhibition buildings, Massey Hall, Old City Hall, Osgoode Hall, Pantages Theatre, Toronto General Hospital, and numerous University of Toronto buildings such as Hart House, Trinity College, and Convocation Hall.—[17] These buildings are now icons of Toronto's built heritage. Much of the city's historical building stock utilized brick sourced from the Don and Scarborough beds.

15 McIllwraith, *Looking for Old Ontario*, 40.

16 S.E. Yundt and D.B. Augaitis, *From Pits to Playgrounds: Aggregate Extraction and Pit Rehabilitation in Toronto—A Historical Review*. Prepared for the Ontario Ministry of Natural Resources (Toronto: Queen's Printer for Ontario, 1992).

17 Metro Parks and Culture, *Don Valley Brick Works*, 1997, retrieved on May 27, 2010 from the Toronto Archives, Fonds 220, Series 773, File 188.

Archaeological research conducted on the Spit reveals a landscape littered with brick that was sourced from within the city and from sites where clay, sand, and limestone were excavated along the periphery of the city.—[18] Marked bricks tie the Leslie Street Spit to a number of historical (now nonoperational) and active brickyards.

18 Schopf and Foster, "Buried Localities."

Toronto Brick pit, located south of Felstead Avenue and East of Greenwood Avenue, 1928. This site has since been filled to the street level shown in the background of the photo and rehabilitated as Monarch Park.

In the late nineteenth century, much of the brick used in the city was sourced within the current city limits from sites such as the Don Valley Brickworks or the brickyards in the vicinity of Greenwood Avenue (between Danforth Avenue and Dundas Street East).—[19] At least twenty-five brickyards were located within Toronto's current city limits at the beginning of the twentieth century. By 1992, a total of eighty-two historical aggregate sites were identified within the Toronto city limits.—[20] As the city expanded and these mineral extraction sites were exhausted, they were absorbed into the urban fabric of the city and were "rehabilitated" to serve other land uses. Of the eighty-two aggregate sites identified within the current city limits, sixty-five have been rehabilitated as parks, golf courses,

19 Heidy Schopf, "The Leslie Street Spit: Ruins of a City and its Surrounding Landscape" (Masters thesis, York University, 2010). Historical, southern Ontario brickworks located outside of Toronto represented at the Leslie Street Spit include the Cooksville Brickyard (Mississauga, Ontario), Cheltenham Brickworks (Cheltenham, Ontario), Streetsville Brick Plant (Mississauga, Ontario), Canada Brick (Ottawa Plant), Phippen, Quinlan & Roberston (Belleville Location), the Milton Pressed Brick Co (Milton Heights), and the Ontario Terra-Cotta and Pressed Brick Co (Campbellville, Ontario). Currently operational brickyards that produced materials now located at the Leslie Street Spit include Hanson Brick (Streetsville, Aldershot, and Burlilngton locations) and Canada Brick (Streetsville, Aldershot, and Burlington locations).

20 Yundt and Augaiyis, *From Pits to Playgrounds*.

and schoolyards, as well as residential, commercial and industrial developments. The majority of these sites are located in the city's central core.—[21]

While brick constitutes the building material for most nineteenth- and early twentieth-century structures, concrete is now the predominant building material for buildings and infrastructure, such as sidewalks, bridges, culverts, and telephone poles. Concrete was used for Toronto's New City Hall in 1960 and has since become a building material that is symbolic of Toronto's progressive modernism and willingness to break with traditional architecture in order to be viewed as an up-to-date and "world-class" city.—[22] Many of Toronto's most emblematic buildings are concrete, including the CN Tower, the Bata Shoe Museum, the Skydome (also known as the Rogers Centre), and the Eaton Centre. The construction of concrete buildings boomed during the nineteen-eighties, when Toronto experienced a great deal of development, particularly in the form of high-rise office towers in the downtown core.—[23] This coincided with rapid population growth, which was accompanied by intense demand for housing and resulting suburban sprawl.—[24] More recently, concrete has been widely used in the construction of new condominium towers throughout the city.—[25] The widespread use of concrete as a construction material is evident at the Leslie Street Spit where concrete rubble mixes with clay bricks to form the foundation of the landscape.

As buildings in Toronto were deemed no longer useful, desired, or economically appropriate, they were demolished and dumped at the Leslie Street Spit. In the past, demolition materials would have been buried in brickyards or dumped along the city's lake edges to extend its land base. The Spit was designed to serve two key purposes: to provide a sheltering breakwater for the harbor while accepting unwanted building materials. The materials comprising the Spit are a well-recognized archive of Toronto's built form, but they also point to lesser-known stories of slum clearance and urban dispossession.

21 Ibid.

22 Schopf and Foster, "Buried Localities."

23 Pierre Filion, *Rapture of Continuity? Modern and Postmodern Planning in Toronto* (Oxford: Joint Editors and Blackwell Publishers, 1999), 432.

24 Frances Friskin, "The Toronto Story: Sober Reflections on Fifty Years of Experiments with Regional Governance," *Journal of Urban Affairs* 23, no. 5 (2001): 513–41, 527; Larry S. Bourne, "Designing a Metropolitan Region: The Lessons and Lost Opportunities of the Toronto Experience," in *The Challenge of Urban Government: Policies and Practices*, ed. Mila Freire and Richard Stren (Washington, DC: The World Bank, 2001), 27–46, 35.

25 Ute Lehrer, "Urban Development and the Creative Class in a Neoliberal Age: Two Case Studies in Toronto," in *Neoliberal Urbanism and its Contestations: Crossing Theoretical Boundaries*, ed. J. Künkel and M. Mayer (Palgrave, 2011), 99–118.

Concrete mixing plant in Toronto, 1922.

One study coupling archaeological visual survey with fire insurance and planning records finds household debris and personal artifacts mixed with brick and other construction materials in one of the earliest portions of the Spit.—[26] This corresponds with dumping and development approval records for slum clearance in Alexandra Park, the removal of heritage buildings along the cluttered downtown Yonge Street, and the destruction of arcades, low-end hotels, and dwellings that were located at the site now occupied by New City Hall.—[27] Officially, the Spit is composed of clean fill in the form of inert construction debris and dumping permits are restricted to such materials. Later sections of the Spit feature clean fill, including rebar, concrete, and tile. But this is not the case in the earlier portions. Once deposited at the Leslie Street Spit, these materials were gradually subsumed into the landscape to create a space that is part nature preserve, part urban archive, and part active dump.

26 Schopf, "The Leslie Street Spit."

27 Schopf and Foster, "Buried Localities."

Colonialism, Creative Destruction, and Uneven Development

The following key dynamics can be traced through the migration of materials to the Leslie Street Spit: the landscape imprints of Canada's colonial legacy; the cloak of capitalism, modernism, and neoliberalism as rationale for broadscale creative destruction; and the experience of uneven development in Toronto.

The Leslie Street Spit is a contemporary product of Toronto's colonial legacy. Its mineral base descended through Toronto as a result of development processes activated by settlers from England, Scotland, and Ireland beginning in the nineteenth century. But the experience of colonialism spans into the present. Human inhabitation of Canada prior to colonial contact is often neglected in popular historical accounts, and the experiences and even existence of Aboriginal peoples are frequently erased from contemporary interpretations of Canadian heritage and politics—a "habit of thinking"—[28] that is prevalent in interpretations of environmental phenomena nationwide.

28 B. Willems-Braun, "Buried Epistemologies: The Politics of Nature in (post)Colonial British Columbia," *Annals of the Association of American Geographers* 87, no. 1 (1997): 3–31.

The extraction of clay and its rendering into buildings is a critical act of functional and representational colonization, wherein the landscape itself is altered and reconfigured to accommodate Western dominion over what was typically considered tabula rasa—terrain that is vacant and unclaimed. As Jon Johnson explains,

> This myth of an empty, wild continent has, not coincidentally, often been used to justify the seizure of Indigenous people's lands for the use of Euro-Canadian and Euro-American settlers. Local histories of North American places often begin with the arrival of Europeans to the area, thereby contributing to the erasure of the Indigenous historical accomplishments and contributions within these locales."—29

29 Jon Johnson, "The Indigenous Environmental History of Toronto, 'The Meeting Place,'" in *Urban Explorations: Environmental Histories of the Toronto Region*, ed. LA Sandberg, S. Bocking, C. Coates, and K. Cruikshank (Wilson Institute for Canadian History, 2013), 59–69.

The extraction and movement of minerals was the material alteration that hardened the colonial claim in many ways, and the buildings that were constructed present an architectural entitlement to reconfigure this "new" landscape. From the time of early colonial settlement of Toronto (or York, as it was known in early colonial times) to the present, the spatial extent of the city has expanded and its edges have grown through and beyond the pits and quarries from which Leslie Street Spit minerals were extracted. These pits and quarries, long exhausted of viable building materials, are now configured into green open space, such as parks, golf courses, ski facilities, and nature reserves. Their legacy as extraction points is all but forgotten in the popular imagination.

Yet, the buildings and structures that house these minerals are often only temporary settings. Urban development processes driven by the combined forces of capitalism and modernism have fuelled the removal of large tracts of Toronto's postwar urban landscape and replaced them with towers that signal a new era in the city's growth. The city's gleaming towers—including the financial district and Toronto's City Hall—are located on lands that had existing occupants, the majority of whom were not central to the modernist project. The processes of creative destruction enabled the city to recast itself in the image of modernity and as a center for capital accumulation as the city embraced an entrepreneurial, pro-growth temperament beginning in the nineteen-sixties.—[30] Removing unsavory communities was an important strategy for spatial reconfiguration of Toronto's modern future.

30 S. Kipfer, and R. Keil, "Toronto Inc? Planning the Competitive City in the New Toronto," *Antipode: A Journal of Geography* 34, no. 2 (2002): 227–63.

As particular neighborhoods are removed, certain residents experience the uneven effects of creative destruction. The financial gains of these projects are indisputable, but only enjoyed by those invested in Toronto's neoliberal economic globalization. As a play for position in competitive capital markets, this transformation has produced space that serves the needs of some, but diminishes the livelihoods of others.—[31] It is a logic of urban development that escalates land prices, treats space as a commodity, and as Smith explains, produces cities as "an expression of the image of capital."—[32] Building on Henri Lefebvre's conception of the production of space as essential to class struggle,—[33] spatial production is not just a physical process but is absolutely bound to the production and reproduction of spatial meaning, concepts, and consciousness. In the case of the demolition of buildings that now form the base of the Leslie Street Spit, the spatial transformations served to fortify social difference and reify the power of capital,

31 Smith, *Uneven Development.*

32 Ibid.

33 H. Lefebvre, *The Production of Space* (London: Blackwell, 1997).

dispossessing lower and working-class Torontonians of their homes and communities to satisfy the demands of capital accumulation.

The Leslie Street Spit raises vexing questions about the relationship between colonialism, capitalism, and nature. Some relate to the conditions and experiences of flora, fauna, and biophysical existence beyond humans; others to the question of who benefits from urban transformation and the aesthetic appeal of nature in the city; while still others to the form and function of sustainability in places like Toronto.

What are the ethics of creating habitats in landscapes that are known to be contaminated? When city developers began dumping construction debris into Lake Ontario in the nineteen-fifties, they wanted to get rid of unwanted urban material and shelter the harbor from ships. They were not envisioning ecologically significant terrain. If it remained denuded of flora and fauna, the civic objectives of the Spit would still be satisfied. But colonies of birds, fish, trees, mammals, amphibians, reptiles, plants, and insects quickly found it and settled into space that fulfilled their biological needs. Six decades later, dumping continues and the landscape is a vegetation and wildlife magnet. The nooks and crannies between cement blocks form coyote dens, the cottonwood tree stands are strategic lakefront stopover points for migratory birds, fish find protected backchannels for spawning, and reptiles find hibernacula.

The habitat opportunities are endless, and certainly would not exist without the continuous movement of mineral matter through the city in mutable form. But this movement accrues more than just the minerals from the edges of the city. Agglomerated into the mix are known hazards to wildlife health, such as the flame retardant brominated diphenyl ether (Penta-BDE)—a bio-accumulating toxin that affects hormone levels in the thyroid gland and is linked to reproductive and neurological risks in gulls.—[34] A report from Environment Canada finds an immediate vulnerability among the Leslie Street

34 Foster, "Toronto's Leslie Street Spit."

Spit herring gulls caused by proximity to the city.—[35] Other noxious materials are purposely transported to the Spit. The *Great Lakes Water Quality Agreement* prohibits dumping toxic materials into Lake Ontario's open water, so sedimentary matter that collects as the city surface water drains—a sludge containing oils, heavy metals, and PCBs—eventually finds its way to the Spit. These continuously accumulating sediments block the nearby Keating Channel and fill Toronto Harbour, then are endlessly dredged and deposited into the "retention cells" on the Spit. And aside from the physical materials that endanger wildlife bodies, there are hazards associated with the Spit's connectivity to an urban metropolis. For instance, coyote that leave the Spit and utilize the vast range of green corridors linking the Spit to other open spaces are less protected and often killed.—[36] The Spit may be ecologically vivacious, a "happy accident" that delights humans, but it does not necessarily herald health and safety for its inhabitants. Understanding the complexity of this unique landscape is paramount, and this includes building knowledge derived from the natural sciences and natural history into aesthetic conceptualizations of nature, as advocated by philosophers (such as Saito) and landscape architects (such as Nassauer).—[37]

Who benefits from the urban transformation processes that define the Leslie Street Spit? The context within which the Spit is formed—unceasing destruction and reconstruction—is well defined as Toronto continually reconstitutes itself and competes to attain status as a "global city." But the economic expansion and transformation of the city from colonial backwater to a modernist exemplar is wed to neoliberal economic commitments that do not benefit the city's residents equally. Much of the material that has been transferred to the Spit comprises the homes of poor and working class Torontonians whose communities were in the way of modernist ideals. Although officially labeled "clean fill," archaeological exploration of the Spit reveals household artifacts and personal possessions.—[38] A form

35 R.J. Norstrom, M. Simon, J. Moisey, B. Wakeford, and D.V. Weseloh, "Geographic distribution (2000) and temporal trends (1981–2000) of brominated diphenyl ethers in great lakes herring gull eggs," *Environmental Science and Technology* 36, no. 22 (2000): 4783.

36 Foster, "Toronto's Leslie Street Spit."

37 See Y. Saito, "Appreciating nature on its own terms," *Environmental Ethics* 20 (1998): 135–39; Y. Saito, "The aesthetics of unscenic nature," *The Journal of Aesthetics and Art Criticism* 56, no. 2 (1998): 102–11; J.I. Nassauer, "Messy ecosystems, orderly frames," in *Theory in Landscape Architecture: A Reader*, ed. S. Swaffield (Philadelphia: University of Pennsylvania Press, 1995); J.I. Nassauer, "Cultural sustainability: Aligning aesthetics and ecology," in *Placing Nature: Culture and Landscape Ecology*, ed. J.I. Nassauer (Washington, DC: Island Press, 1997).

38 Schopf and Foster, "Buried Localities."

of creative destruction, the demolition of people's homes and communities and replacement with gleaming towers is not without sociocultural cost, and this portion of the Spit's story is little known. The dumped materials are not "clean fill." Beyond their questionable biophysical qualities, they also constitute the displacement of particular people's lives, people whose homes were expropriated and whose histories erode from the established civic chronicle.

The third set of questions raised by the Leslie Street Spit focuses on the mutability of urban landscape as a function of the relationship between capital and nature. In a period of overall ecological decline, what are the implications of a celebratory posture concerning cycles of material displacement, reconstitution, destruction, disposal, disregard, and then spontaneous ecological inhabitation? If nature is able to lay claim to human detritus, should we be concerned about the pace of destruction that precedes ecological colonization? When wastelands are able to self-heal, to aesthetically dissociate humans and functionally dissociate flora and fauna from the scars of destruction, have we lost the incitement to halt or slow the destruction itself? If ecosystems are so adept at recovery, if they are able to thrive in the wake of intense ravage and spoil, why protect them in the first place? It is not difficult to envision a line of reasoning that boosts the momentum of capital accumulation as a potential ecological benefit, or at least as something that might inspire new and ecologically interesting urban spaces. But the emergence of novel ecologies in places like the Leslie Street Spit does not warrant suspension of critical ecological analysis. Much the opposite: these are the very types of spaces that offer a window into the patterns and processes that we should be most concerned about. If we are willing to look beyond the aesthetically pleasing surface qualities, if we are willing to think about the historic journey of the materials rather than simply admire the juxtaposition of verdant nature springing from ruins, then perhaps we can think seriously about the ecological and social justice dimensions of sustainability.

“Making the North”: Mines and Towns of the Labrador Trough

Alessandra Ponte and Stephan Kowal

> ... working in the North does not necessarily imply the northward veering of the worker’s mind.—[1]
>
> The blackflies and the drizzle and the snows are still there and Cain’s legacy, the treasure trove of iron ore, continues to yield its wealth to people of vision and determination.—[2]

Canada is home to 75 percent of all global prospecting and mining companies. Because of the staggering presence of the mining industry, Canada has been named an extraction empire. Nevertheless, the Premier of Québec, Philippe Couillard—guilty of brazenly inviting foreign companies to take advantage of the potentially rich mineral deposits in the north of the province—has been recently reproached for acting as a “colonized” leader.—[3] Historically, Canada’s economy has been based on the extraction and exportation of natural resources: beaver pelts beginning in the seventeenth century; fish, timber, pulp, and paper in the eighteenth and nineteenth centuries; minerals, hydropower, and oil during the twentieth and twenty-first centuries. Canada’s economic development has long been characterized by heavy dependence on foreign markets and imperial control. After being subject to colonial rule first by the French Empire and then by the

1 “... le travail nordique ne s’accompagne pas nécessairement d’un anordissement mental du travailleur” (translation by the authors). Louis-Edmond Hamelin, “Un système zonal de primes pour les travailleurs du Nord, un exemple de géographie appliquée,” *Cahiers de géographie du Québec* 33 (1970): 314.

2 Richard Geren and Blake McCullogh, *Cain’s Legacy: The Building of Iron Ore Company of Canada*, (Sept-Iles: Iron Ore Company of Canada, 1990), 331.

3 Patrice Bergeron, “Plan Nord: Philippe Couillard a une culture de colonisé, dit Amir Khadir,” *La Presse*, April 9, 2016, http://www.lapresse.ca/actualites/politique/politique-quebecoise/201504/09/01-4859620-plan-nord-philippe-couillard-a-une-culture-de-colonise-dit-amir-khadir.php (accessed June 13, 2016).

Panoramic view of Route 389 passing through the town of Gagnon, March 2014.

British Empire, Canadians began to recognize—already by the nineteen-thirties—the threat of being crushed by the empire south of their border: the markets and economy of the United States (U.S.) now dictating the kind of staple or "matter" to be extracted and the rhythm of exploitation. Today, other forces and new international actors control the mining of Canada's natural resources. Canadians have been systematically confronted with—and have reflected upon—relations between centers and peripheries, international market trends, unbalanced systems of power, and colonization strategies. The singularity of the Canadian case permits one to address and understand—in novel geographical, political, and economic terms—the effects of the worldwide distribution of matter extracted from specific locations: the mines and towns of the Labrador Trough, for example, providing a new reading of the Chinese building boom and of the new urban landscapes of South Asia.

In February 2015, the Fraser Institute, a conservative—or, more precisely, right-libertarian—Canadian public policy think tank, published its annual worldwide report on mining companies for the year 2014.—[4] Built on the estimations of mining industry officials and administrators, the Fraser Institute's survey monitors the investment climate in 112 national and sub-national

4 Fraser Institute Annual Survey of Mining Companies: 2014, February 24, 2015, http://www.fraserinstitute.org/studies/annual-survey-of-mining-companies-2014 (accessed January 4, 2016).

"mining jurisdictions"—countries or provinces, territories, and states in the cases of Canada and the U.S.—in order to evaluate how mineral potentials and public policy factors, such as taxation and regulatory uncertainties, influence investment. The Fraser report ranked five Canadian provinces among the top ten mineral jurisdictions: Saskatchewan (number two, after Finland), Manitoba (number four), Quebec (number six), Newfoundland-Labrador (number eight), and Yukon (number nine). Such a massive presence of Canadian mineral sub-jurisdictions at the top of the list is partially explained by Alain Deneault and William Sacher, the authors of an alarming investigation about the status and role of the mining industry in Canada. Published in 2012, the inquest profiles Canada in general, and the province of Quebec in particular, as "mineral states," an unflattering and troubling definition inspired by the so-called narco-states: "areas that have been taken over and are controlled and corrupted by drug cartels and where law enforcement is effectively non-existent."—[5] According to the same authors, eight features typify mineral states: high geological potential; public institutions designed to favor the channeling of public nonrenewable resources and profits generated by their extraction to a minority of private corporations; state's use of legislation to guarantee unlimited accesses to mineral

5 Alain Deneault and William Sacher, *Imperial Canada Inc.: Legal Haven of Choice for the World's Mining Industries* (Vancouver: Talonbooks, 2012), 128.

deposits to private actors; the presence of state-financed infrastructures to facilitate the mobility of human and material resources; banking systems favoring the easy transfer of profits to other countries and the absence of rigorous tax appraisals; low standards applied to environmental laws and working conditions; inexpensive access to energy sources; and the massive influence of the mining industry on public officials and governing bodies.

The province of Quebec ranked first on the Fraser Institute's list from 2007 to 2010, dropped to fifth position in 2012, hardly reached eleventh place in 2013, to reappear, as mentioned above, in sixth position in 2014. In a statement released after the 2014 report, Kenneth Green, Fraser Institute Senior Director of Energy and Natural Resources, attributed Quebec's rebounding mining reputation to the "province's proactive approach to mining policy and its Plan Nord strategy to encourage investment and mineral exploration in northern Quebec."—[6] Green explained the previous year's dramatic drop in ranking by the introduction of a new provincial Mining Act and a proposed increase in royalties to the province. More specifically, according to Green, investors appeared to be discouraged by the uncertainty surrounding the delimitation of wilderness zones, parks, and archeological sites; the pledges to protect 12 percent of Quebec's northern territory; and the introduction of drastic limits to areas for industrial use. Green concluded his remarks with a warning: "As mining companies shift investment to more attractive and stable jurisdictions, skilled workers, employment opportunities, wealth creation, and government revenues will be lost."—[7]

A number of voices questioned Green's assessment, in particular the Canadian Boreal Initiative (CBI), a conservation group advocating that the new mining bill accommodate Aboriginal rights, promote best practices, ensure both environmental protection and economic predictability, as well as land use and planning strategies. In addition, CBI published a poll that uncovered growing

6 "The Fraser Institute: Quebec's Mining Reputation Rebounds in International Mining Survey," http://www.marketwired.com/press-release/fraser-institute-quebecs-mining-reputation-rebounds-international-mining-survey-1994262.htm (accessed January 4, 2016).

7 Alana Wilson, Project Director Kenneth Green, "Quebec's Mining Policy Performance: Greater Uncertainty and Lost Advantage," Fraser Institute (December 2013): viii, http://www.fraserinstitute.org/sites/default/files/quebec-mining-policy-performance.pdf.pdf (accessed January 4, 2016).

hostility to mining in Quebec, while other activists pointed out how the number of jobs created—like the revenues from the industry profits—are in fact negligible.—8 Moreover, a survey conducted by Quebec's provincial statistics agency attributed the effective drop in investment in the mining sector—from $5.13 billion in 2012 to $3.25 billion in 2013—to the decrease of gold prices and the fluctuation in demand from China and other new markets.

The 2015 Fraser Institute report has been received with great skepticism and discredited by an article published by *Press Progress*. Tellingly titled "Now Ordinary Canadians can Skew Fraser Institute's Data from Home," the commentary exposed the highly dubious data collection methods practiced by the institute and highlighted some of the most egregious findings of the 2013 report—including the hilarious factoid that 41 percent of the respondents to the survey "were deterred by Quebec's political instability, which was higher than [that of] Ethiopia, Ghana and Saudi Arabia."—9

The mining industry's insignificant contribution to the wealth of Quebec was recently confirmed by a blog post by Michel Pepin on the ICI Radio-Canada website. According to Pepin, for the fiscal year 2013–2014, the owners of the twenty-four active mining sites in the province contributed a total of 23,650,000 CAD dollars to the public treasury. In fact, the commentator suggests, it seems rather plausible to assume that the province of Quebec has paid mining companies to exploit its nonrenewable resources for the year 2013–2014.—10 This state of affairs does not appear to discourage the current Premier of Quebec, Philippe Couillard—a member of the Quebec Liberal Party—from enthusiastically endorsing the "sustainable development" of his version of Plan Nord: a strategic scheme to facilitate the exploitation of natural resources in the north, which the province has been trying to implement since 2011. Couillard, who clearly is not troubled by the incongruity of the plan he is proposing—it is difficult

8 "News Release: Quebec Polls Show Little Public Support for Mining Industry—Canadian Boreal Initiative Calls for Substantive Reform of Mining Practices," *Republic of Mining*, March 6, 2013, http://www.republicofmining.com/2013/03/06/news-release-quebec-polls-show-little-public-support-for-mining-industry-canadian-boreal-initiative-calls-for-substantive-reform-of-mining-practices/ (accessed January 4, 2016).

9 "Now Ordinary Canadians Can Skew Fraser Institute's Data from Home," *PressProgress*, September 24, 2014, http://www.pressprogress.ca/en/post/now-ordinary-canadians-can-skew-fraser-institutes-data-home (accessed January 4, 2016). Interestingly, according to the same report Botswana outperformed Manitoba, Ontario, Nova Scotia, and British Columbia in the survey's "Policy Perception Index."

10 Michel Pepin, "Moins d'un million de dollar par mine," *ICI Radio-Canada*, May 1, 2015 (5:24 p.m.), http://blogues.radio-canada.ca/politique/2015/05/01/moins-dun-million-de-dollars-par-mine/.

to imagine a sustainable extraction of nonrenewable resources—confirms and extends what has been Quebec's vision of the extraction industry for a long time. For Quebec's leaders, the exploitation of natural resources—as a source of local employment opportunities and generator of associated service activities—is the main (and often the only) engine propelling the fragile economies of the province's sparsely populated, remote, northern regions.

Northern regions represent most of Quebec's territory, as demonstrated by the gigantic area covered by Plan Nord. The development scheme encompasses all the land north of the 49th parallel and the Gulf of Saint Lawrence—measuring 1,200,000 square kilometers in total—and includes the regions of Nunavik, Nord-du-Québec, the northern portion of Saguenay–Lac-Saint-Jean, and almost the entirety of Côte-Nord. To better understand Plan Nord's geographic meaning, it is worth recalling that the 49th parallel also defines 3,500 kilometers of the border between Canada and the U.S., and that Paris, France—the largest city more or less on the same latitude—is situated only fifteen kilometers south of it. The declared need to develop Quebec's territory north of the 49th parallel categorizes 70 percent of the province as subject to harsh climate, difficult to access, sparsely settled, and, according to recent studies, typified by an economy in a devolution phase. In fact since its inception, Plan Nord's designers have eagerly validated its strategies by comparing them to other attempts to (literally) colonize Quebec's impervious territory. Marc-Urbain Proulx, the author of an early, extended commentary on Plan Nord, states that the initiative represents the fifth *front nordique* (northern front) opened by Quebec in the course of its history.—11

The first, linked to the fur trade, began in the seventeenth century. It was followed, in the early nineteenth century, by a program designed to relieve the demographic pressure and discourage emigration to the U.S. This second front targeted mainly the French Canadian Catholic population and promoted permanent

11 See, Marc-Urbain Proulx, "Le nouveau front en périphérie nordique du Québec," *Cahier de recherche, UQAC, Centre de Recherche sur le dévéloppent territorial* (2012): 1–26; for a more recent appraisal, see also a television interview with Marc-Urbain Proulx on the North of Québec, August 2015, https://www.facebook.com/rdieconomie/videos/410858409099703/ (accessed July 5, 2017).

settlements—in the Saguenay, the Lac-Saint-Jean, the Haute-Côte-Nord, and the Témiscamingue—sustained by an economy based on subsistence agriculture and forestry. In 1888, under a nationalist government, this movement culminated in the establishment of the Ministère de l'Agriculture et de la Colonisation (Ministry of Agriculture and Colonization), which was soon renamed Ministère de la Colonisation et de Mines (Ministry of Colonization and Mines, 1897), thus reflecting the new economic drive behind the settlement and development of Quebec's northern regions. This third stage—characterized by growing investments in hydroelectric power, pulp and paper manufacturing, and mining—triggered a massive population influx in the region of Abitibi-Témiscamingue, due to the opening of rich mines of gold, copper, and nickel. It ended in 1929 with the crash of world markets. The fourth phase began at the end of the Second World War and initially involved the forbidding Côte-Nord where iron mining began at an unprecedented scale under the impulse of private ventures, and later the equally remote and harsh Bay James region where Quebec's government invested heavily in the exploitation of hydropower. This booming moment, which saw the creation of permanent settlements in the north, came to an end in the nineteen-eighties, in response to an oversupply of minerals in the world markets.—[12] The development of both regions took place in a climate of rising francophone nationalism, which culminated in the Quiet Revolution.—[13] The nationalism—which was already embedded in the second "agricultural" wave of colonization and again sought to root the French Canadian Catholic populace in its northern lands—acquired a new meaning during these decades, when developing the north was considered essential in order to inaugurate economic autonomy and reaffirm francophone identity.

In 2011, Premier Jean Charest presented Plan Nord, epitome of the fifth front of colonization, under the slogan *"Faire le Nord"* (Making the North). Charest's aim was to legitimize what from the beginning appeared

12 For a history of the mining industry in Québec, see Marc Vallières, *Des mines et des hommes: Histoire de l'industrie minérale québécoise des origines à aujourd'hui*, Ministère des Ressources naturelles, (Gouvernement du Québec, 2012).

13 During the nineteen-sixties and seventies, Quebec experienced a period of important reforms and redefinition of the traditional francophone Canadian nationalism.

Schematic map of Labrador Trough: borders of Plan Nord, towns, railroads, roads, dam, and power plants.

to many to be a dubious scheme, by inscribing it in the triumphant nationalist myth surrounding the opening of the fourth Nordic front. In fact, the expression "Faire le Nord" was borrowed from the eminent geographer Louis-Edmond Hamelin, who founded the Centre d'études nordiques (Center for Northern Studies) in 1961 at Laval University in Quebec. Intensely preoccupied by what he saw as the northern destiny of his country and its people, Hamelin, a linguist, deliberately appropriated the word *nordique* (Nordic), which in French previously defined only Scandinavian countries, to describe the north of Canada.—14 As for the slogan "Faire le Nord," Hamelin borrowed from the slang of the miners employed in the extraction sites in the north. The miners, predominantly born and raised in the Saint Lawrence valley, defined the work as "faire du Nord," which can be unflatteringly translated as "serving time in the North."—15

14 See the interview with Hamelin describing the adoption of the words *nordique* and *nordicité*: "Nord, nordique, nordicité," in *La nordicité du Québec: Entretiens avec Louis-Edmond Hamelin* by Daniel Chartier and Jean Désy (Québec: Presse de l'Université du Québec, 2014): 29–45.

15 Denis Lessard, "Louis-Edmond Hamelin: 'Faire le Nord,'" *La Presse*, May 14, 2011, http://www.lapresse.ca/actualites/politique/politique-quebecoise/201105/13/01-4399289--louis-edmond-hamelin-faire-le-nord.php (accessed January 4, 2016).

Hamelin, recently described as one of the great thinkers—[16] of the Quiet Revolution in Quebec, presented his theses on the Canadian north—and Quebec's north, in particular—in the canonic *Nordicité canadienne.*—[17] The book's aim was to transform the immense and uncharted Canadian north into a series of manageable regions open to transformation. To achieve this aim, Hamelin introduced the concept of "nordicity," an expression of the degree of "northernness," calculated on the basis of ten geographical and human factors: latitude, summer heat, annual cold, types of ice, precipitation, vegetation cover, land or sea accessibility, air service, population, and economic activity. Following these criteria, Hamelin defined four distinct zones in the Canadian north: extreme north, far north, middle north, and near north. Additionally, he identified processes of "nordification" and "denordification" tied to the introduction or abandonment of economic activities—in general, extraction processes—in any given area. Finally, Hamelin spoke of a *nordiste* stance, defined as the ensemble of mental attitudes or actions expressing an engagement in favor of the north.—[18]

Hamelin participated enthusiastically in the elaboration of massive governmental hydroelectricity projects in the James Bay region—acting, among other things, as a vigorous champion of the First Nations—and closely monitored the activities of the mining industry in the area of the Labrador Trough on the border between Quebec and Labrador. The construction of the huge system of dams and power plants on James Bay started in 1973, while the exploitation of the Labrador Trough began in earnest in the early nineteen-fifties.—[19] Thus, it is safe to assume that the Labrador Trough, with its mining activities, served as a laboratory where Hamelin could test and develop the ideas introduced in *Nordicité canadienne.* This hypothesis is confirmed by a number of articles, related directly or indirectly to the region, written by Hamelin before the publication of *Nordicité canadienne.*

16 Daniel Chartier and Jean Désy, *La nordicité du Québec*, 3.

17 Louis-Edmond Hamelin, *Nordicité canadienne* (Quebec: Éditions Hurtubise HMH, 1975).

18 Ibid., 81–121. In particular section 3, "Limites, dimensions et variations du Nord."

19 On the James Bay project, see Alessandra Ponte, "Journey to the North of Quebec: Understanding (McLuhan's) Media," in *The House of Light and Entropy* (London: Architectural Association Publications, 2014), 135–168.

The Labrador Trough, situated in the Côte-Nord district, is still the theater of important exploitation processes. International mining corporations—attentively watched by the Quebec government, which has included the Côte-Nord in Plan Nord as an area of particular interest—have flocked to the region since the beginning of the last decade in response to an upsurge in the world's mineral markets.

The Labrador Trough is a vast geological formation—1,600 kilometers long and 160 kilometers wide—spanning the Labrador-Quebec border. It contains a large iron ore belt developed on banded iron formations with low levels of contaminants, which makes it a favorite for steel manufacturers. Described by Jacques Cartier—the first European explorer to send reports on Labrador and the Côte-Nord—as "the land that God gave to Cain,"—[20] the region was exceptionally difficult to access, hostile, and still uncharted when prospecting began in the nineteen-twenties. Plans and investors who were prepared to develop the area materialized only in the nineteen-forties, when the diminishing iron reserves of the U.S.—depleted by the war effort—made the exploitation of the Labrador Trough inviting, despite the massive infrastructure financing required to extract the ore. The Iron Ore Company of Canada (IOC), incorporated in 1949 as a result of a partnership between the U.S. and Canada, was the first to undertake the construction of an extremely costly system. It was composed of a 580-kilometer railroad with connected hydroelectric dams and power plants (the Quebec North Shore and Labrador Railway), a deep-water harbor at Sept-Iles on the Saint Lawrence River, and a new town (Schefferville) near the extraction site in the north. Mining began in 1954 when the railroad was completed. The Premiers of Quebec and Newfoundland, Maurice Duplessis and Joseph R. Smallwood respectively, attentively followed the whole operation. Both were moved by the nationalistic intent to claim the wealth and economic activities promised by the exploitation of the huge iron deposit. Duplessis (Premier from 1936–1939 and 1944–1959) was

20 Richard Geren and Blake McCullogh, *Cain's Legacy*, 4.

pursuing his long-term policy of privileging the private industry as a generator for the development of Quebec, while Smallwood (Premier 1949–1972) was enthusiastically following a similar approach in Newfoundland (renamed Newfoundland-Labrador in 2001), which had just joined the Canadian Confederation and was disputing its borders with Quebec.

Duplessis had the satisfaction of seeing a "modern" town, Schefferville, built in the icy desert of the Quebec's north, while, in the early nineteen-sixties, Smallwood saw the construction of an even larger settlement, Labrador City, in the wilderness of Labrador's interior. Situated 200 kilometers south of Schefferville, Labrador City was built to exploit a vast deposit of low-grade ore that necessitated the construction of a concentrator, additional tracks connecting the new exploitation site to the main railroad line, a dam together with a power plant, and new facilities in the Sept-Iles harbor. Soon afterwards, a competing company—a joint Canadian/American/ European venture—founded the twin city of Wabush, where the region's main airport is located, to extract iron from what turned out to be the largest continuous geological formation of low-grade iron in North America. The IOC built Schefferville—where Duplessis died during a visit in 1972—and Labrador City following the model of the typical North American community designed for the automobile. An incongruous choice not just in relation to the climate, but also because the cities were not accessible by car. Even today, Schefferville can only be reached by plane or by train—which, thanks to governmental negotiations, also provides a sparse passenger service—while the road connecting Labrador City to Baie-Comeau on the shore of the Saint Lawrence River in Quebec, and to Goose Bay in Labrador, was completed decades after the town's incorporation. While this state of affairs did not discourage inhabitants from adopting cars as the habitual means of transportation, it apparently did amplify feelings of frustration and isolation. Dismal accounts from the nineteen-sixties describe how Schefferville's inhabitants spent their leisure time driving in endless circles around town. In order to insure the "stability" of the settlements, the IOC also implemented for decades the policy of promoting single-family home ownership and a conventional organization of the households, with husbands employed by the mining company—in an exclusively male environment—and wives at home performing domestic chores and taking care of the children.—21

21 See Jane Hammond, "Gender, Labor, and Community in A Remote Mining Town," in *Mining and Communities in Northern Canada: History, Politics, and Memory*, ed. Arn Keeling and John Sandlos (Calgary: University of Calgary Press, 2015), 117–135.

Next to the IOC, the second major player in the development of the Labrador Trough region was the Compagnie Minière Québec Cartier, which was created by the United States Steel Corporation (U.S. Steel) in 1957. The company began mining at Lake Jeannine in 1959 and founded the town of Gagnon the following year. The operation again necessitated huge investments in order to build a concentrator and a hydroelectric dam and plant next to the city

Road to Labrador City and Wabush. Smoke and steam clouds over the mining sites.

of Gagnon. In addition to this, there was the construction of a 306-kilometer railway line as well as a new harbor and servicing town of Port-Cartier on the Saint Lawrence River. Gagnon was accessible only by train or by plane. In the early nineteen-seventies, depletion of ore at Lac Janine forced the Quebec Cartier Company to move activities to Mont Wright, 130 kilometers to the northeast. The transfer required the construction of an additional 150 kilometers of railway track, a new concentrator, and eventually the creation of the new city of Fermont located twenty-seven kilometers from Labrador City in 1974.

While Gagnon, like Schefferville and Labrador City, was planned following an ill-adapted suburban model of the south and designed for the automobile, Fermont was built according to the decision of the Compagnie Minière Québec Cartier to create an ideal northern community. To develop the concept for the new city, they employed an expert of architecture in Nordic regions, Ralph Erskine, a British architect practicing in Sweden, in collaboration with Montreal-based firm Desnoyers-Schoenauer. Early design proposals for Fermont considered reusing homes from Gagnon: a study was made to relocate 441 houses, fourteen four-unit row houses, and thirty-three duplexes; as well as to move the recreational center, either by sleigh on winter routes specially built for the purpose, or by rail, hovercraft, or helicopter. It was eventually decided that it would be more profitable to start anew.

The plan of Fermont features a 1.3-kilometer "wall" or windscreen. The structure—a five-story, climate-controlled pedestrian megastructure—shelters the rest of the town from the dominant winds. The wall, which actually forms a slight angle to the north, contains split-level apartments, civic and cultural facilities (town hall, school, library, health facility, and fire station), a commercial mall, and a hotel. The town itself includes a series of townhouses and semidetached houses that were prefabricated in Montreal and transported to the site. They sit on a slight slope surrounded on two sides by a lake. The settlement faces south to benefit from passive solar radiation, which creates microclimates between the buildings. Streets are short and narrow, forming T-intersections to slow down automobile circulation and avoid the use of traffic lights. A parallel pedestrian system was incorporated into the project. Snow and wind studies were made to test the windscreen, roof slopes, and snow accumulation patterns.—22

22 On Fermont, see Adrian Sheppard, "Fermont: The Making of a New Town in the Canadian Sub-Arctic," Paper delivered at the Architecture Symposium Ion Mincu School of Architecture and Urbanism, Bucharest, Romania, July 11, 2007, 1–13, https://www.mcgill.ca/files/architecture/Fermont.pdf (accessed September 9, 2015); Martin Simard and Carl Brisson, "L'industrie minière et le développement urbain en milieu nordique: l'exemple de Fermont au Québec," *Cybergeo: European Journal of Geography, Espace, Société, Territoire* 637 (2013), https://cybergeo.revues.org/25817 (accessed July 5, 2017). See also papers and other reports collected in the Norbert Schoenauer Collections, John Bland Canadian Architecture Collection, McGill University Archives, Montreal, in particular Ralph Erskine,"QCM Report after discussions and visits February 1970," Box 12; and Surveyer, Nenniger & Chênevert Inc. "Concept Development and Cost Estimate Mount Wright Townsite," Volume 1 prepared for USS Consultants of Canada Limited, Box 12.

The unprecedented scale of intervention and the colonizing drive of mining companies operating on extremely difficult and uncharted terrain captured Hamelin's attention. In 1970, he published a fascinating analysis of the labor market in Canada's northern regions; it was presented as an example of applied geography and had a twofold objective. The first was an accurate description of the availability, mobility, and qualification of the work force in the north, together with the disparities in incomes defined by ethnicity (indigenous workers had lower

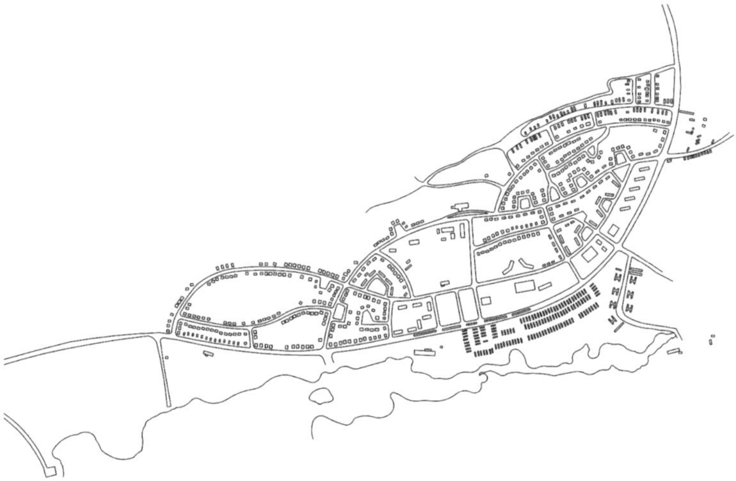

Redrawn map of the City of Gagnon.

salaries than Euro-Canadians), the wild fluctuations of job offers, and the degree of nordicity in the region where employment was offered. The second was an examination of the effectiveness and fairness of the monetary incentives already adopted by private industries and governmental bodies to attract variously qualified personnel and to assure (hopefully) prolonged engagements and the establishment of permanent settlements in the north. Two maps were included to illustrate the results of Hamelin's research: one traced the borders of the many different "norths" of Canada, while the other defined the isolines determined by the monetary incentives applied by the

Canadian government. The similarity between the two maps is rather striking. The first was republished five years later as a key document to sustain Hamelin's main thesis in *Nordicité canadienne*. However, in the 1970 study, Hamelin sadly concluded that the majority of the "migrants" or southern workers transported to the north were far from developing a nordiste attitude or a desire to settle. The things they remembered best, wrote Hamelin, were the feeling of adventure and the good pay.—[23]

23 Louis-Edmond Hamelin, "Un système zonal de primes pour les travailleurs du Nord, un exemple de géographie appliquée," 314.

The 1982 iron crisis profoundly affected the entire Labrador Trough region. The IOC ceased production at Schefferville and abandoned the city. Gagnon, kept alive until then by a different mining company—Sidbec-Normines through the exploitation of Lac Fire—was closed and demolished in 1984. Mining activities continued near Fermont and Labrador City, keeping the cities alive, while the First Nations inhabitants from nearby reservations slowly occupied the remains of Schefferville. In 1988, during the iron and steel market crisis, Richard Leclerc

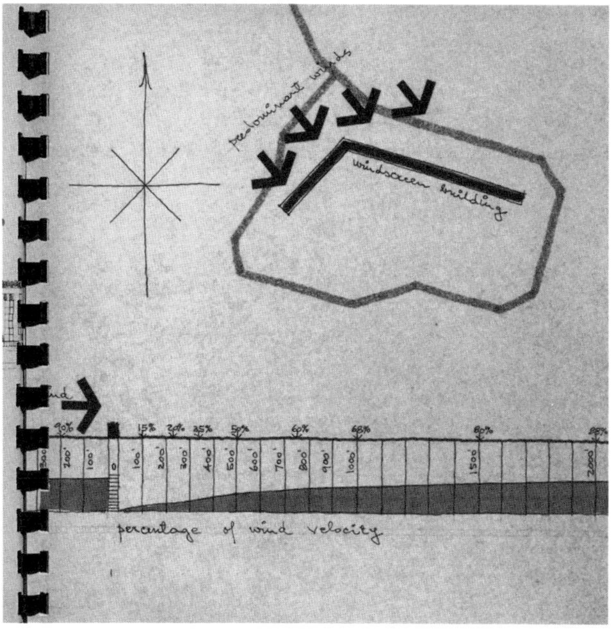

Windscreen study for the town of Fermont. Desnoyers Schoenauer Architects, Townsite of Fermont Project Summary, undated sketch book.

remarked—in a geographic study devoted to the railroad infrastructure of Quebec-Labrador, in which he quoted Hamelin's earlier essay on the same topic—that the daring and costly construction of two important railroads in the region did not engender (as was hoped) enduring posts or settlements along the tracks, or, in other words, the colonization of the area. The hostility of the land and its poverty could only sustain the sparse communities required by mining. Isolated in a geographical enclave, these communities suffered the vicissitudes of a mono-product economy responding to the fluctuations of the world market.—24

24 Richard Leclerc, "L'infrastructure ferroviaire du Québec-Labrador," *Annales de Géographie* 543(1988): 578–92, http://www.persee.fr/doc/geo_0003-4010_1988_num_97_543_20703 (accessed January 5, 2016).

Fermont seen from Mont Daviault.

Since 2000, the growing demand for iron ore in steel production by emerging economies, in particular China and India, has generated a new wave of mining investment in the Labrador Trough. Multinational corporations—such as New Millennium Iron Corp., Tata Steel, ArcelorMittal, Cliffs Natural Resources, and Rio Tinto—have been prospecting and opening new exploitation sites in the region. During this new upsurge of activities and investments, corporations, in most cases, opted to build temporary camp structures instead of permanent settlements to house the workers, while still investing heavily in transport infrastructure to facilitate the processing and transfer of iron ore and personnel. Increasingly, the mining companies adopted the so-called fly-in fly-out (FIFO) model, in which employees are flown in by company planes and work on a schedule of two or three weeks of twelve-hour days alternating with a corresponding period of rest in their hometowns. The system appears better adapted to the new investment boom that started in 2005, as well as to the life span of a mining site, whose uncertain futures do not justify the colossal investment and social costs implied by the constructions of company towns. This model puts an end to the vision of a permanent francophone, Euro-Canadian colonization of the Quebec's north.

Testing Ground

Mining in the Labrador Trough was the research topic for a design studio that took place during the 2014 winter semester in the School of Architecture at the University of Montréal. Titled *Testing Ground*, the studio was intended to develop analytical tools to explore and test architecture's agency in extreme situations. Two of the main companies currently working in the region agreed to present their operations to students and tutors involved in the studio: ArcelorMittal, which is currently exploiting the mines of Fire Lake and Mont-Wright near the city of Fermont; and New Millennium, part of the giant Tata Steel, which is now in the process of opening a new mine in the proximity of Schefferville. At the end of February 2014, the imbalance between the cost of exploitation and the market price of iron and steel led to the permanent suspension of operations of a mine in Wabush and the layoff of nearly 400 workers employed either in Wabush or Sept-Iles. At the time, the price of iron was 120 US dollars a ton, a significant drop from the 187 US dollars in 2011, but nothing compared to the rapid plunge of the following months: in September 2015, iron was valued at about 56

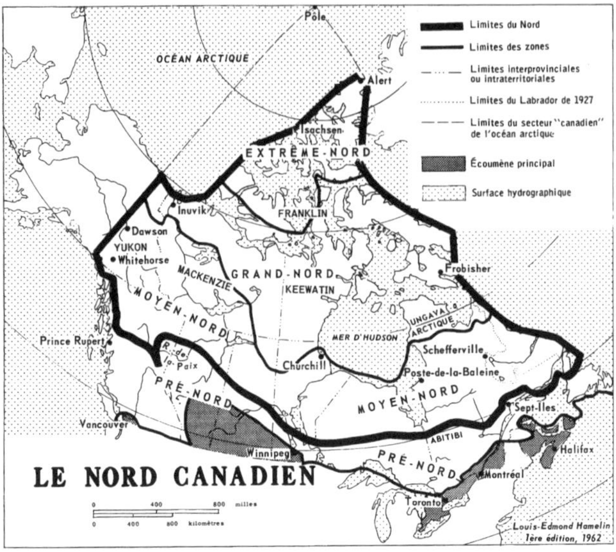

"The Canadian North," first published by Louis-Edmond Hamelin in 1962. The map shows the limits of the Extreme North, Far North, Middle North, and Near North, interprovincial or "intra-territorial" borders, the frontier of Labrador, and of the area of the Arctic Ocean controlled by Canada, also indicated, are the Ecumene (or inhabited lands) and the hydrography.

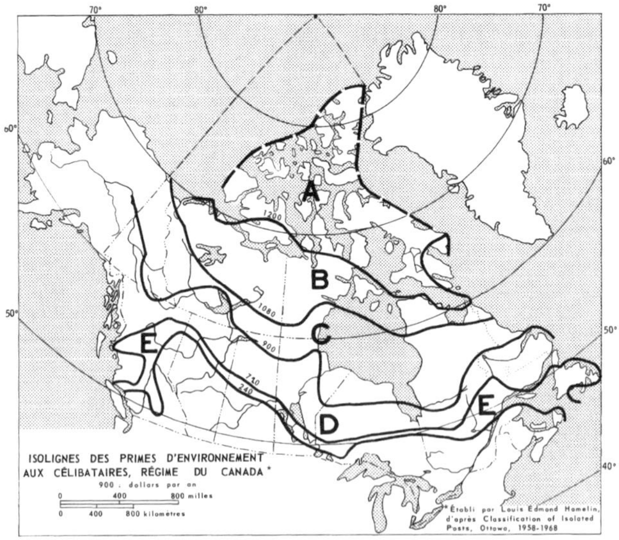

"Isolines of environmental premiums for single [men], Government of Canada." Map shows increments of 900 CAD dollars per year, as established by Louis-Edmond Hamelin following the governmental Classification of Isolated Posts, Ottawa, 1958–1968.

US dollars a ton.—[25] In 2015, ArcelorMittal and Tata Steel continued to function despite the ruinous decline of iron prices. They seem to prolong the policies described to us during the meetings in February 2014, when they explained, for example, how their companies found the FIFO model detrimental to production in addition to being a source of tension within the established communities. These assertions were confirmed during the field trip that took place after the encounters. Corroboration was found even in the renaming of the personnel from FIFO to permanent nonresident (PNR) to indicate a more stable relation with the mining company and the locals. Moreover, the Senior Director for Government and Stakeholder Relations of Tata Steel Minerals Canada strongly underlined company investment in building fitting relations with members of the First Nations inhabiting the reservations in and near Schefferville and Sept-Iles. Efforts to date have included the restoration of the hockey arena in Schefferville and the commitment to train and employ Aboriginals in 30 percent of the jobs in the mining site near Schefferville and in the harbor facilities at Sept-Iles.—[26] Recent newspaper articles confirm the relatively optimistic climate surrounding extraction activities both in Fermont and Schefferville.—[27]

The conversations with the delegates of ArcelorMittal and Tata Steel also revealed the tremendous difficulties involved in operating in extreme climatic conditions and remote sites. Challenges to humans, machines, and infrastructures were worsened by the especially severe winter months of 2014 and 2015. We experienced the same rigors and trials during the field trip that took place the first week of March 2014. The high cost of flying to the small and distant cluster of towns in the Labrador Trough, together with the desire to truly understand the scale of the territory and of the infrastructures servicing the mining industry convinced us to charter a bus and cover more than 3,000 kilometers, most of them on icy and difficult roads. It proved difficult to find a company and a

25 http://www.indexmundi.com/commodities/?commodity=iron-ore&months=60 (accessed January 5, 2015).

26 A more nuanced reading of the Aboriginal relations with mining companies in the Labrador Trough region with a particular focus on Schefferville is provided by Jean-Sébastien, Boutet, "The Revival of Quebec's Iron Ore Industry: Perspective on Mining, Development and History," in *Mining and Communities in Northern Canada*, 169–206.

27 See Isabelle Grégoire, "La deuxième vie de Schefferville," *L'actualité*, April 6, 2015, http://www.lactualite.com/societe/la-deuxieme-vie-de-schefferville/?utm_source=Facebook&utm_campaign=Echobox&utm_medium=Social (accessed January 5, 2016); Fanny Lévesque, "Tata Steel Minerals Canada: un géant tranquille," *Le Soleil*, June 6, 2015, http://www.lapresse.ca/le-soleil/affaires/les-regions/201506/05/01-4875717-tata-steel-minerals-canada-un-geant-tranquille.php (accessed January 5, 2016).

driver willing to accompany us in what was considered by all to be a risky venture. The journey started in Montreal, and from Quebec City we followed the north shore of the Saint Lawrence River to the small port town of Baie-Comeau, an eleven-hour drive in the middle of a snowstorm. Route 389 starts in Baie-Comeau and is the only road linking the Labrador Trough mining region to the Saint Lawrence port towns. Construction began on the first part of the road in 1959 to serve the gigantic complex of dams and power plants of the Manicouagan-Outardes project, culminating in the erection of the spectacular Manic-5, a concrete multiple-arch buttress dam. The rest of Route 389 was completed much later in exceptional circumstances. It now reaches Fermont and Labrador City, an eight-hour drive, and is used mainly by eighteen-wheelers servicing the towns and the mines. Our perilous bus ride was an intense and unforgettable way of experiencing the infinite, hypnotic landscape of the taiga, which is intersected by a gigantic hydroelectric infrastructure and traversed by endless trains transporting loads of iron or untreated ore to the far shores of the Saint Lawrence. It was watching the passage of these trains through the mud-spattered windows of our bus that we began to think of the region as the "land of the moving mountains." We spent four days visiting Fermont, Labrador City, and Wabush. Schefferville, further north and reachable only by plane or by bi-weekly passenger train, remained inaccessible during this trip.

As the public relations representative of the IOC/ Rio Tinto in Labrador City succinctly put it, the mining process can be summarized with the sentence "We blow it up, we crush it, and we ship it." It is possible that she was consciously echoing Smallwood, who famously said in 1962, while setting off the blast inaugurating the homonymous mine, "What a blast! I have always wanted to move mountains."—[28] Dynamite, we learned to our surprise, represents the greatest expense in the running of an iron mine. And indeed the mining companies in the

28 Richard Geren and Blake McCullogh, *Cain's Legacy*, 287.

region are in the business of moving mountains: from shipping the ore, first to the ports on the Saint Lawrence and then to India and China, to building new mountains out of waste, or displacing them as needed. The mayor of Fermont explained how ArcelorMittal complied with her request to remove a mound of residue encroaching on the city, while, at Labrador City, the IOC is contemplating the opportunity of taking over the hill now serving as ski resort to open a new pit.

The visit to the Mont-Wright's mine and to the wall of Fermont represented the culmination of the field trip. Yet, it was the stop on the way back to look at the howling void that has taken the place of the disappeared city of Gagnon—still mourned on Facebook as a lost paradise by its former inhabitants—which left a stark impression. It reminded us of the precarious and risky existence of the communities we had just visited and of the troubling comment we heard in Labrador City about a plan to close down the town if mining were to cease. Labrador City and Wabush have a population of about 10,000 inhabitants, whose livelihoods are strictly dependent on one industry. The risks associated with the mono-product economy dominating the region were clearly perceived in all of the towns, including Fermont, which was desperately trying to develop tourism, and Sept-Iles, which was also struggling to foster alternative solutions.

The field trip produced an incredible wealth of photos, videos, sound recordings, cartographies, geotagged information, and images of historical documents and plans gathered in the national archives of Sept-Iles. But even more testing are the memories of conversations overheard in miners' bars populated by strippers (also part of the FIFO workforce—[29]); or the image of a group of workers breakfasting very early in the morning already fully geared to cover, for recreation, the seven-hour snowmobile trek from Fermont to Schefferville at minus thirty-eight degrees; or the unbearable sadness of having to resort to "Italian cuisine" served by waiters from the Philippines

29 Mitchell Sunderland, "Life as a Stripper in a Subarctic Indoor Mining Town," July 2, 2015, https://broadly.vice.com/en_us/article/life-as-a-stripper-in-a-subarctic-indoor-mining-town (accessed January 5, 2016).

hired with low wages for two-year contracts, who lived in overcrowded, miserable conditions; or of visiting the gloomy but vaunted mall of Labrador City.—[30] We cannot repeat or make use of any of these experiences or the overload of recorded and unrecorded information of the most incredible landscapes: the glaring lights at night and, during the day, the steam blowing out of the mines against mountains covered with snow and ice; the biting winds and frozen lakes; and always the cold—burning and stinging, freezing engines, stopping machineries.

30 The hiring of temporary workers from developing countries began in the 2000s to compensate for the scarcity of labor for service or menial jobs that could not offer salaries comparable with those offered by mining companies. See Jane Hammond, "Gender, Labour, and Community in a Remote Mining Town."

Cold, remote, isolated: a frozen solitude in winter, a sea of mud and melting ice on the muskeg in spring, an inferno of mosquitos and black flies in summer. Traveling to the Labrador Trough was a reality test. But what was tested? Subjects and objects of experimentation multiplied, became interchangeable: the stability of world markets, the resilience of the mining industry, of its personnel and infrastructure, the inhabitants and their policing, the researchers and their tools, actors human and nonhuman, urban planning and architecture's agency or complicity. Have we been witnesses, should we produce the collected evidence for it to be tested, can the experiment be repeated, should its pressing ethical and political issues be addressed or reformulated? Is a viable stance available when confronted by the draining of Quebec's natural resources?

The plummeting of investments and activities in the Labrador Trough has been used to question the wisdom of Premier Philippe Couillard's relaunching of Plan Nord in 2015. Couillard's response to such questioning was that the wild fluctuations of the world markets are a "reality," which should not deter the government from heavily investing public money in infrastructure and research in the north to facilitate mining ventures, in order "to ensure the prosperity of Quebec."—[31] Couillard describes Plan Nord as an "ambitious social project," an innovative experiment in territorial governance that will involve indigenous communities, create thousands of employment opportunities, and generate millions of dollars in revenues. Moreover,

31 Alexandre Shields, "Plan Nord: Couillard mise sur les mines," *Le Devoir*, April 9, 2015, http://www.ledevoir.com/environnement/actualites-sur-l-environnement/436710/plan-nord-couillard-mise-sur-les-mines (accessed January 15, 2016).

his new version of the plan promises that 50 percent of the land covered by Plan Nord will be exempted from industrial activities, while 20 percent will consist of protected areas. However, only 30 percent of the territory has been "minimally explored," meaning that a huge amount of information still needs to be collected in order to establish the mineral potentials—and hopefully the biodiversity and ecologies—of the gigantic region, in order to establish the area to be protected from the one to be developed.—[32]

32 Robert Dutrisac, "Développent durable et mines éphémères," *Le Devoir*, April 11, 2015, http://www.ledevoir.com/non-classe/436941/plan-nord-developpement-durable-et-mines-ephemeres (accessed January 16, 2016).

In terms of investments and revenues from the mining industry, Couillard's forecasts and those of the other Plan Nord authors appear optimistic, to say the least, and are objects of unceasing readjustments. Past experiences have taught indigenous groups—who are now involved in the process of negotiation at the opening of new exploitation sites—to mistrust promises of prosperity and land remediation at the closing of the mines on their territories. As for the creation of thousands of jobs, according to a study published in June 2015, the Quebec mining sector will offer 10,192 employment opportunities for a decade from 2015 to 2025 to offset retiring personnel, employees changing occupation, or workers leaving the province altogether. The figure corresponds to 59 percent of the total of job offers in the mining industry for the decade. It disproves previous projections that estimated a higher demand in the sector: in general, employment in mining will diminish rather than increase. Furthermore, the same study foresees that 45 percent of the workers active in the mines in the north will come from the southern areas of the province, while in 2010, the projection came in at 26 percent.—[33] In other words, the local, mainly Aboriginal, communities in the north will profit even less from the extraction of nonrenewable resources, while carrying the heavy burden of pollution and social disruption inevitably linked to the short lives of mines.

33 Comité sectoriel de main-d'œuvre de l'industrie de mines, "Estimation des besoin de main-d'œuvre du secteur minier au Québec pour 2015-2025," June 4, 2015, http://explorelesmines.com/nouvelles/nouvelles-corporatives/1050-estimation-des-besoins-de-main-d-oeuvre-du-secteur-minier-au-quebec-pour-2015-2025.html (accessed January 16, 2016).

Quebec's policy in relation to the north and the mining industry is exceptional in the Canadian context, only because of the francophone nationalism expressed by

Hamelin's nordiste dream. Quebec, like the federation's other provinces, has pursued what is essentially a colonial project. The editors of a recent study on mining communities in Canada's north observe:

> Our research has found, similar to cases in the developing world, that the southern Canadian perception of the North as both an underdeveloped territory and as potentially rich resource frontier underwrote industry-friendly government policies and subsidies for infrastructure, including dams, townsites, roads and railways, all of which further affected Native communities and territories.—34

34 Arn Keeling and John Sandlos, "Introduction: The Complex Legacy of Mining in Northern Canada," *Mining and Communities in Northern Canada*, 7–8.

Quebec Cartier's train containing Iron ore crossing Route 389 between Mines of Fire Lake and Mount Wright March 2014.

At the closure of the volume, which documents a dismal chain of ecological and human catastrophes across the Canadian north, the same editors reflect on the ambiguous character of mining activities and our collective (and growing) demands for raw materials and natural resources. They conclude by inviting southern Canadians and international mining companies and foreign governments—which are in turn obviously encouraged by Canadian governmental policies to colonize the country—to share the burden and to be accountable as individuals and as a society. To respond to such an invitation we need a novel geophilosophy in order to redefine our geopolitics.

The present investigation represents the outcome of findings and arguments developed in the context of a design studio held at the School of architecture of the University of Montreal during the winter semester 2014. Titled *Testing Ground: The Labrador Trough*, the studio was directed by Alessandra Ponte in collaboration with Stephan Kowal, Olivier Jacques and Son Nguyen. The studio included a field trip to visit the mines and mining towns of the region. Many thanks are due to the students enrolled in the studio for the enormous enthusiasm and talent they deployed in support of the project: Bianca Arciero, Marie-Emmanuelle Auger, Marilène Blain-Sabourin, Kassandra Bonneville, Laurianne Brodeur, Dale Byrns, Sébastien Carzunel, Jérôme Descheneaux, Kateri Dozois, Josiane Gemme-Guimond, David Gilbert, Pierre Olivier Jacques, Emmanuelle Lauzier, Marc-André Laniel, Catherine Alexandre Lacombe, Maude Ledoux, Érick Soulière, and Audrey Touchette.

City forester Jacob H. Prost looking at a damaged tree, 1910.

“Tree Doctor” vs. “Tree Butcher”: Material Practices and Politics of Arboriculture in Chicago

Sonja Dümpelmann

In *Nature's Metropolis*, historian William Cronon uncovers and makes palpable the nineteenth-century connections and mutual dependencies between the city of Chicago and its hinterland. Cronon's study focuses on the flows and networks of natural resources, their transformation into commodities, and their consumption. It is premised upon and critiques the common nineteenth-century spatial and rhetorical distinction between the country as “nature,” the land of cultivation and extraction of natural resources, and a virtuous pastoral idyll, and the city center as the location of business, consumption, and moral corruption. The twentieth-century story of Chicago's street trees, of which a small part is told here, shows how this spatial distinction between natural resources outside the city, and their transformation inside the city—even for the nineteenth century an artificial construction at best—became increasingly blurred. In fact, the history of Chicago's street trees reveals the dissolution of the separation between nature and the city or culture, and of the distinctions between nature and production outside, and culture and consumption inside the city.

Short parts of this article derive from Sonja Dümpelmann, “Seeing Trees: Street Trees in New York City and Berlin” (New Haven and London: Yale University Press, forthcoming).

In 1909, Chicago was among the earliest metropolitan centers in the United States (U.S.) to hire a city forester, Jacob H. Prost. Years later, in the nineteen-seventies, the city also became a pioneer and case study for turning what by this time had come to be called the “urban forest” into a sustainable timber resource.—[1] In the early twentieth century, city foresters tended to make clear distinctions between urban and forest trees, and the way they were treated and managed: urban trees were primarily an aesthetic and climatological asset, whereas forest trees were grown for timber. Yet, by the nineteen-seventies, global and local ecological, political, and economic developments had led urban foresters to argue for a local and more systematic adoption of forestry practices in the city. Studies were undertaken to turn Chicago's street trees into a productive urban forest that could be harvested and turned into revenue. The city was not only the site of both nature and culture, but it was also the site of production and consumption.

1 See, for example, H. Ken Cordell and Thomas W. Clements, "Urban Waste Wood: A National Perspective," in U.S. Department of Agriculture, *Urban Waste Wood Utilization, Proceedings of a Conference on Alternatives to Urban Waste Wood Disposal, Forest Service General Technical Report SE-16, March 26–28, 1979, Charleston, South Carolina* (Asheville, NC: Southeastern Forest Experiment Station, September, 1979), 3–13. Other notable cities that experimented with alternative wood waste disposal options were Minneapolis MN, Madison WI, St. Paul MN, Portland OR, Burlington VT, Lansing MI, Atlanta GA, and Toledo OH.

"Tree butchering" of rows of poplars in Chicago, circa 1914.

"Tree Doctor" vs. "Tree Butcher"

Tree experts like early city forester Jacob H. Prost, who on occasion were also called "tree doctors" or "tree surgeons" as a result of the age-old anthropomorphization of trees, accused the "tree butchers" of mutilating trees.—[2] Often the tree butchers were linemen and other men working

2 See, for example, Ephraim Porter Felt, *Our Shade Trees* (New York: Orange Judd Publishing Company, 1938), 51.

for electric, gas, and telegraph firms, and streetcar lines, who injured trees by laying new pipes and wires and indiscriminately cutting branches. Thus, the many arboricultural manuals and bulletins that were published in the early twentieth century always also gave instructions on how to properly prune trees. Care had to be taken in determining the correct location and angle of the cut and in choosing the appropriate tools for the job. To prevent the cut wounds from being susceptible to insects and fungi, they were to be covered with an impermeable, antiseptic protective layer of coal tar. While pruning enhanced the trees' vitality, it could also improve a street's aesthetic and spatial effect. Prost argued for uniformity in planting street trees. This implied the planting of the same tree species along a straight line throughout one street as well as equal distances between the individual trees. It also meant that trees should be trimmed to the same, symmetrical form and size. According to Prost, it was this uniformity that inspired public admiration and refinement.—3

To produce vital street trees of the same form and dimension in big numbers, Prost's colleagues—Charles Sprague Sargent, Bernhard E. Fernow, and William Solotaroff—suggested the employment of a new optical instrument: the dendroscope. This handy contrivance came from France, where it had been invented in the eighteen-sixties by Count Amédée Joseph de Pérusse Des Cars. Presented at the 1867 World's Fair in Paris, it also captured the attention of foreign foresters.—4

Holding the dendroscope—a cardboard with a hole in the shape of a tree in it—at the level of the eye while moving around the tree, its operator, could give instructions to the pruner to achieve this desired tree shape. Des Cars suggested four different crown shapes and crown to trunk ratios, depending on the tree's age. Young tree crowns were to be egg-shaped, or an elongated oval that should measure two-thirds of the tree's entire height. In contrast, an old tree's crown should have a more rounded

3 J. H. Prost, *Trees and Lawns for the Streets,* Special Park Commission, Pamphlet No. 6 (April, 1914), 1. Also see J. H. Prost, *Street Tree Planting for Illinois,* Illinois Outdoor Improvement Association Pamphlet No. 2 (April, 1910): 6; J. H. Prost, "Reforestation of a Great City," *The World To-Day* 19 (1910): 735–740, here 738–739.

4 Charles Sprague Sargent, "Introduction," in *A Treatise on Pruning Forest and Ornamental Trees*, by A. Des Cars, transl. from the seventh French edition. 3rd ed. (Boston: Massachusetts Society for the Promotion of Agriculture, 1894), 19–27; Bernhard E. Fernow, *The Care of Trees in Lawn, Street, and Park* (New York: Henry Holt and Company, 1910), 105–106; William Solotaroff, *Shade-Trees in Towns and Cities* (New York: John Wiley and Sons, 1911), 128–129. For early advice on the use of the dendroscope, also see The Massachusetts Forestry Association, *Practical Suggestions for Tree Wardens* (Boston, 1900), 7; J. Wesseln, "Vorwort," in *Das Aufästen der Bäume*, by A. Des Cars (Köln: Verlag der M. Dumont-Schauberg'schen Buchhandlung, 1868), v–viii.

The dendroscope invented by A. Des Cars and its use.

outline and could have a height half as high as the entire tree. By cutting the tree into the shape that was projected onto it through the dendroscope, three-dimensional nature was made to copy the ideal shape on the two-dimensional picture plane. Through the use of the dendroscope, street trees could be "forced" into shape.

Although the dendroscope had been invented to assist in the pruning of forest trees for economic ends so that their vitality and consequently their wood production would be enhanced, Des Cars had argued that the tree outlines used in his dendroscope were also the most beautiful. They were the shapes that "nature gives the most perfect and most beautiful trees."—[5] Like their French colleagues Adolphe Chargueraud and Jules Nanot—who by the eighteen-nineties were promoting the dendroscope's application to the trees of Paris and street trees in general—Sargent, Fernow, and Solotaroff sought to apply the dendroscope to the context of urban America.—[6] It could help to economize arboriculture and standardize tree shape and urban beautification. While it remains unclear how many tree experts and tree pruners used this device, the fact that it was presented in all prominent manuals at the time suggests that it could have found at least some application, including perhaps in Chicago.

A practice that was certainly used widely in this city and elsewhere was the filling of tree cavities in order to preserve more or less mature trees. Tree experts considered fillings to be not only a cosmetic treatment, but also a necessary functional and lifesaving one that could enhance stability and slow decay. It was this particular treatment, based on "the science of doctoring trees," that turned tree experts into tree doctors and tree surgeons and that frequently also led to comments anthropomorphizing trees.—[7] Observing some tree work in 1876, one Chicago citizen commented on the tree doctor's activity that reminded him "of a surgeon engaged in removing a tumor from the human frame, or a dentist excavating a tooth preparatory to filling."—[8] Indeed, in the first decades

5 A. Des Cars, *A Treatise on Pruning Forest and Ornamental Trees*, 21.

6 See Adolphe Chargueraud, *Les arbres de la ville de Paris. Traité des plantations d'alignement et d'ornement* (Paris: J. Rothschild, 1896), 107–109; Jules Nanot, *Guide de l'ingénieur pour l'établissement et l'entretien des plantations d'alignement d'arbres fruitiers, forestiers et d'ornement sur les routes, boulevards et avenues* (Paris: Librairie central d'agriculture et de jardinage), 220–22.

7 See, for example, "The Science of Doctoring Trees," *The New York Times*, July 31, 1910, XI.

8 "Treatment of Trees," *Chicago Daily Tribune*, March 25, 1876, 10.

of the early twentieth century, similar analogies were frequently drawn to illustrate the importance of expert knowledge and trained men for the treatment of trees. Yet, still in the nineteen-thirties, the professional status of the arboriculturist was not accepted widely,—[9] causing the entomologist and tree researcher Ephraim Porter Felt to argue, that "the tree expert may well be compared in a professional way with the dentist, surgeon, or physician. Men engaged in other learned professions establish a reputation, which they cannot afford to jeopardize. The same is true of the tree expert."—[10]

9 Felt, *Our Shade Trees*, 50–51.

10 Ibid., 46. By 1939, only six or seven states had laws requiring licenses for tree surgeons. See Wilbur H. Seubert, "Ounce of Prevention Theory Is Effective in Tree Surgery," *The New York Times*, April 2, 1939, 56.

"Filling a large cavity of an elm tree."

In 1911, one of the most well-known tree doctors in the nation, John Davey, lectured in Chicago on occasion of the Real Estate Show.—[11] As "brother to the trees" Davey pleaded to the audience that "trees are almost human.… When one is sick it must be doctored."—[12] In his lectures and in his illustrated book *The Tree Doctor*—which was sold for one dollar so that it would "be within reach

11 See "Teachers to see exhibit," *Chicago Daily Tribune*, May 1, 1911, 13.

12 Davey quoted in "Veterans will be Guests at the Real Estate Show," *Chicago Daily Tribune*, May 3, 1911, 24.

of all"—Davey popularized expert tree knowledge and care. Having emigrated from his native England in 1873, he built a business around trees in Kent, Ohio, where he founded the Davey Tree Expert Company in 1880, followed by the Davey Institute of Tree Surgery in 1908. Among his early patents was a new "Process of Treating and Dressing a Bruise or Wound in the Trunk or Live Branch of a Live Tree," which he filed together with his sons Martin and James Davey in 1908.

"Cement stump—Result of Poor Tree Work."

Although the filling of tree cavities has been found to be detrimental to trees and is no longer used, by the early twentieth century it already had a long history reaching back millennia. Yet, in the late nineteenth and early twentieth centuries when Davey's business took off, the filling of cavities with cement, concrete, or "cementitious material" was widely considered an innovative method and state of the art. The practice, like the material itself, became internationally known and was employed in many major cities with notable street tree systems.

According to Davey and other tree experts at the time, "the repair of tree cavities [was] very much like the process of filling a tooth,"—[13] leading some to not only

13 Solotaroff, *Shade-Trees*, 220.

talk of "tree surgery," but even of "tree dentistry."—[14] The edges of cavities were to be cut smooth and even, and decomposed matter and debris were to be removed from the interior. A coating of coal tar was to be applied to the surface of the cavity before it was filled with cement, or with a mixture of cement, broken stone, and brick. In order to facilitate the healing callus to overgrow the filling, the cement plug was to stop at a depth just below the bark and was to be shaped to follow the contour of the tree.—[15] Davey's "improved" treatment included a narrow pipe that could drain any effluent from the interior of the tree, and a metal shield that covered and overlapped the filling. Other more elastic materials and methods of filling were used and tested in the subsequent decades, including magnesite, rubber, and asbestos fiber. The sectional filling of the cavity was thought to prevent cracks, a common occurrence in the monolithic cement plugs. As Davey's son Paul reported in 1939—when some other tree experts were already questioning the benefit of fillings in the first place—if applied in sections, the modern material could "bend with the natural movement of the trunk." This was a vital characteristic given that in long cavities concrete often "made the trunks so rigid that in high winds, the branches blew off in all directions."—[16] According to Paul Davey, sectional concrete cavity fillings were the best given their durability, longevity, flexibility, inexpensiveness, easy installment, and antiseptic effects.

For decades, cement had been hailed as the material of choice, replacing the simple wooden boards that had often been employed previously. Used profusely in the increasingly standardized building industry during this time, arboriculture provided yet another, seemingly unlikely use for this ubiquitous material that began to be produced in the U.S. in the eighteen-seventies. Despite its existence for millennia, around the turn of the century cement began to be considered a modern and progressive material that would transform "nature … ourselves, and our relationships with each other."—[17] In trees, concrete became

14 See "The Care of Trees," *American City* 4 (1911): 92.

15 Solotaroff, *Shade-Trees*, 220–25.

16 Paul R. Davey, "The Use of Concrete Fillings for Tree Cavities," *The New York Times*, July 9, 1939, 42; Seubert, "Ounce of Prevention Theory."

17 Adrian Forty, *Concrete and Culture* (London: Reaktion, 2012), 14.

part of nature, yet stood in contrast with the vernacular qualities embodied by the tree. The material differed from the living plant that had grown in a location and was in danger of losing stability in a variety of ways. Their material properties were opposites: wood is warm, concrete is cold; trees and their wood are living and porous; concrete is inert, compact, and non-porous. Whereas trees and wood can burn, concrete is fireproof. Concrete stood and often still stands for modernity, progressiveness, and ubiquitousness; it was the quintessential material of the international style that opposed ornament. The tree is rooted in the ground in a particular location; it stood and still stands for the vernacular, for nature, and for ornament. Yet, through the application of concrete—and other maintenance and management practices outlined above—trees became increasingly standardized and urbanized in the early twentieth century, while cities became naturalized.

Broken Standards

By the late nineteen-fifties, the Bureau of Forestry and Parkways in Chicago was publicly announcing its efficiency principles and labor economy. In pursuing its mission to provide and maintain "a forestry program for the propagation and preservation of community trees in City parkways," the Bureau emphasized the fact that it only planted, cared for, and managed, trees in "sections" and not individually, thus promoting tree monocultures along long stretches of road.—[18] Paradoxically, the Bureau was announcing this wholesale and comprehensive management regimen at a time when the first negative impacts of the strategy were being observed. Since the time of city forester Prost, American elms had been considered one of the best and most beautiful trees for wide streets in Chicago, despite the realization that they attracted a range of potentially harmful insect species—such as the tent caterpillar and the Tussock moth, which

18 City of Chicago Bureau of Forestry and Parkways, "The Functions of the Bureau of Forestry and Parkways" (Chicago, 1959).

had caused Prost a lot of grief in his first years in office. Furthermore, the Bureau was growing American elms in its nursery even in the nineteen-sixties, when Dutch elm disease (DED), spread by the elm bark beetle, was already ravaging the area.—[19]

19 See Prost, *Street Tree Planting for Illinois*, 11; Prost, *Trees and Lawns for the Streets*, 11; Justin Fishbein, "The Mod Woodsman who Spared Chicago's Trees," *Chicago Tribune*, August 18, 1974, A1.

DED had been imported to the U.S. from Europe, where an epidemic had first been detected in the Netherlands in 1920. In 1931, the disease was initially discovered in isolated spots near Cleveland and in Cincinnati, followed by 600 infected trees found within a thirty-mile radius of New York City in 1933.—[20] The disease spread to the state of Illinois in the nineteen-fifties, and the first affected elms in

20 See Thomas J. Campanella, *Republic of Shade* (New Haven and London: Yale University Press, 2003), 147–48; R. Kent Beattie, "How the Dutch Elm Disease Reached America," *Ninth National Shade Tree Conference, Proceedings of Annual Meeting* (1933): 101–05; R. P. White, "The Dutch Elm Disease in New Jersey," *Ninth National Shade Tree Conference, Proceedings of Annual Meeting* (1933): 105–10.

Clarence Hines, spraying trees for the eradication of Dutch elm disease, 1958.

Chicago were reported in 1956.—[21] Although the city had been spraying trees with a dichlorodiphenyltrichloroethane (DDT) solution since 1950, sixteen elm trees had to be removed from different locations in the city in 1956. Comprehensive treatment and protection against the disease no longer meant the conservation, but instead the eradication of trees and its fungus. The *Chicago Daily Tribune* reported that after tree removal, the city sprayed "the surrounding area to kill any fungus remaining."—[22]

21 "Illinois Dutch Elm Disease Peril Spreads," *Chicago Daily Tribune*, November 14, 1956, 3; "Creeping Plague of Fatal Dutch Elm Disease Invades Tree Lined Streets of Southwest Suburbs," *Chicago Daily Tribune*, August 5, 1956, SW1.

22 "City Forester Reports 16 Trees Infected With Plaguing Dutch Elm…" *Chicago Daily Tribune*, Aug. 16, 1956, W3. In the nineteen-sixties, this practice included the spraying of all trees within a 1,000-foot radius of the diseased tree. See Chicago Public Works, *92nd Annual Report, Fiscal Year Ending December 31, 1967* (City of Chicago, 1967), 14.

Early scientific experiments and warnings about the chemical's harmful effects on wildlife and humans—which had already begun in the nineteen-forties and reached the biggest publicity through Rachel Carson's *Silent Spring* in 1962—were disregarded until 1969 when the Bureau of Forestry, Parkways, and Beautification finally abandoned the use of the harmful chemical and replaced it with methoxychlor, then thought to be less harmful.—[23] The newspaper argued that the protection campaign against DED was better than any other investment of public funds.—[24] However, to ensure all affected trees could be treated, and if necessary felled, legislative measures were also necessary. An amendment to the municipal code, unanimously adopted by the City Council in November 1958, declared all trees affected by DED a public nuisance and gave the city's Bureau of Forestry and Recreation the authority to intervene on private property if the owner herself did not undertake the spraying, removal, and burning of the tree.—[25]

By the nineteen-sixties, municipal governments in the Chicago region were felling hundreds of elm trees each year, replacing them with sugar maples or other elm varieties that were not affected by the disease.—[26] In 1970, the disease killed 50,000 elms in the city,—[27] and in the years leading up to 1973, work crews removed 137,000 trees from Chicago's streets.—[28] The death and removal of this quantity of trees led to the consternation of many citizens who mourned their shade and aesthetic effect.

Street Trees Fuel Recycling

Plant scientists and the city's foresters not only had to curtail the disease and promote the development of disease-resistant varieties and species, but Chicago's urban foresters also had to deal with the practical consequences of the disease: the disposal of an unusually large amount of wood from the felled trees. Wood from diseased trees was piling up. The situation was exacerbated by

23 See Chicago Department of Public Works, *1969 Annual Report* (City of Chicago, 1969), 20.

24 "The Fight on Dutch Elm Disease," *Chicago Daily Tribune*, April 10, 1956, 18.

25 See *Journal of the Proceedings of the City Council of the City of Chicago*, Illinois, November 7, 1958, 8524–525; "City Council OK's Hyde Park Renewal Plan," *Chicago Daily Tribune*, November 8, 1958, 3; "New Law Aids Against NW Elm Blight," *Northwest News*, November 20, 1958.

26 Charles Leininger, "Suburbs Report Dutch Elm Disease," *Chicago Tribune*, August 28, 1966, M1.

27 Sally Wagner, "Dutch Elm Disease Runs Out of Trees," *Chicago Tribune*, August 12, 1971, W4.

28 See Charles A. Stewart, "Wood Waste Disposal," Paper held at the 29th Meeting of the Midwest Chapter of the International Shade Tree Conference, February 1974, St. Louis, Missouri, 8. Also see "Dutch Elm Disease is on Upswing in Chicago," *Chicago Tribune*, August 22, 1974, W2.

the fact that the City's Municipal Code and the Illinois State Environmental Protection Act now also prohibited Chicago's foresters from disposing of wood by open burning. However, when the *Chicago Tribune* argued in 1971 that, "overcoming the blight also will mean a new timber variety,"—[29] it was not only alluding to the city's wood disposal problem and the search for new urban tree species. By the early nineteen-seventies, a contingent coincidence of global, national, and local circumstances made Chicago's urban foresters and city officials appreciate street trees as a renewable timber resource. Indeed, these particular circumstances instigated Chicago's urban foresters and in particular the young urban forester Charles A. Stewart—who would become Assistant General Superintendent of the City's Bureau of Forestry, Parkways, and Beautification—to reconsider their profession's roots in eighteenth- and nineteenth-century scientific forestry.

The elm bark beetle carrying DED had spread unchallenged across the continent throughout the nineteen-fifties, sixties, and seventies. At the same time, domestic energy politics caused a lack of spare production capacity and a shortage of refinery capacity, while the 1967 Air Quality Act fueled oil consumption. The country's dependence on oil imports increased—a situation that was exacerbated further by particularly cold winters in the early nineteen-seventies, and the 1973 oil embargo by the Arab oil-producing countries. The oil embargo in particular contributed to a heightened environmentalism and it induced national, state, and local leaders to call for measures to conserve energy and draw attention to alternative, renewable energy sources.

Local political issues also created a climate prone to change. In the nineteen-sixties, Chicago's street trees were not well maintained, and the Bureau of Forestry was discovered to be a hotbed of corruption. The Bureau came under fire when the Better Government Association revealed that citizens' tax dollars were spent on "loafing"

29 "War on Dutch Elm," *Chicago Tribune*, January 30, 1971, W_A20.

30 See, for example, Stan Ziemba, "Forestry Bureau Shift Approval Expected Soon," *Chicago Tribune*, December 14, 1969, N13; "Move Forestry Unit—Daley," *Chicago Tribune*, December 3, 1969, A7; Edward Schreiber, "Daley Denies Tree Waste," *Chicago Tribune*, November 29, 1969, 1; Michael Kilian, "City Tree Scandal Told," *Chicago Tribune*, November 28, 1969, 1; "City Forest Bureau Defended by Daley," *Chicago Tribune*, November 5, 1969, A4; "Daley Orders Probe of Forestry Bureau," *Chicago Tribune*, October 28, 1969, 3. "Taxpayers Loss Estimated at 1 to 2 Million: Shows films as 'proof,'" *Chicago Daily Tribune*, August 3, 1962, 1; George Tagge, "City Forestry Bureau: Taxes Lost in Trees," *Chicago Daily Tribune*, June 24, 1962, 31; "B.G.A. Proof on City Idlers Is Presented," *Chicago Daily Tribune*, June 13, 1962, 1.

31 Wood debris had been burned or dumped in landfills since the early years of the twentieth century. During City Forester Prost's time, debris and wood waste from trees was "cut into convenient lengths and disposed of…" Prost, *Trees and Lawns*, 5. The dumping of wood debris in landfills was regulated by the 1965 Solid Waste Disposal Act, which also called for the conservation of natural resources by reducing solid waste disposal. The 1967 federal Air Quality Act laid the foundation for further clean air legislation beginning in 1970 on the federal and state levels. It prohibited the large-scale burning of wood debris in urban areas.

workers. Democratic Mayor Richard J. Daley, who publicly backed the Bureau and declared the accusations to be politically motivated, was forced to suspend several workers and to order an investigation. To address the manifold problems, budgets were redistributed and in 1969, the Bureau of Forestry was eventually moved from the Department of Public Works into the Department of Streets and Sanitation. Motivated by concerns of economy and efficiency, the development also reflected street trees' increasing perception as an element of street furniture best handled by a department dealing with road construction and waste disposal, rather than with the urban park lands and recreational facilities.—[30]

Given the Bureau's restricted budget, the pending energy crisis, and the piles of wood from diseased trees, Chicago's foresters sought to make a virtue out of necessity. City officials began to understand street trees as a renewable resource.—[31] Hence the problem was less one of "disposal of a nuisance," but one of recycling or "recovery of a resource," as Charles A. Stewart explained at a 1974 Shade Tree conference.—[32] Turning wood that was a liability into a diverse array of products, including fuel, was a new business idea. Stewart and his colleagues undertook some market research and soon discovered an increasing demand for woodchips. By selling round wood from dead trees, the city was able to invest in larger chipping machinery and by 1974 it was selling woodchips from urban trees to local roofing felt mills and composition board plants.

In the city's first pilot project in 1972, the Bureau of Forestry removed 21,000 dead trees and turned an estimated 15 to 20 percent of this wood into woodchips, leading to a gross earning of $22,000.—[33] This was a very small sum when compared with the City's 1973 budget estimate for the management of street trees, which was $9,150,197. Nevertheless, hopes were high that with further development, the tree recycling project would ultimately contribute significantly to solving the

32 See Stewart, "Wood Waste Disposal," 1, 10. The Bureau of Forestry, Parkways, and Beautification was in charge of all trees along public parkways, boulevards, and streets. Park and forest preserve trees fell under the jurisdiction of other government agencies.

33 Paper producers in the Chicago area were reported to be looking into the city's trees as a resource for the production of cardboard. See Frederick Hartmann, "The Chicago Forestry Scheme," *Natural History Special Supplement* (Nov. 1973): 72–73, here 72. Other cities in the Midwest sought to follow Chicago's example, but the initiatives either did not succeed in the first place, being opposed by preservationists (as in Dayton OH), or they did not prove to be sustainable in the long term as in the city of Chicago itself. For Dayton OH, see Anne Whiston Spirn, *The Granite Garden* (New York: Basic Books, 1984), 174; James A. Schmid, *Urban Vegetation: A Review and Chicago Case Study*. University of Chicago, Department of Geography, Research Paper no. 161 (Chicago: The University of Chicago, 1975), 96–99.

"wood disposal problem." After all, one of the project's advantages was that the resource, its transformation, and subsequent market were all in the same location, thereby largely eliminating transportation needs.

Perhaps it was Stewart's inkling that the hopes would not be fulfilled after all that soon led him to expand his call for tree recycling to include the vision of a self-sustainable urban energy supply system, which was based on urban solid waste, including tree wood and debris.—[34] Indeed, after a decline of the use of wood fuel in the nineteen-fifties and sixties, environmental concerns and the oil crisis in the nineteen-seventies led many industries to consider wood the renewable fuel of the future. It could help conserve fossil fuels and save costs.—[35] For example, General Motors began using pellets and wood scraps to supplement other fuels at its Pontiac, Michigan assembly plant.—[36] High fuel prices also motivated many home-owners to begin using wood as fuel, promoting a boom in the wood stove industry.—[37] In 1979, *The New York Times* reported on a nationwide increase of the use of woodstoves in private households from 250,000 in 1972 to two million in 1977.—[38]

It was the use of wood and tree debris as fuel that was finally considered the best and most promising use of Chicago's dead and diseased street trees. It was also the only safe measure to prevent DED from spreading. This was the result of a cooperative study on "Municipal Wood Utilization," which was published in 1978 and carried out by Chicago's Bureau of Forestry, Parkways, and Beautification and the United States Department of Agriculture (USDA) Forest Service. The study, which had been initiated by the 1976 National Forest Management Act and the 1977 Food and Agriculture Act and its Title XIV, suggested that farm and forest products and residues be used as substitutes for nonrenewable fossil fuels. The USDA and the Forest Service were eager to identify unutilized wood resources for a comprehensive national energy program.—[39]

34 See Stewart, "Wood Waste Disposal," 8–9.

35 "Wood Viewed as Fuel of the Future," *Chicago Tribune*, November 13, 1975, S2; "Wood Making Comeback as Fuel for Industry," *Chicago Tribune*, December 27, 1978, D2. Also see James R. Geiger, *Utilizing Urban Tree Debris: An Analysis of Alternatives for Chicago* (Broomall, PA: Dept. of Agriculture, Forest Service, 1978), 23.

36 See S. Ager, "Wood Making Comeback as Fuel for Industry Boilers," *Chicago Sun-Times*, September 4, 1977, 78.

37 Geiger, Utilizing Urban Tree Debris, 24. Also see "Wood-burning stove making comeback," *Chicago Tribune*, November 8, 1973, N14; "Wood-burning stove a hot item," *Chicago Tribune*, December 13, 1973, W10; John Shuttleworth, "Stoke up the ol' fireplace with economical wood fuel," *Chicago Tribune*, March 2, 1975, N_A9.

38 Agis Salpukas, "Wood Heat: Cutting Free of the Fuel Crisis," *The New York Times*, December 20, 1979, C8. Also see Joan Lee Faust, "Another Log on the Fire: Which Wood Burns best," *The New York Times*, January 1, 1978, CN8; Verna Tomasson, "Chopping Fuel Expenses with a Wood-Burning Stove," *The New York Times*, September 30, 1979, WC2.

39 See U.S. Congress, National Forest Management Act of 1976. 90 Stat. 2949. Public Law 94–588; Geiger, *Utilizing Urban Tree Debris*, 57.

Once before, in 1914—five years after the institution of Prost as the first city forester with insufficient funds—Chicago's city government proposed the idea of using urban trees as a source of timber and firewood, which would in turn generate revenue for tree planting and maintenance. German cities with municipal harvesting of street trees were used as an example. There, tree culture was a source of income, the *Chicago City Manual* explained. Through the "judicious and non-destructive harvesting of the timber of the municipal domain," German city forestry departments were able to maintain their grounds and pay for salaries and expenses.—[40] This resonated in a city where almost 36 percent of the citizens were German-born. Yet Chicago streets had already become a timber source in the economically challenging years of the late nineteenth century, albeit as part of an unplanned and informal economy. Then, it was not the recently planted street trees, but the wooden plank sidewalks that provided precious kindling wood. As in many other cities, in late nineteenth-century Chicago, wood was still the predominant material used for the paving of streets and sidewalks—either in the form of cedar blocks on the roads or pine and oak planks on sidewalks.—[41] While many sidewalks were being "improved" and more and more were gradually covered in concrete, their former planks became objects of speculation. In 1892, one North Side resident was reported to have sold a sidewalk to a woodman for six dollars. Without handling it, the latter soon sold it for $107 as kindling wood.—[42]

By 1978, the "Municipal Wood Utilization" study was able to report that whereas Chicago's urban tree debris was an unsuitable source for wood products, it had a high potential for use as fuel. Not only did wood contain less sulfur pollutants than coal, but the annual harvest of tree debris also yielded 252 billion BTU that could replace $536,210 worth of coal, $785,454 worth of fuel oil, and $701,195 worth of natural gas.—[43] The study recommended private investment in the construction of a facility

40 *Chicago City Manual 1914* (Chicago: Bureau of Statistics, 1914), 214.

41 See, for example, *Eleventh Annual Report of the Department of Public Works to the City Council of the City of Chicago, for the fiscal year ending December 31, 1886* (Chicago: M. B. Kenny, 1887), 57, 186–187, 190–191, 216. Still in 1908, 28 percent of all paved streets and alleys were paved with cedar blocks, at the time the second most widely used paving material in the city after macadam. See *Chicago City Manual 1909* (Chicago: Bureau of Statistics and Municipal Library, 1909), 220.

42 See "Notes," *Garden and Forest* no. 232 (August 3, 1892): 372.

43 Geiger, *Utilizing Urban Tree Debris*, xiv, 57–58, 67.

to produce energy from Chicago's tree debris. In addition, it proposed an energy task force to study the long-range potential of incorporating tree debris into a total solid waste energy recovery program.—44

44 Ibid., xv, xiv.

One of the principal reasons for the unsuitability of urban tree debris for woodchip production and other wood products was the highly inefficient production process. Due to its varying quality and size, tree debris had to be sorted. As a result of tree preservation efforts and the methods of tree surgery used until the nineteen-seventies, a large amount of tree debris had imbedded metal and concrete, crotches and limb stubs, or it was simply rotten. Metal and cement fillings, in particular, often harmed the chipping machines and made frequent repairs necessary, causing very high operating costs. Thus, the tree surgery methods that had been considered vital in the establishment and conservation of a functional urban forest in the first place were now largely prohibiting turning the trees into a multiple-use, sustainable-yield urban forest.

The City as Sustainable Forest

Charles A. Stewart, who led the Bureau of Forestry's initiatives from 1970 until 1974, when he left to become a private consultant on urban forestry, had argued for including recycling in the urban forest management plan. Since the beginning of more widespread and systematic planting initiatives for street trees in U.S. cities in the nineteenth century, wood production had not been part of the planting objectives. In contrast to scientific forestry, in urban forestry trees were planted first and foremost for their aesthetic, microclimatic, and health functions. They were "ornamental" or "shade trees." Chicago's street tree recycling project acknowledged the trees' multiple uses, adding their value as a timber resource. After all, Stewart argued, trees should not be planted in cities "merely for the sake of planting trees." Implicitly drawing a parallel to the recent 1960 Multiple-Use Sustained-Yield Act that had required the Forest Service to manage forests for both timber production and other uses—such as recreation, watershed protection, and wildlife management—Stewart argued that timber production could be integrated into the management of urban forests. The urban forest was also to be a multiple-use forest. To turn street trees into timber, Stewart also introduced into urban forestry the management practice of "sustainable yield." This practice had first been developed in eighteenth- and nineteenth-century German scientific forestry as a reaction to the depletion of the country's wood resources by the mining industry. It built upon forest management practices first enacted in the French 1669 forest ordinance. Sustainable yield introduced the time factor to forestry science. By the seventeenth century, it had become clear that foresters needed to predict and plan ahead so that they could achieve a maximum, yet equal yield each year. In the late nineteenth century, the German forestry principle of sustainable yield was adopted in professional forestry in the U.S.

Similar long-term planning and management would be required in Chicago if wood production were to be introduced into urban forestry and urban land-use planning. The aim was to establish a sustainable-yield system in which the revenues earned from tree harvesting would pay for the removal and replacement of dead trees. In Stewart's eyes, foresters had an important role to play in "Urban America."—[45] Scientific forestry applied to urban forestry meant that "optimum stocking levels" needed to be determined, rotations established, and the timber harvested at an optimum time—i.e., before the trees' maintenance costs rose.—[46] To reduce overall maintenance costs, the choice of site-specific species would be preferable. Stewart suggested mixing three or four fast-growing species of trees with quality hardwood species. This way, sizeable trees could be retained along streets and in front of homes, while others were harvested when their maintenance costs were still low and they provided the

45 Charles A. Stewart, "Forestry Considerations in Land Use Planning: The Role of the Urban Forester," (1972), 9.

46 Stewart, "Wood Waste Disposal," 8–9.

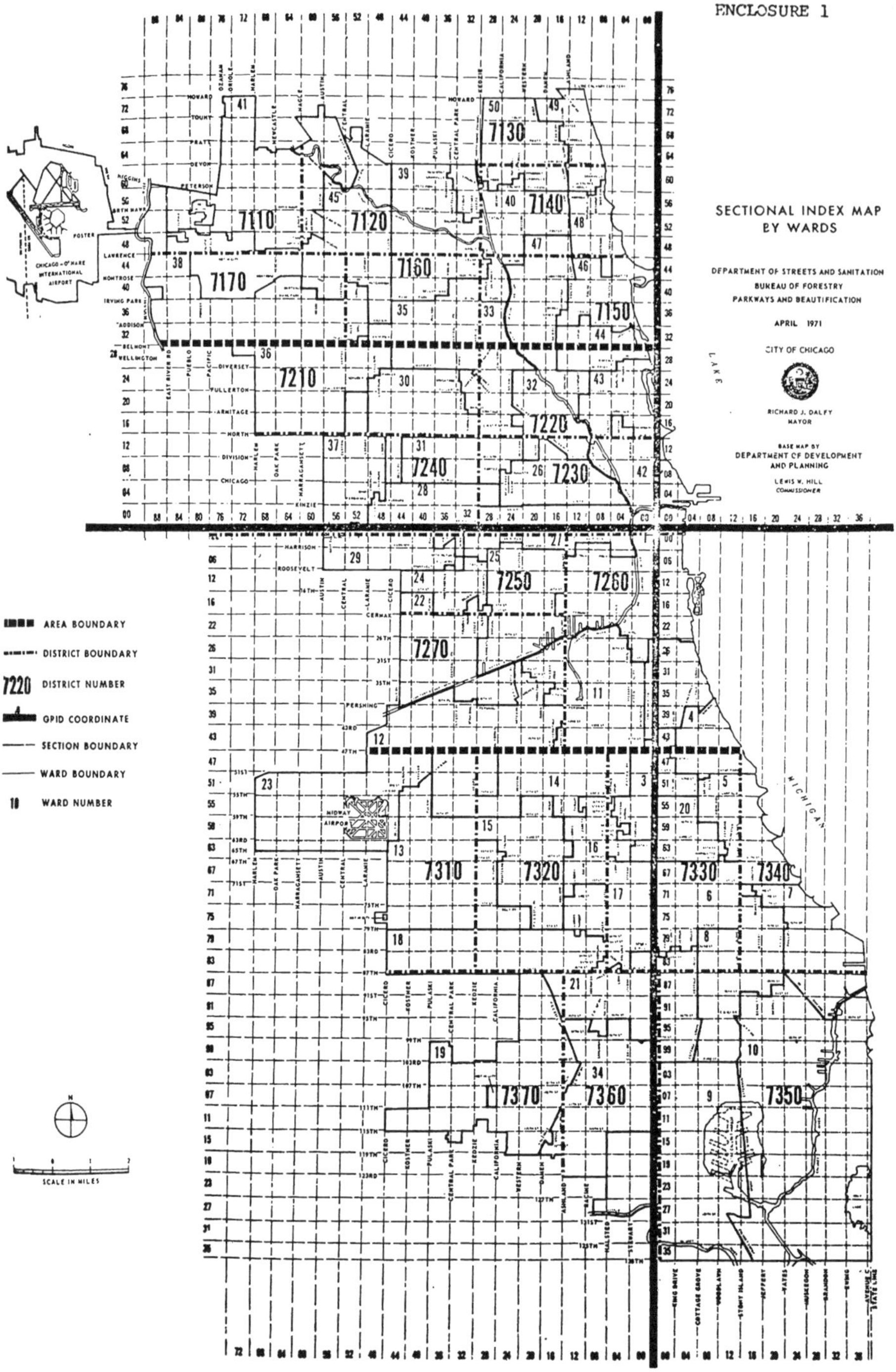

Chicago's city map overlaid with a grid of 160-acre units for urban tree management, 1972.

best market value timber. Mixing species also safeguarded against the effects of epidemics like DED.—[47]

47 Fishbein, "The Mod Woodsman."

Years later, urban forestry specialist Denice F. Lobel at the University of California at Berkeley elaborated on similar ideas. Like Stewart, she argued for long-range planning in urban forestry. To her mind, further adaptations of forestry concepts should also include the establishment of an uneven-aged structure and the establishment of a diversity of species, objectives that went hand in hand given that the life span of different species varies.—[48] Like Stewart, Lobel also attributed urban foresters with a role in urban landscape design; after all, a variable species and age structure also added "visual diversity in form, color, and texture" and an aspired aesthetic value of the urban forest.—[49]

48 See Denice F. Lobel, "Managing Urban Forests Using Forestry Concepts," *Journal of Arboriculture* 9, no. 3 (1983): 75–78.

49 See Ibid., 77; Stewart, "Forestry Considerations," 6.

For the purpose of turning Chicago into a productive, sustainable, and self-sustaining forest and "to maximize efficiency,"—[50] Stewart indiscriminately overlaid it with a grid of management units measuring 160 acres, or one-quarter square mile each. The grid disregarded political units and census tracts. It turned Chicago's street trees into an urban forest and a layer of nature that was both imposed upon the urban fabric and intersected with it. The grid served the Bureau of Forestry, Parkways, and Beautification to efficiently manage the urban forest. The Bureau's objective was to program and conduct work by sections established by the grid. This meant that all dead trees in one section would be removed before the work crew moved on to the next section. Trimming was also to be carried out by section and in a five- to seven-year rotation, thus establishing a cyclic trimming program throughout the city. Trees were also to be planted by section, depending on the need. The latter would be determined on the basis of the number of open planting sites, diseased trees, tree stumps, and citizen requests for trees in a particular section.—[51] Thus, certain principles—such as rotation and optimum stocking level—were to be adopted from forestry and adapted to the management

50 See Richard J. Daley, Mayor, City of Chicago, and Lewis W. Hill, Commissioner, Department of Development and Planning, *Community Appearance Report, City Trees, Guidelines for Selecting and Maintaining Trees in an Urban Setting* (City of Chicago: September, 1974), 28.

51 See Ibid., 29–30.

of the urban forest. The question of when trees were to be harvested had long been an issue; was it to be at the rotation age that was most physically productive or most profitable for landowners? In the nineteenth century, foresters and economists answered this question differently. In general, however, by the middle of the nineteenth century rotation cycles that stipulated the harvesting of trees before they reached full maturity were considered

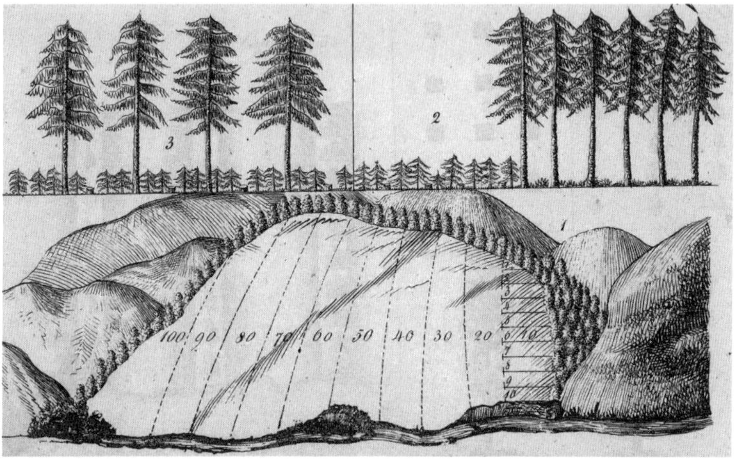

Illustration of nineteenth-century forestry rotation in Switzerland and Germany.

most profitable, promoting the establishment of even-aged, monocultural forests. In the urban environment of the twentieth century, it also appeared that a timely felling of mature trees would keep maintenance costs at bay.

However, despite the arguably profitable adoption of forestry methods in the management of the urban forest, the urban environment was, of course, uncontestably different than any expansive forest outside of cities. For example, the urban forest lacked equal density and a clear gradation of age. The proposed methods for the management of the Chicago urban forest can therefore perhaps best be compared to some of the early European forest management practices. They adhere closest to the amended, mid-seventeenth-century, French *method à tire et aire*, rather than the sectional clear cutting of forests that followed in the nineteenth-century German states (where forest sections with trees of the same age were subject to rotational cutting). In contrast, the *method à tire et aire* retained seed-bearing trees on lots to guarantee natural regrowth; in late eighteenth-century Prussia the method was amended, confining treatment to the *thinning* of sections which meant only the removal of "*bad* wood and … *matured* wood, or trees upwards of 70 and 80 years of age."—[52] Even though Chicago's foresters overlaid the city with a rigid, uniform grid and treated and planted trees by sections, they still needed to deal with trees of different species and ages in each section, which prohibited their wholesale treatment. After all, despite the shift to perceive all urban trees in their entirety as an urban forest, the city foresters' work was still grounded in arboriculture, meaning that it was grounded in the culture and management of individual trees for shade and decorative purposes, rather than in silviculture, the culture and management of entire forests for timber yield.

52 See the comments on the French and Prussian system in John Croumbie Brown, *French Forest Ordinance of 1669* (Edinburgh: Oliver and Boyd, Tweeddale Court, 1883), 42, emphasis in the original.

Yet, the shift to understanding and dealing with the urban forest as a whole—as well as the increasing techno-scientific development of urban planning—led the city of Chicago to include a computerized tree inventory in its long-term plans. Computer inventories that listed individual trees by species, age, and condition began to proliferate in U.S. cities in the late nineteen-seventies, replacing the old list and index card systems that some cities with foresters like New York City had begun to try and implement in the nineteen-tens.—[53] In their adoption of computerized systems, U.S. cities followed the early model of Washington, D.C. In the capital, Hans J. Johannsen—chief of the tree division in the city's Department of Highways and Traffic—had presented the Management Information System for Street Trees (MISTRE) in 1974. Computer inventories were considered able to provide a comprehensive and unbiased insight into the condition of street trees and to be an efficient management tool that facilitated care and accelerated adequate

53 For New York City's card catalog of urban trees, see Wayne C. Holsworth, "Street Tree Planting in its Relation to City Planning," *Parks & Recreation* 7 (January–February 1924): 1–32, here 20.

responses to disease and damage.—[54] Urban foresters were hoping that the new computer systems would improve the urban tree systems. Data collected about individual trees in the computer system would produce statistics that could show the trends of the urban forest as a whole, turning it into a more tangible entity that could be managed and controlled in its entirety. Due to the computer system's velocity and flexibility, urban foresters considered it particularly ideal as a tool for managing dynamic nature.

54 See Michael Kieran, "DC Logs Profile of Its Trees," *Washington Star-News*, April 11, 1974, A3; Hans J. Johannsen, "Municipal tree survey and urban tree inventory," *Journal of Arboriculture* 1, no. 4 (1975): 71–74; David E. Cramer, Frederick J. Deneke, and Gene W. Grey, "Computer Use in City Tree Inventories," *Journal of Arboriculture* 2, no. 10 (1976): 193–96; Franklin J. Chan and Gwen Cartwright, F.A. Chan "Tree Management Aided by Computer," *Journal of Arboriculture* 5, no. 1 (1979): 16–20.

In Chicago, it was clear that the wood debris problem would continue indefinitely beyond DED, because of the "dynamic nature and inherent characteristics of the urban forest."—[55] It was this dynamism of nature that city officials thought they could control, or at least manage, more successfully with a computerized tree inventory. They envisioned the replacement of the city's urban forest ravaged by DED with a new, productive urban forest. In many urban foresters' eyes, the computer system could lead to a faster replacement of trees with a greater variety of pest- and pollution-resistant as well as fast-growing species.—[56] Thus, the assumption was that computers could also help to render the city's urban forestry unit self-sufficient and contribute to an overall self-sufficient energy system for the city.

55 Geiger, *Utilizing Urban Tree Debris*, 69.

56 See Frederick Hartmann, "The Chicago Forestry Scheme," *Natural History Special Supplement* (Nov. 1973): 72–73, here 73.

At a time of severe energy crisis, the idea that wood could play a decisive role in the establishment of a self-sufficient city with a self-contained energy supply system was very attractive for many citizens. The ideas from the nineteen-seventies for a street tree recycling program in Chicago recall related ideas from centuries before. In the sixteenth century, the walls in the Tuscan town of Lucca were planted with fast-growing poplars. Besides the tree roots' ability to fasten and stabilize the soil, quite literally fortifying the city even further, the planting effort also provided the city with an important timber resource in times of siege. Similarly, during the energy crisis in the nineteen-seventies and the short-lived attempt by the

U.S. to obtain energy independence, Chicago's street trees provided a welcome fuel source and "biomass," as the proponents of alternative energy and self-sufficiency would begin to say in these same years.—[57] In contrast to Chicago's nineteenth- and early twentieth-century park and forest belts—which were attributed with recreational, educational, and aesthetic functions and were still largely conceived of as antidotes to the city that encircled the urban core—street trees were interspersed throughout most parts of the entire city and quickly became an integral component of the urban fabric. By the nineteen-seventies, their use as fuel and timber had been added to their generally accepted aesthetic and climatological functions. Chicago's pioneering ideas to turn the urban forest into a sustainable timber resource illustrates how the common nineteenth-century dichotomy between nature and the city—as well as nature and production outside, and culture and consumption inside the city—further dissolved during the twentieth century. From the beginning, Chicago's street trees and its later living urban forest were at the same time separate from the inanimate, constructed architecture of the city and entangled within it. Nature—i.e., street trees providing timber—was inside the city, rather than outside and separate from it.

57 First used by ecologists in the nineteen-thirties when describing living organisms as a comprehensive and calculable entity, the term "biomass" began to be applied to organic material regarded as a fuel source in the nineteen-seventies.

Saint Louis, Brick City

Jane Wolff

Saint Louis is a brick landscape. The city made bricks, and one by one, bricks made the everyday surfaces of the city. They're everywhere, laid three wythes thick—[1] in almost every building wall and stretched continuously just below the asphalt in the streets. They're so ubiquitous—so *visible*—that they might not seem remarkable. But those common bricks and face bricks and ornamental bricks and firebricks and glazed bricks and paving bricks are more than objects. Artifacts of geology, economics, technology, craft, politics, law, and custom, they're persistent evidence of a negotiation between cultural intentions and forces and processes that people don't control. Considered in the contexts of time, space, and place, they offer ways to trace the environmental history of the city. And because looking back is also a way of thinking ahead, their story might call forth ideas about what the city could be next.

1 A wythe is a continuous line of bricks laid one thick.

The story of the brick city begins in a conflagration. The story before the story begins in 1811 with the first voyage of a steamboat from Pittsburgh to New Orleans. In the years and decades that followed, traffic up and down the Mississippi grew exponentially. The steamboats changed the meaning of the landscape. They turned the river into a highway, and because they ran on wood, they made the forests into fuel.—[2] Up and down the Mississippi Valley, trees were cut into logs, and logs were stored in the holds of the boats. Saint Louis was the most important port in the middle reaches of the river, and by mid-century, steamboats were lined up for more than a mile along the waterfront.—[3]

On the evening of May 17, 1849, fuel stored in the hold of the steamer *White Cloud* caught fire. The fire spread to the next boat, to boats up and down the waterfront, and to the buildings on and inland from the river's bank. Fifteen city blocks were destroyed in eleven hours. Property damage was estimated at 5.5 million dollars.—[4] The fire produced a law that changed the landscape's meaning again: a new city code said that buildings had to be made from brick.—[5] Resource values shifted. The clay soils that lay beneath the ground were suddenly worth more than the trees that grew above the surface. Wealth had been created by the port and destroyed by the fire. Now it would come from clay mines and brick factories. History had intersected with geology: a moment in time created the demand for a material formed three hundred million years earlier.

2 F. Terry Norris, "Where Did the Villages Go? Steamboats, Deforestation, and Archaeological Loss in the Mississippi Valley," in *Common Fields: an environmental history of St. Louis*, ed. Andrew Hurley (Saint Louis: Missouri Historical Society Press, 1997), 80. Norris notes that in one day of travel, a single large steamboat burned enough wood to build fifteen small frame houses.

3 Ibid., 79.

4 S.L. Kotar and J.E. Gessler, *The steamboat era: A history of Fulton's folly on American rivers, 1807–1860* (Jefferson, NC: McFarland & Co., 2009), 256–57.

5 Thos. C. Chester, Revisor, *The Ordinances of the City of St. Louis, State of Missouri, Digested and Revised by the City Council of Said City, in the Years 1855-6* (St. Louis: George Knapp & Co., 1856), 428–32.

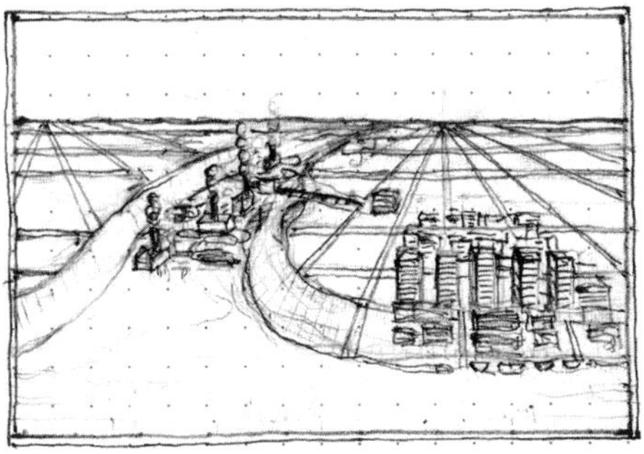

Geology and geography shaped the infrastructure and economy of the brick city. After the fire, the blocks along and above the crowded port were reconstructed in brick. Saint Louis's origins were there, just downstream from the confluence of the Mississippi and Missouri Rivers, and its financial and commercial centers stayed close to the waterfront. But the sources from which the city was built lay west and south of the port, where a geological feature called the Cheltenham syncline—[6] had preserved seams of shale, coal, and fire clay from the Pennsylvanian period beneath layers of limestone and common clays.—[7] The syncline offered all the material necessary to a brick city. Fire clay—[8] could withstand high heat, and so it offered suitable material for the construction of kilns; surface clay could be used to form the bricks themselves; and coal provided the fuel to heat the kilns. By the early eighteen-fifties, the mining and manufacturing of clay and clay products had been undertaken on a large scale in the wide, shallow valley of the River des Peres. Clay was extracted in underground mines, from the walls of the valley, and from open pits on slopes. It was dried and cured, made into bricks, pipes, and tiles, and fired. Beside the factories and kilns, sheds stored finished products. In 1852, a railroad through Mill Creek Valley was built to carry bricks ten minutes east to a terminal downtown. From there, they went into the great buildings of the city.—[9]

The landscape of brick production wasn't far from the landscape of brick consumption, and the two places were closely tied by economics and material. But they were separated by purpose and topography. Hidden in the valley of the River des Peres, mines and factories produced the wealth—and the bricks—on display in the

6 N.M. Fenneman, "Economic Geology: Clay," in *USGS Bulletin 438: Geology and Mineral Resources of the St. Louis Quadrangle* (Washington: Government Printing Office, 1911), 49–53; Bill Streeter, *Brick by Chance and Fortune: The Story of Brick in St. Louis*, dir. Bill Streeter (2011; St. Louis: Independent Production, 2011).

7 The common clay of the region is a loessial clay deposited in the floodplains of the river valleys of the Mississippi and the Missouri. Fenneman, "Economic Geology," 53–54.

8 Fire clay is also known as refractory clay.

9 Lewis F. Thomas offers a detailed discussion of the landscape of brick manufacture in "The Sequence of Areal Occupance in a Section of St. Louis, Missouri," *Annals of the Association of American Geographers* 21, no. 2 (June 1931): 75–90, http://www.jstor.org/stable/2560754.

monumental buildings above the Mississippi. Central to the city's existence, peripheral to its consciousness, making and moving bricks took place out of the sight of bankers and capitalists.

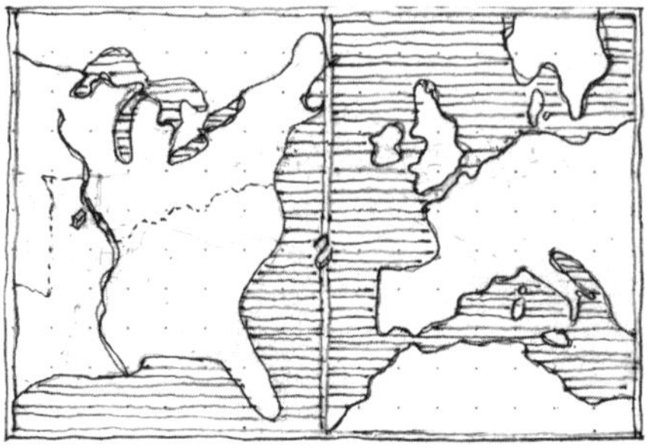

The brick landscape developed at an intersection among natural resources, technology, and labor. Economics, politics, and culture shaped networks of transfer and migration: bricks and other clay products were sent all over the central and eastern United States (U.S.), and workers came from as far away as across the Atlantic.

The brick industry grew rapidly, and by the early twentieth century, there were more than one hundred companies mining clay and manufacturing finished goods—bricks, pipes, and terra cotta—in and around the River des Peres valley.—[10] Refractory clay suitable for building kilns and ovens is a rare material, and its abundance in the Cheltenham syncline made Saint Louis a national source for the infrastructure needed to make clay products. The city was also the largest manufacturer of face brick and ornamental brick in the U.S., and the vertically integrated Hydraulic Press Brick Company became the nation's single largest brick supplier. Founded in the eighteen-sixties, the company refined hydraulic machinery to mold and press brick that was significantly stronger than brick made by hand.—[11] The hydraulic process made it possible to produce an extraordinary range of patterned brick—standard or customized—and in the late nineteenth century, as steel-frame construction led to the design of increasingly elaborate brick façades, demand for ornamental brick escalated. In 1868, the Hydraulic Press Brick Company made five million bricks. By 1904, it

10 G.E. Ladd identifies forty-six manufacturers of clay building materials in "The Clay, Stone, Lime, and Sand Industries of St. Louis and County," *Bulletin of the Geological Survey of Missouri*, no. 3 (St. Louis: 1890). Scott K. Williams identifies fifty-two clay mines operating between the end of the Civil War and the American entry into the First World War in "Underground Coal and Clay Mines in the City of St. Louis" in *UsGenNet*, http://www.usgennet.org/usa/mo/county/stlouis/underground_stl.htm (accessed November 13, 2007); Malcolm Gay offers a tally of more than one hundred plants in "Thieves Cart Off St. Louis Bricks," *The New York Times*, Sept 19, 2010, http://www.nytimes.com/2010/09/20/us/20brick.html (accessed May 4, 2017).

11 Mimi Stiritz, "Hydraulic Brick Company: The Early Years," in *Brick by Brick: Building St. Louis and the Nation* (St. Louis: Saint Louis University Museum of Art, 2004), 26.

operated eleven plants in Saint Louis and fourteen more around the country, and it had the capacity to produce three hundred million bricks per year.—12

12 "Introduction," in *Brick by Brick*, 8, 38.

The bricks that left Saint Louis were made by people who came to the city in search of work. Unemployment and the failed revolution of 1848 brought masons and skilled laborers from Germany. Blacks freed by the Emancipation Proclamation left the Deep South for jobs as clay miners. Poverty and the turmoil of the *Risorgimento* delivered Italian peasants to work in the mines and the brickyards. Distant turmoil provided the work force to exploit local geology.

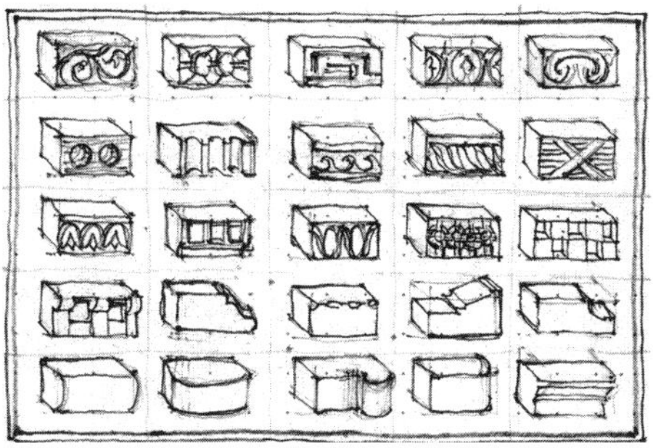

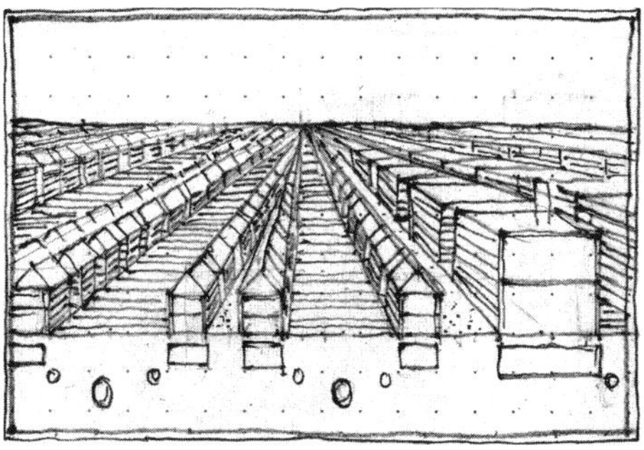

Bricks are standard units, but they're not all the same. Common bricks are used to build the internal structure of a wall; face bricks are used for outside surfaces; glazed bricks have a ceramic coating; refractory bricks can withstand high heat; paving bricks can support traffic. Hydraulic manufacturing produced bricks with a huge range of patterned surfaces, and the variety of the units was expanded by the variation in their assembly. The brick city is homogenous in its material and heterogeneous in its expression.

The brick city is an assembly: it's an accumulation of parts, an accretion of labor, a web of conduits. Imagine its beginning with one trowel in the hand of one mason. How many bricks could that mason lay in a day? How many bricks could his hod-carrier bring him in one load? How many loads were there per palette of bricks? How many masons and how many carriers were at work on any given day? For how many days and weeks and months and years? How many bricks did they lay, three wythes thick, in how many walls?

The aggregation of bricks changed the landscape and its ecology. Brick by brick, incremental growth produced new systems. Density demanded streets and sewers. Paving bricks were laid on the surfaces where people traveled, and clay pipes ran below ground to carry water away from all the buildings and roads.

How many bricks are there in the houses on a street? How many make up a block's worth of pavement? How many pipe sections add up to a mile of sewer? Units become networks: construction that starts at the scale of the body becomes infrastructure at the scale of the city.

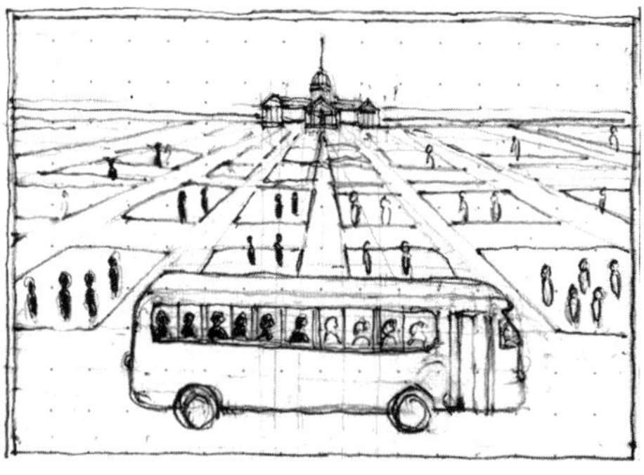

Laws and customs are also units of construction: their aggregation shapes the actions of a community. Tied together by material assemblies, the brick city was pulled apart by social practices. Race defined space.

The Mississippi River formed the border between slave and free territory, and Saint Louis lay on the slave side.—13 On the steps of the Old Courthouse, overlooking the river, slaves were sold at auction for work on plantations further south. In 1847, in the same courthouse, the Saint Louis Circuit Court denied freedom to Dred Scott,

13 In the Missouri Compromise of 1820, Missouri was admitted to the Union as a slave state and Maine as a free state.

who sued for his release from slavery after having lived for years in free territory. Upheld by the Supreme Court, the case helped to propel the nation into the Civil War. When the conflict ended, the Emancipation Proclamation and the Thirteenth and Fourteenth Amendments granted blacks and whites the same status under the law. Then *Plessy v. Ferguson* ruled that the Constitution allowed separate facilities for blacks and whites as long as they were equal. In 1916, a Saint Louis city ordinance forbade blacks and whites to live on the same block. When the law was overturned by the Supreme Court a year later, whites turned to restrictive covenants, private agreements to keep blacks out of their neighborhoods. In *Shelley v. Kraemer*, a 1948 case that originated in Saint Louis, the Supreme Court ruled against those agreements, and in 1954, in *Brown v. Board of Education*, it decided that separate was inherently unequal.

But the *Brown* ruling didn't end division. The city of Saint Louis had been separated from Saint Louis County in 1876. Federal mortgage policies made it easier for whites to buy new houses in the county than old ones in the city; suburban towns zoned for large lots and single-family dwellings made it hard for blacks to follow; and the Federal Highways Act of 1956 built fast roads for commuters. Between 1950 and 1970, nearly 60 percent of the white population of the city of Saint Louis moved out.—[14]

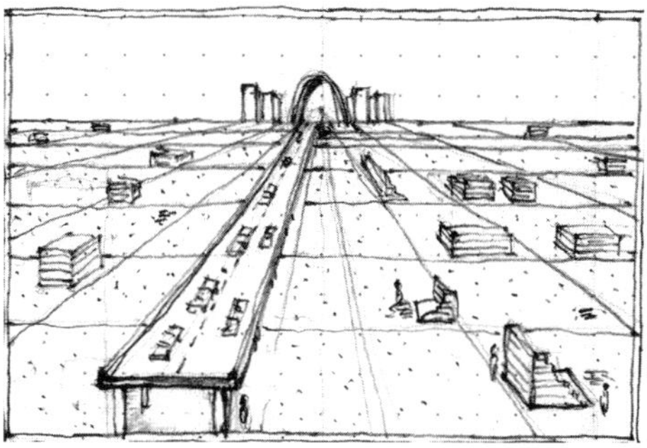

The U.S. Census recorded the population of Saint Louis at 856,796 in 1950. In 2010 it was 319,294.—[15] The exodus has produced a slow catastrophe, a collapse played out over decades.

14 Colin Gordon, *Mapping Decline: St. Louis and the Fate of the American City* (Philadelphia: University of Pennsylvania Press, 2008), 25.

15 Richard L. Forstall (ed.), "U.S. Bureau of the Census: Missouri Population of Counties by Decennial Census: 1900 to 1990," *United States Census Bureau*, https://www.census.gov/population/cencounts/mo190090.txt (accessed May 4, 2017); "2010 Census Interactive Population Search," *United States Census Bureau*, https://www.census.gov/2010census/popmap/ipmtext.php?fl=29 (accessed May 4, 2017).

The disassembly of the brick city, foreshadowed by federal urban renewal projects before and after the Second World War,—[16] gained steam in the nineteen-seventies. Vacant commercial buildings were torn down. The city government began to demolish abandoned houses,—[17] and thieves carried on the work. The market for used bricks started in the suburbs, but common brick from inner wythes didn't weather well in Saint Louis's cold winters. The brick thieves became exporters, sending whole blocks, brick by brick, to growing cities further south. Accelerated by hard financial times after the crisis of 2008, the illegal deconstruction and sale of the city's brick buildings made *The New York Times.*—[18] It's a violent process, the opposite of the meticulous work of bricklaying. Some thieves drive trucks into walls whose mortar has been loosened. Others set buildings on fire, and the fire department is forced to knock them down. After the buildings have been reduced to piles of brick, the thieves sort through the rubble and sell what they collect to dealers who ship them out of town. A new brick economy of disassembly and sale recapitulates what existed a century ago: an impoverished labor force does the hard work of gathering material, growth in other cities creates a marketplace, and transportation networks make exports profitable.

16 Federally funded demolition of large tracts of land began in the nineteen-thirties, when the Works Progress Administration and the Public Works Administration cleared eighty-two acres along the riverfront for the National Jefferson Expansion Memorial; starting in the nineteen-fifties, a number of significant residential neighborhoods were replaced by federal public housing projects. For an analysis of the city's postwar transformation, see Mark Abbot's essay, "The 1947 *Comprehensive City Plan* and Harland Bartholomew's St. Louis" in *St. Louis Plans: The Ideal and the Real St. Louis*, ed. Mark Tranel (St. Louis: Missouri Historical Society Press, 2007), 125–33.

17 Michael R. Allen, "Brick Theft in North St. Louis: A Preservation Crisis," *Preservation Research Office*, http://preservationresearch.com/news-2/brick-theft-in-north-st-louis-a-preservation-crisis/ (accessed May 3, 2017).

18 Gay, "Thieves Cart Off St. Louis Bricks."

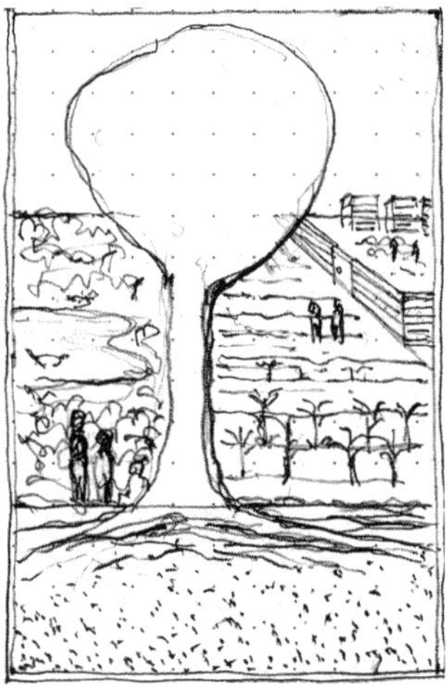

A brick's essential qualities—its size and its place in a system of units—allowed the construction of the city, and they also allow its disassembly. Deconstruction reverses the processes of building. Walls and houses built piece by piece fall as a whole, and the rubble becomes a new kind of mine. Thieves steal what has value, and their actions point toward new possibilities.

The story of the brick city is about the transformation of material and meaning. Catastrophe produced regulation; one resource replaced another as a source of wealth; raw materials became manufactured goods; and units became systems. Now, as robbers, racial politics, and industrial decline pull the city apart, assemblages have become pieces, and land once crowded with buildings stands empty. At present there are 25,000 vacant lots in Saint Louis.—[19] The city owns just under 12,000 parcels, most of them without structures—[20] and all of them mowed periodically at an annual cost of 1.3 million dollars.—[21]

It's time to take stock of the landscape, to make an inventory of what it offers and to ask what could happen next. In the age of the Anthropocene, open ground affords a means to mediate environmental difficulty. Left unpaved, it can hold water. Left unmowed, it can support plant life that sequesters carbon, mitigates heat, and provides habitat. Cultivated, it can feed people. And as the thieves know, bricks in buildings that no longer house anyone can be reused somewhere else. If the mowers stopped across Saint Louis, how many wetlands and forests and farms might be created? If all the bricks in all the buildings and streets where no one lives were harvested, how could they be reassembled to frame a new urban landscape? Could that landscape, managed and inhabited as productive infrastructure,—[22] become the ecological heart of the metropolis sprawling around it? What if we measured the brick city not by what it has lost, but by what it might promise?

19 Mike Faulk, "Study explores reducing city's share of vacant properties," *St. Louis Post-Dispatch*, February 23, 2017, http://www.stltoday.com/news/local/metro/study-explores-reducing-city-s-share-of-vacant-properties/article_0873d63f-6a1b-5689-a73c-4f32d2d6f536.html (accessed May 3, 2017).

20 Walker Moskop, "Fewer properties go unwanted at St. Louis tax auctions," *St. Louis Post-Dispatch*, December 21, 2016, http://www.stltoday.com/news/local/govt-and-politics/fewer-properties-go-unwanted-at-st-louis-tax-auctions/article_143fd702-5df8-575b-9268-85be135caff2.html (accessed May 3, 2017).

21 Maria Altman, "St. Louis takes a new look at old problem: What to do with vacant land and abandoned buildings," *St. Louis Public Radio*, June 15, 2016, http://news.stlpublicradio.org/post/st-louis-takes-new-look-old-problem-what-do-vacant-land-and-abandoned-buildings#stream/0 (accessed May 5, 2017).

22 For a thoughtful discussion of the hybrid ecologies of urban wilds, see Jill Desimini, "Deciphering the Urban Wild: Remnant and Re-emergent," in *Urban Landscape*, Volume 4, ed. Anita Berrizbeitia (Abingdon, Oxon: Routledge, 2015), 163–70.

Nine African American men posed, standing along fence. Thomasville, Georgia, circa 1884–1891.

Picturing Modernity: Race, Labor, and Landscape Production in the Old South

Jana Cephas

The prisoners slept all night with their ankles shackled together. Long chains connected each pair of shackled ankles to those of the prisoners in the adjacent bunks. Before dawn, a guard standing at the end of the barracks woke the prisoners and instructed the men to raise their shackles by the chains. Once they were raised, the guard pulled the chain through, momentarily freeing the prisoners from the chains linking them together, though the shackles remained. After a short breakfast of an unidentifiable stew and a tin of coffee, the guards loaded the prisoners, each dressed in black and white striped uniforms, onto the back of flatbed trucks to which they were chained again. Black prisoners were loaded onto one truck and white prisoners onto another, despite black prisoners outnumbering whites at least three to one. A short while later, the prisoners went to work at the roadside site, using pickaxes and sledgehammers to pummel rocks into aggregate to be used for paving roads. After twelve to fifteen hours of this hard labor, the prisoners were transported back to the barracks and chained in for the rest of the evening. Any prisoner attempting escape was either chased down by hounds or shot on sight. Although sentences to this road labor crew ranged from one to twenty years, the chain gang prisoners commonly considered their plight a death sentence from which there was no escape.—[1]

1 See the following for first-person narratives describing life on the Georgia chain gang: A Georgia Negro Peon, "The New Slavery in the South: An Autobiography," *The Independent*, February 25, 1904; Robert Elliot Burns, "Escape to Prison," in *Georgia: History Written by those Who Lived It* (Savannah, GA: Beehive Foundation, 1995); Robert Elliott Burns, *I Am a Fugitive from a Georgia Chain Gang!* (New York: Grosset & Dunlap, 1932); Sasha Smalls, *Hell in Georgia* (New York: International Labor Defense: 1939); John Louis Spivak, *Georgia Nigger* (New York: Brewer, Warren and Putnam, 1932); and John Louis Spivak, *On the Chain Gang*, International Pamphlets, Vol. 32. (New York: International Pamphlets, 1932).

The practice of chaining together prisoners as they labored on roads, farms, and public infrastructure projects occupied a portion of United States (U.S.) history that most Americans would rather forget. Although chain gangs were prevalent throughout the North and South in the nineteenth century, by the early twentieth century the "gang" system had largely fallen out of favor in the industrialized North; yet it persisted throughout the southern states. Georgia, in particular, was known for having the greatest number of chain gangs, the most brutal gangs, and an impassable system of laws railroading even the most minor offender into the gang system for up to twenty years.

The presence of mostly black, chained prisoners working the Georgia landscape as part of early twentieth century modernization projects produced visualizations of race, space, and modernity alongside the production of roads, bridges, and agricultural goods. While on the surface, the use of chain gang labor was said to rehabilitate the men through outdoor physical labor, gangs tied race to landscape practice by reinforcing associations of black bodies with agricultural and infrastructural production. In the early twentieth century, Georgian politicians and businessmen encouraged the building of roads and other critical infrastructure, believing that they would bring great wealth and prosperity to the struggling South. But while modernization in the North meant challenging imposed economic and social disparities between whites and blacks, modernization in the South relied upon reinforcing those disparities, in part by rooting black labor in landscape practices. In this setting, landscape became more than the place where racial subordination was enacted; rather, landscape provided the very means through which the racialization of labor was constructed—primarily by reinforcing landscape and labor ideals that positioned the black body as best suited for outdoor work.

Chain gang laborers were a recurrent feature of landscape production in the American South. Landscape production refers to the commodity products of a "worked" and constructed landscape, such as the yield of agricultural production and infrastructures like roads, sewers, bridges, ditches, and utility networks. Yet, the working of landscape to extract materials and goods for consumption also yields a new conceptual landscape—a spatial imaginary—that itself becomes a product for consumption. Landscape has been defined as the scope of land visible within a glance, such that landscape production also results in landscape scenography and imagery.—[2] Accordingly, a spatial imaginary of landscape scenes, territories, topographies, and geographies emerged as both the byproduct and progenitor of landscape commodity production and the cultural and visual consumption of landscapes.

2 See: James Corner, "Recovering Landscape as Critical Cultural Practice" in *Recovering Landscape: Essay in Contemporary Landscape Architecture*, ed. James Corner (New York: Princeton Architectural Press, 1999); Denis Cosgrove, "Iconography and Landscape" in *The Iconography of Landscape*, ed. Denis Cosgrove (Cambridge: Cambridge University Press, 1988); Deryck W. Holdsworth, "Landscape and Archives as Texts" in *Understanding Ordinary Landscapes*, eds. Paul Groth and Todd W. Bressi (New Haven: Yale University Press, 1997).

Forced prison labor was less efficient and more expensive than paid labor, which made it economically counterproductive. As such, the persistence of chain gang labor throughout the South reflected two conflicting positions—the anti-modern condition of the chained laborer in the landscape coupled with the drive for a highly modernized southern economy. These contradictory conceptions of labor, landscape, and modernity served to fix the image of the South in three important ways.

First, rather than view modernization as a fundamental change in economic and social relations, Georgian officials presumed a continuation of existing relations. Second, idealizing labor rooted in southern agrarian practices, they privileged outdoor work and linked southern identity to landscape labor. Finally, they believed that effective punishment must be both public and publicized and that hard physical labor was good for the soul. By putting public work on public display, southern officials situated the landscape as the literal grounds for both punishment and reform.—[3] Each of these conceptions of labor, landscape, and modernity further drew upon and reinforced racial practices that worked to define blackness in relation to landscape production.

3 Elsewhere I discuss how public work on public display can also serve a liberatory function, notably in the case of urban farmers in Detroit at the turn of the twenty-first century. See: Jana Cephas, "Agricultural Urbanism in Detroit," in *In the Life of Cities…: Parallel Narratives of the Urban*," ed. Mohsen Mostafavi (Cambridge, MA: Harvard Graduate School of Design, 2012).

Racializing Labor

Before the Civil War, both black slaves and white prisoners built and maintained Georgian roads. Black slaves often constructed the roads in and around the plantations on which they labored. Beyond the private plantations, crews of prisoners constructed the public town and county roads. These prison work crews were almost entirely white because the institution of slavery served as the de facto penal system for blacks, thus leaving few black prisoners in the state penal system.—[4] In either case, the building and maintenance of roads did not exist as a distinct, specialized form of work, though it came to be seen as the work of black slaves and white criminals. During the Civil War, however, Georgia governor Joseph Brown ordered the release of the state's white prisoners to fight for the Confederacy, and when General Sherman's army destroyed the state's single penitentiary at Milledgeville in 1864, the state was left with neither a prison nor a prison population for road building.

4 United States Prison Industries Reorganization Administration, *The Prison Labor Problem in Georgia, A Survey* (Washington, DC: United States Prison Industries Reorganization Administration, 1937), 2.

The association of road building with blacks and criminals meant that law-abiding whites were uninterested in working the roads. Thus after the war, town and county charters stipulated that all able-bodied men must volunteer a specified number of hours per month to build and maintain county roads or otherwise pay a fine.—[5] Those who could afford it opted for the hefty fine, which left largely free blacks and poor whites working on the roads. Poor whites felt that road work was not proper for free white citizens. Because they resented being made to work the roads alongside blacks, poor whites increasingly paid the fine while others flat out refused to work.—[6] This left the counties with fewer laborers than necessary for building roads. As the prison population slowly built up again after the war, towns and counties turned once again to prison labor for roadwork. This practice was sanctioned by the state through laws that regulated such "convict

5 See: State of Georgia, *Acts and Resolutions of the General Assembly of the State of Georgia* (Atlanta, GA: State of Georgia, 1908).

6 Alexander C. Lichtenstein, *Twice the Work of Free Labor: The Political Economy of Convict Labor in the New South* (London; New York: Verso, 1996), 163.

leasing" for work on a range of public and private projects, including farming, road building, and factory work. Most of these prisoners were former slaves who were either unable to procure employment or lacked the means to head northward after the war and were subsequently rounded up by local constabularies on account of "vagrancy."

By the early twentieth century, the work of building and maintaining roads was so thoroughly associated with blackness that it was not considered a viable form of work for white residents, despite the rise in unemployment as agricultural production declined. To create more jobs for whites, the state of Georgia abolished the convict leasing law in 1908—a move backed by national and local labor unions specifically because the new law disallowed the use of convict labor in competition with "skilled mechanical free labor," namely those laborers who were among the unions' constituents. However, roadwork was not perceived to compete with this "free labor"—that is, the forms of work considered appropriate for non-incarcerated white laborers. The act, titled "Employment of Convicts; System of Penology," stipulated that convict labor could exist only outside of industrial labor processes.—[7] As one highway construction professional noted in 1913: "considering the scarcity of labor in our rural sections, this is one employment of convict labor which for many years to come will not in any way be in competition for free labor."—[8] In other words, white refusal to work on roads ensured that (black) convict labor in roadwork would not compete with any jobs that white laborers might desire.

While local and national labor unions fought to abolish convict leasing, in Georgia the Georgia Farmers Union, the International Association of Machinists – Atlanta Lodge No. 1, and the Atlanta Federation of Trades sought to replace the lease system with publicly managed prison road gangs to limit chain gang work to public landscape projects. The Atlanta Federation of Trades announced its position in an editorial in the *Atlanta Journal*:

7 State of Georgia, "Employment of Convicts; System of Penology" in *Acts and Resolutions of the General Assembly of the State of Georgia* (Atlanta, GA: State of Georgia, 1908).

8 Joseph Hyde Pratt, "Convict Labor in Highway Construction," *Annals of the American Academy of Political and Social Science* 46, (March 1913): 78–87.

> We believe the administration of penal laws through the leasing of private parties is fundamentally wrong and is necessarily accompanied by abuses which should be eliminated. We respectfully suggest that the convicts of the state might be put upon the public roads without producing unfair competition with anyone.

Furthermore, Samuel Gompers, then President of the American Federation of Labor, urged the Federation to support both the abolition of convict leasing and the institution of road gangs to build the nation's highways.—[9]

With support from industrial labor unions, prison reformers led the way in justifying the use of convict labor by arguing that work—hard labor in particular—contributed to the personal growth of the prisoner. Charles Richmond Henderson, a University of Chicago sociologist and prison reform professional, assembled a collection of reports made by the delegates attending the International Prison Congress in Budapest in 1905, including his own, which he then later used to advise officials on the benefits of prison labor.—[10] Henderson's report was specifically addressed to Governor C. S. Deneen of Illinois, but as a collection of the Congress's papers, the report reflected professional attitudes regarding convict labor in the U.S. in the early twentieth century.

According to Henderson, the International Prison Congress concluded that prison labor was necessary for both the penal and moral reform of the convict. Outdoor labor, especially road work, was seen as a particularly constructive and "healthful occupation" for physical and moral health.—[11] Henderson noted the difficulty of employing convicts in outdoor labor in the North: "The majority of our convicts [are not] negroes, [and thus not] easily subdued and tractable under white overseers."—[12] Henderson doubted that the primarily white prisoners in the North would be as well suited to outdoor labor as the black prisoners in the South. Not only did the white convict lack the "natural docility" that Henderson attributed to black prisoners, but the white convict would be

9 See: Sydney Wilmot, "Use of Convict Labor for Highway Construction in the North," Proceedings of the Academy of American Political Science in the City of New York 4 no. 2, Good Roads and Convict Labor (January 1914): 6–68.

10 The report is based on reports from commissioners of various European prisons as well as reports generated by studies of prisons across the United States, including in Georgia. See: Charles Richmond Henderson, *Outdoor Labor for Convicts: A Report to the Governor of Illinois* (Chicago: University of Chicago Press, 1907).

11 Pratt, "Convict Labor," 81.

12 Charles Richmond Henderson, *Outdoor Labor for Convicts: A Report to the Governor of Illinois* (Chicago: University of Chicago Press, 1907), xii.

unduly exposed to the humiliation of public labor. While Henderson was an advocate of outdoor labor for black prisoners, he ultimately opposed it for white prisoners.

Henderson suggested that the public display of white working prisoners had detrimental social impacts:

> Nothing can be more degrading to a [white] prisoner, nothing more hardening to public feeling, than the public punishment of convicts. It is to be hoped that our towns and rural communities will never permit themselves to grow accustomed to spectacles which constantly suggest crime.—[13]

13 Ibid.

Henderson's distinction between the easily subdued black convict and the easily humiliated white prisoner exemplified the practice of racializing outdoor prison labor. Still, Henderson was eager to test the healthful benefits of outdoor prison labor on white convicts. Thus he suggested the placement of district workhouses in isolated parts of the rural landscape, which would allow white convicts to work in the outdoors without being seen by others.—[14]

14 Ibid., xiii.

Like Henderson, other prison reformers and labor advocates widely accepted convict labor on prison farms and in public works among. Outdoor labor was perceived as the healthiest and most productive, prompting even trade unions to use this argument as they lobbied both federal and state governments to restrict convict labor in manufacturing while encouraging the use of chain gangs for outdoor labor. John Frey, the editor of *International Molders' Journal*, affirmed in 1913 the trade union position on convict labor:

> For years the trade-unions have endeavored through legislative efforts, to have the convicts employed out of doors as much as possible, where the sunshine and pure air would build up the physical man and give that rugged health which would enable the unfortunates upon their release to have clear heads and strong bodies, instead of being the pallid wrecks which so often leave the prison door, nerveless, dejected and unfit to undertake the task of reclaiming their places as useful members of society or to properly support themselves through their labor.—[15]

15 John P. Frey, "The Trade-Union Attitude Towards Prison Labor," *Annals of the American Academy of Political and Social Science* 46 (March 1913): 135.

With the relegation of black prisoners to roadwork and the prioritization of new road construction in the nineteen-tens as part of the modernization of the new South, road work had progressed from being an expected civic duty to an emblem of racial denigration. Despite the devastating effects of the decline of agriculture on the local economy in the early twentieth century, black prisoners continued to be the preferred labor source for the construction of new roads. Additionally, the abolition of convict leasing in 1908 did little to curb the use of convict labor in roadwork. Advocated by the national Good Roads Movement, which was spearheaded by the U.S. Department of Agriculture's Office of Public Roads, the use of chain gang labor for the construction of southern roads and highways was instead seen as a model of moral progress.—16

16 The Office of Public Roads was located in the Department of Agriculture until it was moved to the Department of Commerce in 1949 then to the Federal Highway Administration Department of Transportation in 1966.

Public Work on Public Display

By the time Charles Richmond Henderson raised his concerns at the International Prison Congress about how the display of white prisoners could raise social anxiety about crime and punishment, there was already a long history in the U.S. of using public display as a punishment geared to shame and embarrass the prisoner, while also reinforcing social inequity and racial difference. As early as the eighteenth century, white criminals unable to pay a fine could be displayed in the stocks or in a public cage, where they would be jeered at or spat upon by townspeople.—17 By the twentieth century, chain gangs became the modern form of public humiliation. While Henderson cautioned against the public display of the white convict, he and others considered the visibility of the black convict as necessary to the institution of punishment. The presentation of the black convict worker in the public eye as a member of the road gang working on public projects suggested a double meaning of "public works." The road gang was both limited to the work of the "public"—that

17 David J. Rothman, "Perfecting the Prison: United States, 1789–1865," in *The Oxford History of the Prison: The Practice of Punishment in Western Society* (New York: Oxford University Press, 1995), 122.

is, the state—while at the same time the work of the gangs was necessarily made public and put on display.

The public display of black working bodies served several purposes. The first was an affirmation of the belief that black workers were immune to the humiliation normally associated with chain gang work. One federal road engineer for the Office of Public Roads stated:

> Personally, I favor the employment of convicts [only] in the Southern States in the building of public roads as in this section of the country the convicts are largely made up of negroes, who are benefited by outdoor manual labor." The assistant director of the Office of Public Works further affirmed this position by stating: "The negro is accustomed to outdoor occupations ... [is] experienced in manual labor ... [and] does not possess the same aversion to working in public ... as is characteristic of the white race.—18

18 Alex Lichtenstein, "Good Roads and Chain Gangs in the Progressive South: 'The Negro Convict Is a Slave,'" *The Journal of Southern History* 59, no. 1 (February 1993): 106.

Both of these highway construction professionals exhibited precisely the same attitudes demonstrated by Henderson in his report from the International Prison Congress. The presumption that black laborers lacked the shame associated with public work and therefore could not feel humiliation was widespread in the road construction industry.

Second, the display of chained laborers toiling in the landscape served as a reminder to black southerners of the two options available to them: either the farm or the "gang." As the South continued to rely on its agricultural base, even as that base was declining, blacks found themselves confined to a pool of labor that was both highly competitive and poorly compensated. Iron shackles and striped shirts and pants made the prisoners nearly impossible to miss in the landscape, while also casting the group of individual prisoners as a mass. Most new roads constructed in Georgia during this period—and thus worked by chain gang crews—were routed through predominately black areas. The new roads cut across the old plantation districts where most blacks were concentrated as sharecroppers and tenant farmers. Thus the dual option of "the farm or the gang" was visibly present in the working lives and landscapes of southern black communities—the livelihood of black laborers was inextricably tied to the landscape. By 1915, 629 white convicts and 6,222 black convicts worked on the roads in Georgia, a racial disproportion that further reified roadwork as black work.—[19]

19 United States Prison Industries Reorganization Administration.

Finally, the display of chain gang laborers in the landscape served as a not-so-veiled threat against escape from the rural south. A full-page spread in the *New Orleans States* in 1923 exemplified white anxieties surrounding the growing migration of black workers from the rural south. The spread displayed two images: one showed a black man walking, suitcase in hand, away from a farm where his wife and child called after him from the farmhouse porch. The other image showed presumably the same black man shivering in front of a store window in a city, contemplating the high prices of fuel, food, and clothing as displayed in the shop window signs. The caption under the first image read, "Should you leave your happy, sunshiny home in the South…" and continued under the second image, "…to face the hard comforts and high cost of living in the north?" The images were followed by a full page "argument" for the South:

> Colored people of the South are facing the most serious crisis in the history of their race. Many of them are leaving their homes and the homes of their forefathers, breaking family ties and association[s] with kin and lifelong friends to settle among unfriendly people…. All that Northerners want out of you is your labor and they do not care what becomes of you outside of that. There is no age-old sentiment in the breasts of the white people of the North towards you, such as held by the Southern white people towards the Negro…. Your advancement is much quicker and easier in the South than it would be in the North.—[20]

20 "Look at This Picture—A Scheme of the South to Keep You in Bondage," *Chicago Defender* (Chicago, IL), August 18, 1923.

This message, echoed in other southern newspapers, urged southerners to dismiss the attractions of an industrial, and thus not land-based, economy and stem the flow of black agricultural workers northward. The spread in the

New Orleans States does not mention the chain gang, but for most black men like the one depicted in the images, the gang loomed not far behind sharecropping. Increasingly, black understanding of true emancipation focused not just on escape from the South, but escape from land-based work.

From the end of the Civil War until the turn of the twentieth century, blacks made up at least 90 percent of the prison population in Georgia. But this number steadily declined to about 75 percent in the nineteen-thirties as more white prisoners joined the ranks.—[21] Despite the increasingly racialized work of the chain gangs and its public display, the number of white laborers on the gang grew. Prisons across the South were segregated by race, as were the housing units at the road gang campsites and the transportation to and from the worksites. Yet the chain gang worksites in Georgia were racially integrated: white and black prisoners worked side by side on the road, although they belonged to racially segregated work crews. In a state so committed to racial segregation in all aspects of life, the integration of the chain gang was not incidental.

21 United States Prison Industries Reorganization Administration.

The integration of the chain gang in the nineteen-thirties reveals the relationship between race, labor, landscape, and the southern penal system. Like the antebellum slave, the convict laborer working on the chain gang was forced into a condition of public servitude from which he had little, if any, recourse. While it is tempting to note white chain gang convicts as an aberration in a system of racialized oppression, it may be more accurate to understand the racialization of chain gang labor as extending to white prisoners such that their mere presence on the (black) chain gang served to degrade their white status in society.

The public association of white prisoners with both black bodies and black work served to further reinforce the racialization of chain gang labor. On the one hand, white status prevented the gang guards and wardens from torturing white prisoners to the same degree as black prisoners. White prisoners were well aware of their relative privilege compared to blacks on the chain gang; as one white prisoner said: "We used to hear their cries and pleas, and we'd say among ourselves, 'Our Lord Jesus had an easy time compared to these poor n——rs.'"—[22] However, similar to the poor whites who resented the road "labor tax" and felt a loss of status by working alongside blacks on the roads, white prisoners on the chain gang were downgraded from full white citizenship. The racialized social politics of the South had constructed the publicly laboring body to be perceived as an actual black body or effectively construed as one. By placing white prisoners within a black milieu, officials threatened white prisoners with the loss, albeit temporarily and incompletely, of the full benefits of white privilege.

22 Myra Page, "Men in Chains," *The Nation* (November 13, 1935): 562.

The appearance of white convicts, including white-collar criminals, on the gangs in the nineteen-thirties reinforced rather than diminished the racialization of labor and landscape in the South. Between 1930 and 1939, the *Atlanta Journal* and the *Atlanta Constitution* ran numerous stories on white criminals sentenced to the chain gang. Many of the stories were linked to violations of the Prohibition laws and advocated outdoor labor for the moral reform of the drunkard. Additionally, corrupt politicians and businessmen were increasingly sentenced to hard labor on the gang. Chain gangs were so prevalent in Georgia that one small town's local claim to fame was that "not a single native of Lincoln county, white or colored, is serving time on the county chain-gang."—[23]

23 "No Citizen of Lincoln in Chain Gang, is Claim," *Atlanta Constitution* (Atlanta, GA), September 17, 1934.

The exposé of the laboring body forcibly working on the chain gang was key to increasing public opposition to chain gang labor. Organized labor unions, many of which were instrumental in advocating for chain gang labor in nonindustrial settings, had by now begun to publicize the demeaning effects of the public display of chain gang work. In 1933, Angelo Herndon, a black labor activist and known communist, was sentenced to eighteen to twenty years of hard labor on the chain gang after he organized an interracial labor march in Georgia. Herndon's case was not unique, but was the most well known in a series of cases where labor organizers were sentenced to the gang for these activities.—[24] Consequently, the labor unions' opposition to the gangs grew and contributed crucially to awareness of the brutality of chain gang labor.

24 Spivak, *On the Chain Gang* (see note 1).

Popular objections to the chain gang gained momentum as the body, exploited and brutalized, was documented in print images. Published in 1932, John Spivak's exposé of the Georgia chain gang was the first major publication on the subject to gain widespread attention. Unlike earlier books and articles, Spivak illustrated his text with numerous photographs of black prisoners being whipped, beaten, and tied to posts. While Spivak's images were likely staged and not real life documentary photographs as he suggested, they nevertheless rallied a public that was unaccustomed to such unimaginable punishments and subsequently convinced by these photographic images of the atrocities of the Georgia penal system.—[25]

25 Spivak, *Georgia Nigger* (see note 1).

Yet outrage over chain gangs stemmed largely from public knowledge of the treatment of whites on the gang through exposés in major newspapers, books, and films. Quickly following Spivak's book, Robert Elliott Burns' book *I Am a Fugitive from a Georgia Chain Gang!*—published in 1932 and adapted into a film in the same year—tapped into simmering discomfort with the chain gang system. Unlike Spivak's book, which focused on the conditions of black convicts, Burns' book and movie focused on himself—a young white war veteran who, facing financial hard times in 1922, had been sentenced to eight to ten years on the chain gang for stealing a little over five dollars. After a short time on the gang, Burns escaped and made his way to Chicago where he became a wealthy and successful magazine editor and publisher. Betrayed to authorities in Georgia by his estranged wife, Burns voluntarily returned to the chain gang in 1929 under the agreement that after ninety days of hard labor his sentence would be commuted. However, the Georgia prison authorities refused to let Burns off the gang when his time was served. Burns escaped a second time about a year later and lived as a fugitive for the next fifteen years, until the governor of Georgia pardoned him in 1945.—[26]

26 Burns, *I Am a Fugitive from a Georgia Chain Gang!* (see note 1).

Burns's imagery of men, black and white, smashing rocks in the Georgia heat, chained together while sleeping, and dying of thirst and exhaustion, captivated a public equally horrified at the dishonesty of the Georgia prison officials as it was at the tribulations of hard labor. While Burns's book and the film adaptation featured both black and white prisoners on the gang, it was his own story of his hard labor as a white man that prompted public inquiry into the conditions of the Georgia chain gang. Only after Burns's book and film did the challenge to chain gang labor enter a broad public debate beyond the black newspapers that had been reporting on chain gang atrocities for decades. Accordingly, his subsequent book documenting the lives and miraculous escapes of black men working on the Georgia chain gangs received little critical attention. Other similar black narratives written both before and after Burns's memoir received almost no attention outside of the black press.

In 1939, the Georgia Legislature abolished the use of chain gangs in the state of Georgia. The law declared county-run work camps illegal and permitted only state-run work camps overseen by the newly formed Prison Commission and the State Highway Board. Prisoners were still expected to do hard labor, but a range of measures were instituted to curb abuses and ensure the health and well being of the prisoners. Additionally, the use of shackles and stripes was declared illegal and the law called for the removal of the phrase "chain gang" from all state and county documents, to be replaced with the more palatable "convict camps." The legal abolition of the gangs, however, did not prevent some counties from continuing to send prisoners out to work the roads in stripes and shackles. Chain gangs persisted in Georgia for several more decades. They were not eradicated from the landscape for good until the county unit system of voting was abolished in 1962, thus overturning the disproportionate allocation of political power to rural areas.

With the official dismantling of the chain gang system in 1939 also came the institution of Georgia's first state-run prison system. Based on recommendations from the federal government via the United States Prison Industries Reorganization Association (USPIRA), Georgia instituted a state prison system complete with a modern prison building within which convicts were expected to work in manufacturing jobs and train in the industrial trades. Journalists, prison reformers, and government officials hailed the new prison at Tattnall as a state-of-the-art facility. The prison complex included a cotton mill, canning plant, shoe factory, printing plant, tobacco processing plant, clothing factory, hosiery mill, metal working plant, concrete pipe culvert plant, and dehydrating plant.—[27] The $1.5 million building was designed to house the majority of Georgia's prisoners with only a select few sent to work at the convict road camps. The USPIRA mandate restructured the new road camps as a privilege for prisoners with good behavior and nearing parole.

The federally mandated replacement of Georgia's penal system with a modern system disrupted the racial conflation of labor and landscape by prioritizing industrialized modes of production and moving labor indoors. The USPIRA continued to advocate for prison labor, but suggested shifting the majority of prisoners from roadwork to manufacturing, which was deemed more "equitable."—[28] Roadwork and agricultural work, however, would remain the chief occupation for those few prisoners still engaged in outdoor labor.—[29]

27 United States Prison Industries Reorganization Administration, 53–55.

28 United States Prison Industries Reorganization Administration.

29 Walter Wilson, "The Twilight of the Chain Gang," *The Nation* (January 13, 1940): 45.

In his 1893 essay, "The Reason Why the Colored American is Not in the World's Columbian Exposition," Frederick Douglass attributed the exclusion of black participation from the 1893 Chicago World's Fair to the growing number of blacks on convict leasing work crews. He argued that blacks were unfairly given long prison sentences for petty crimes in order to replace the free labor lost with the abolition of slavery. Thus, the means and motivations of chain gang labor were already clearly recognized at the time as a continuation of the social and economic practices that had supported the South's slave economy.—30

30 Frederick Douglass, "Introduction," in *The Reason Why the Colored American is Not in the World's Columbian Exposition*, ed. Ida B. Wells (Chicago, IL: Privately published, 1893).

Just over a decade later, in his essay "Following the Color Line," Roy Stannard Baker wrote,

> Many Southerners look back wistfully to the faithful, simple, ignorant, obedient, cheerful, old plantation Negro and deplore his disappearance. They want the New South, but the old Negro. That Negro is disappearing forever along with the old feudalism and the old-time exclusively agricultural life.—31

31 Roy Stannard Baker, "Following the Color Line," in *Georgia: History Written by those Who Lived It* (Savannah, GA: Beehive Foundation, 1995), 273.

Baker aptly described the southern desire for the benefits of modern industry and its technological comforts while still retaining antebellum social relations, which were thoroughly rooted in an almost feudal relationship to the land. The institution of convict labor and the use of chain gangs to build southern roads demonstrated that the realization of a *new* new South with the "old negro" was perhaps impossible to achieve.

Georgia did, however, construct several hundred miles of roads during the chain gang era, linking thousands of rural residents to nearby towns and cities, and bringing black and white residents out of rural isolation. When the Travis County commissioner John E. Shelton asserted, "You can't get a man to get out and do the work that these prisoners on the chain gang do," one indeed wonders whether the South would have gotten their modern roads without chain gang labor.—[32] Not only did Georgia have more miles of paved roads than any other southern state, but counties with the largest chain gang forces in Georgia were consistently the counties with the most miles of new and repaired roads.—[33] Thus, while building a new South with the "old Negro" and a new modern landscape with the old landscape imaginary did result in some measure of modernization of the South's rural landscape, it occurred without the parallel modernization of its social relations.

32 Page, "Men in Chains," 561.

33 Lichtenstein, "Progressive South," 102.

Sitting atop the open waters of the Guanabara Bay, a new plaza's scrim of water reflects the sky, prompting the sensation of floa above the sea. The space at once activates Afro-Brazilian traditions associated with the sea, while offering a microclimate refres ing to urban dwellers in the Brazilian heat, layering ritual with the everyday.

Transatlantic Memory: Material and Immaterial Design at the Valongo Wharf, Rio de Janeiro, Brazil

Sara Zewde

The 2009 announcement of Rio de Janeiro as the host of the 2016 Summer Olympics created an indelible image in Brazilian popular consciousness. The moment marks a period of exceptional optimism and hope for economic growth in the country. Tens of thousands of people—drenched in blue, green, and yellow—gathered at Copacabana Beach and erupted into jubilation as a weeping President Lula declared, "Brazil's moment has arrived!"—[1] Rio would be the first South American city to ever host the Olympics, and the first city in the world to host both the World Cup and the Olympics in the same two-year period.

1 Juliet Macur, "Rio Wins 2016 Olympics in a First for South America," *The New York Times*, October 2, 2009, http://www.nytimes.com/2009/10/03/sports/03olympics.html (accessed April 16, 2017).

The city had won its bid for the Olympics in part because of the proposal to locate facilities in the existing urban core, identifying the downtown Port Zone as one such area that could leverage the reinvestment. With the eyes of the world on Rio, the city began to make major upgrades to its infrastructure, preparing for the growth in tourism and redevelopment. In the process, construction crews working downtown uncovered the vestiges of a structure six feet below Barão de Tefé Street. A team of archeologists from the Brazilian National Museum quickly confirmed that these were in fact the ruins of the Valongo Wharf—arguably the Transatlantic Slave Trade's busiest port—incredibly well preserved and intact.—[2] An estimated 22 percent of all Africans brought to the Americas via the Transatlantic Slave Trade passed through Rio de

2 Somine Candida, "Tania Andrade Lima, a arqueóloga que desenterrou a história do Cais do Valongo," *O Globo*, September 21, 2014, https://oglobo.globo.com/rio/tania-andrade-lima-arqueologa-que-desenterrou-historia-do-cais-do-valongo-14002079 (accessed May 1, 2017).

Janeiro.—[3] The Valongo Wharf was the arrival point for millions of them.

3 Simon Romero, "Rio's Race to Future Intersects Slave Past," *The New York Times*, March 8, 2014, https://www.nytimes.com/2014/03/09/world/americas/rios-race-to-future-intersects-slave-past.html?_r=0 (accessed April 13, 2017).

At the time, I was a resident of Rio de Janeiro and read about the discovery in the local newspapers. Local activists pressured the city to mark the significance of the site in some way. In response, Mayor Eduardo Paes announced the city would "design something here to represent the Black experience in Brazil." Over the course of the next six years, I would work with the Mayor's Office of Rio de Janeiro and the instigating community activists to develop a site design for the Valongo Wharf region, as well as a methodological framework through which to do it.

The industry of buying and selling Africans would be the central, centrifugal force of the formation of the city of Rio de Janeiro.

The Tradition of the Typology: Memorial as Object

In his 1910 essay entitled "Architecture," architect Adolf Loos identified the monument and the tomb as the only "true moments of architecture."—[4] He posits that monuments stand outside the time and functions of everyday life, and thus form an "ascendant mode as paradigm for the architect."—[5] Memorials are often fashioned around the notion of an isolated, discrete event—a war, a hero, a triumph, or tragedy—existing outside of the everyday.

4 Jeremy Till, "In Time," *Architecture Depends* (Cambridge, MA: MIT Press, 2009), 97.

5 Ibid.

Rooted in classical notions of monumentality, the form of the memorial is intended to overwhelm the human body and trigger a spatial experience outside of the quotidian. Despite the formal trends in architecture over time, the memorial has persisted in reinforcing spatial traditions of distance, stillness, and silence.—[6] The typology of the memorial typifies the notion of architecture as an isolated object—a concept deeply entrenched in Western design traditions.

6 Erika Doss, *Memorial Mania: Public Feeling in America* (Chicago: University of Chicago Press, 2010).

As I reviewed precedents of memorials dealing with the Transatlantic Slave Trade—of which there are relatively few—I found that they also tended to co-opt the formal languages of monumentality, leaving unresolved the fact that slavery was not an event. Rather, it was 400 years of the way the world operated—its effects still present today. This suggested a methodological and formal break from the grand narrative of the memorial as isolated object, *but towards what?*

The Immateriality of Valongo

In maps dating back to the sixteenth century, the Valongo beach is noted as a docking area in the Rio de Janeiro harbor. In 1774, a modest wooden deck was constructed, as the wharf shifted to operate exclusively as a disembarkation point for enslaved Africans. Speculating that slavery might become more lucrative, investors financed further upgrading of the Valongo Wharf to a stone jetty in 1811. This proved to be a sound investment, because the first twenty years of the upgrade saw over one million Africans walk across those stones.—[7]

7 IPHAN, "Proposal for the Nomination of the Valongo Wharf Archeological Site as World Heritage," UNESCO Dossier, 2016, http://portal.iphan.gov.br/uploads/ckfinder/arquivos/Valongo3_VersaoFinal_WEB2.pdf (accessed May 1, 2017).

In 1843, the anticipated visit from Neapolitan Princess Tereza Cristina, wife of Portuguese Emperor Don Pedro II,—[8] triggered a renovation of the wharf. A new layer of paving was laid atop the original stones and an obelisk was erected at the site in her honor. Following the abolition of slavery in 1888, a series of landfill operations modified the coastline, such that the stone jetty was buried below

8 Ibid.

the city fabric and wholly removed from view, creating a distance between the site and the sea of about a quarter of a mile. Each era of urbanization deposited another layer of paving over the top of the stones, such that the excavation of Valongo revealed a multilayered cross-section indexing the city's history of redevelopment.

Over the one hundred plus years between the burial of the wharf and its rediscovery, African cultural memory supported a vibrant consciousness about the wharf that was immaterial. With the wharf hidden from view, cultural production registered material memory of Valongo. Storytelling—a practice emanating from the African oral tradition of griots—kept Valongo's tales alive, as well as the idea that it may still exist below the earth. The priests and priestesses of Candomble, an Afro-Brazilian religion, consistently witnessed spirits in their visions of the neighborhood,—[9] whose streets formed the beating heart of Afro-Brazilian musical and religious rituals such as samba, capoeira, afoxé, and jongo. The trance-like rhythms would carve the psychological space of remembering, the sounds of which are laced with lyrics that give life to the memory of Valongo.

9 Sandra de Sá Carneiro and Márcia Leitão Pinheiro, "Cais do Valongo: patrimonialização de locais, objetos e herança africana," Religião & Sociedade 35, no. 2, (2015): 384–401.

> There in the bosom of Africa, he lived!
> In the lush jungle, the end of his monarchy.
> The warrior died
> On the slave ship!
> … He landed there at the Valongo Wharf,
> In Rio de Janeiro,
> With his tribes coming!—[10]

10 https://www.letras.com/sambas/958872/ (accessed April 29, 2017), translation by the author.

The Salgueiro Samba School chanted these lines in the 1976 carnival. Without the material preservation of the wharf, cultural spatial practices would form the vessel for the memory that archeology and preservation had deemed unworthy. Thus, designing in this context would start with the recognition of cultural production as a registration of spatial vernacular. While memorials are often sought to be a repository of memory, in this case, memory was already actively being retained in the everyday, cultural practices

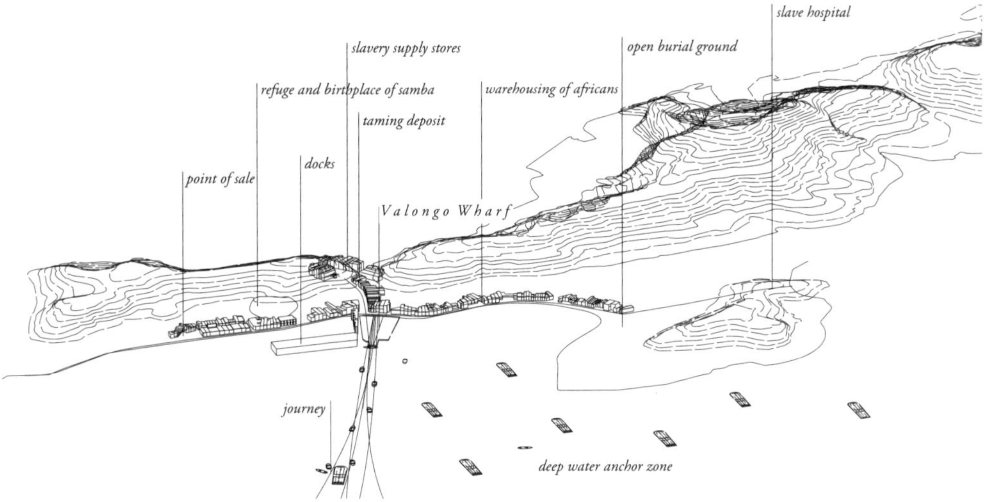

Africans arriving at the Valongo Wharf would have seen infrastructures necessary to ship, store, buy, sell, and trade millions of people.

of Afro-descendants. Thus, it became clear that the design should not exist outside of these traditions of active memory, but serve to highlight and bolster them.

The Material Culture of a Slave Economy

Journalist Brentin Mock reminds us that Africans were the "central, centrifugal force of commerce"; they formed the city, in both its physical construction and the creation of the wealth that built the cities, through their free labor.—11 The architecture of the Port Zone reveals the scale of infrastructures necessary to ship, store, buy, sell, and trade millions of people. Arriving in the Guanabara Bay of Rio de Janeiro, Africans disembarked at the Valongo Wharf. If dead upon arrival, they were dumped nearby in a sprawling open burial ground, the Cemiterio dos Pretos Novos.—12 If ill upon arrival, they were taken to the nearby slave hospital, Santa Casa da Misericórdia, to be treated before their sale. If showing no ostensible signs of physical weakness, they were marched down Camerino Street a quarter of a mile to a plaza called the Largo do Deposito, or the Deposit. Here, they were tamed

11 Brentin Mock, "How Slavery Built Charleston," *City Lab*, July 20, 2015, https://www.citylab.com/design/2015/07/how-slavery-built-charleston/399005/ (accessed April 16, 2017).

12 Júlio César Medeiros da Silva Pereira, *À Flor da Terra: O Cemitério dos Pretos Novos no Rio de Janeiro* (Rio de Janeiro: Garamond, 2007).

and fattened over a two- to three-week period, in order to optimize the price point of the sale. Until their purchase, Africans were stored in warehouses lining the streets of the neighborhood. The end of the taming period culminated in slave auctions held in the array of small streets, marginal spaces, and plazas peppered through the Port Zone. Overlooking these plazas were small retail shops that formed street fronts for whip and chain suppliers.

Much of the infrastructure constructed to support the slave economy still exists in the city. The former slave hospital, the Santa Casa da Misericórdia, is in a new location a mile and a half away and its original hospital building complex remains government-owned property in the same location.—[13] Blocks of residential infill and small shops were constructed atop the open burial ground in the early twentieth century, with no marker of what lies below. When Merced Guimaraes, a local resident, embarked on a home remodeling project in 1993, she found the remains of Africans—mainly teenage boys—below her floorboards.—[14] With no institutional support, she turned her living room into a makeshift museum. The Largo do Deposito plaza remains a plaza, renamed Praça dos Estivadores, or "Plaza of the Workers"—effectively erasing the history of the space as a place of torture. The warehouses once storing humans still line Camerino and Sacadura Cabral streets, and the retail storefronts that once sold whips and chains now are hardware stores, banks, and mechanic shops. The small streets, spaces, and plazas also remain material relics ossified in the city, with little to no telling of their history—their memory largely captured in the neighborhood's storytelling.

It became clear, then, that the architectural tradition of the memorial—singular and discrete—would not speak to the interwoven nature of the history of Valongo with the city around it. The design of a memorial at Valongo would need to expand, explode, and integrate with the city, much like its material culture already had.

13 Flavia Boghossian Kiperman, "Social Housing in Preserved Buildings: The Case of the Valongo Architectural Complex," http://www.paisagenshibridas.com.br/Flavia%20Boghossian%20Valongo%20CICOP%2006W.pdf (accessed April 17, 2017).

14 Merced Guimaraes, in discussion with the author, December 2011.

Time forms a critical fourth dimension in materialist discourses, offering the theoretical grounding of space *in* time.—[15] Materialist scholars who discuss time-space relations invest in defining a matrix of time specific to the individual, the culture, or the society.—[16] In many West African-descendant philosophies, for instance, time is understood to be circular; the future is the future, but composed of pieces of the immediate present and the past.—[17]

15 Henri Lefebvre, *Dialectical Materialism*, trans. John Sturrock (Minneapolis: University of Minnesota Press, 2009).

16 Henri Lefebvre, *Rhythmanalysis: Space, Time, and Everyday Life*, trans. Stuart Elden and Gerald Moore (Norfolk, UK: Continuum, 2004), 51–67.

17 John S. Mbiti, *African Religions and Philosophy* (London: Heinemann, 1990).

Enslaved Africans actively brought seeds aboard ships to reconstruct culinary, spiritual, and cultural traditions where they landed.

Africans in Brazil looked to the landscape to orient their consciousness about time, space, and memory, recognizing that the trading of humans was a large-scale biotic exchange between two continents taking place over four centuries. A geomorphological framing of the Transatlantic Slave Trade further reveals that the Valongo Port touched what is now the southwestern coast of Africa in the early Cretaceous period, about 300 Million years ago. To this day, these lands share similar red, latosollic soil profiles and floristic characteristics.—[18]

18 Robert A. Voeks, *Sacred Leaves of Candomble: African Magic, Medicine, and Religion in Brazil* (Austin: University of Texas Press, 1997).

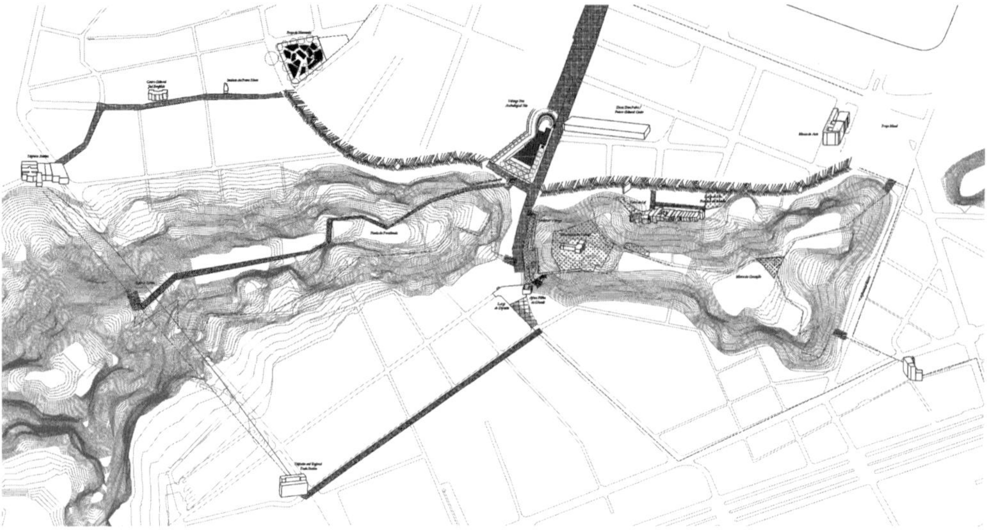

The Circuit of African Heritage repositions the tradition of the memorial as a constellation of designs, interwoven in the everyday space of the city.

Enslaved Africans actively brought plants aboard ships seeking to reconstruct plant-based culinary, spiritual, and cultural traditions wherever they might land. Many of these species hybridized, adapted, and flourished in the Brazilian landscape, including species such as *Sansevieria trifasciata* and *Padanus utili*.—[19] Additionally, plants that evolved flotation devices made the same journey from Africa to Brazil prior to the Transatlantic Slave Trade, and established themselves. According to local legend, when the Africans arrived at the Valongo Port and saw the red latosollic clay soils and the familiar coastal plant species—such as *Ipomoea pres capre* and *Lagenaria siceraria*—they knew their gods were present.—[20]

Over the 150 million years of separation, the two continents had retained their floristic similarities at the genus level, but evolved in distinct ways at the species level. Some species native to Brazil offered similar branching and leaf structures as plants of the same genus remembered from home and were subsumed into Afro-Brazilian rituals, such as Africa's *Bauhinia thonningii* to Brazil's *Bauhinia ovata*.—[21] Another genus native to both continents is the Ficus. Afro-Brazilians believe that the base of this tree is

19 Ibid.

20 Ibid.

21 Judith A. Carney and Robert A. Voeks, "Landscape Legacies of the African Diaspora in Brazil," *Progress in Human Geography* 27, no. 1 (2003): 68–81.

where the ancestors gather and they mark this tradition through a wrapping of white fabric or white walls around the base of the tree.—[22] Much like the Ficus, many of the most revered plants in Afro-Brazilian philosophy are those that grow in the toughest conditions, because they are said to have the most spirit. Afro-Brazilian memory, much like its flora, is not static. Rather, it is active and adaptive—flourishing despite the conditions. The story of the flora of Afro-Brazil is central to the time-space consciousness of the people, and in this way, offered rich ground for design.

22 Ibid.

A bench designed to recall the white wrapping of plants in Afro-Brazilian tradition re-emerges as a motif across the constellation. The bench holds Afro-Brazilian shade trees and vegetation as well as inscriptions about the history of the land.

Expanding the Tradition of the Memorial

As design lead consultant, I worked with the city of Rio de Janeiro's in-house architects to move the design project away from the model of a discrete memorial. Instead, the design for the Circuit of African Heritage repositions the tradition of the memorial as a constellation of designs, inter-woven in the everyday space of the city. By referencing the mayor's redevelopment plan for the Olympics, we identified a constellation of sites the design might act upon, resulting in eight designs that the city could include in their redevelopment plan. Each of the eight sites would incorporate Afro-Brazilian vegetal species and support the spatial traditions associated with them, forming a cohesive, yet disparate, spatial experience to the expanded memorial.—23

23 Images and descriptions of some of these sites accompany this text.

A proposal for the planting of a Baobab tree (*Adansonia spp.*). Afro-Brazilian legend has it that the tree's roots grow underneath the Atlantic Ocean to touch the roots of the Baobobs of Africa.

When my involvement in the project began in 2011, community members sought to leverage the 2014 World Cup and the 2016 Olympics. By the start of the Olympics, however, negligible amounts of the proposal had actually been installed. Two weeks before the Olympic games began, the city planted a few of the proposed plant species, yet no signage accompanies the installation. Hence, the struggle to construct a design supportive of the living history and culture of the Valongo continues. The city of Rio de Janeiro has transitioned to a new mayoral administration, and it remains unclear whether the memorial development at the Valongo Wharf will continue to invest in the proposal's realization. In July 2017, the Valongo Wharf was named a UNESCO World Heritage Site, a designation that could prompt further investment in memorial efforts.

When the Valongo Wharf was discovered below Barão de Tefé Street in 2011, thousands of artifacts associated with African religious rituals—such as beads, stones, and amulets—were found scattered among the stones. Most striking to me were the hundreds of small rings made of West African Raffia palm leaves (Raphia) preserved between the layers of paving.—[24] These rings would have adorned the small, delicate fingers of the teenage boys who landed at Valongo Wharf.—[25] It is clear that the stone jetty of the Valongo Wharf is one of the most significant collections of African material culture in the Americas. Yet, the Transatlantic Slave Trade represents a history so overwhelming in its scale, impact, and inhumanity that its tangible, material presence is often overlooked.

24 Somine Candida, "Tania Andrade Lima."

25 Ibid.

Because of the slave trade's role in the formation of cities across the Americas, its material evidence persists in the urban core. Thus, similar tensions have and will play out on the sacred grounds of cities, making clear that the typology of the memorial requires new formal languages. The interpretation of material and immaterial cultures as design methodology moves us beyond the limits of architecture's cultural assumptions and challenges us to speak directly to the time-space consciousness of memory itself, specific to people and place.

The proposed design of Sacadura Cabral Street, the historic coastline. This street not only touched the sea 100 years ago, but also touched southwest Africa 100 million years ago. The proposed paving pattern, lighting, and Ficus planting speak to the ripping apart and stitching together of the continents.

Documentation of ruderal plants on the site of former Görlitzer Bahnhof, 1965.

Revisiting Görlitzer Park: Material Practices and the Postmodern Landscape

Cornelia Escher and Kim Förster

Görlitzer Park, located in Berlin's formerly countercultural and now trendy and highly gentrified district of Friedrichshain-Kreuzberg, recently entered public awareness through news features on illegal street dealing and drug trafficking. However, the Görli—as the park is affectionately called by its users, who often leave it trashed but love it for its Taiga feel—has been a highly contested urban space, claimed by different actors and institutions, since a participatory planning process on the site of former railway station Görlitzer Bahnhof led to a park design competition in 1984. The winning design by Freie Planungsgruppe Berlin offered postmodern symbolism, drawing inspiration from the strategies of the Internationale Bauausstellung Berlin 84/87 (International Building Exhibition, or IBA for short). By conserving some historical structures and offering invented meaning and traditions, the picturesque scheme promised to mediate between the myriad factions with claims on the park. As a singular scheme, the design was said to unify the conflicting desires of resident groups, the local administration, and experts involved in planning.—1

By analyzing the sociopolitical conditions and the urban context from which the park emerged, the process of planning and design, and the materialization and appropriations of physical space, we offer an alternative reading. We argue that apart from all of the postmodern symbolism

1 An early version of this essay we presented in the context of the conference "Den Protest regieren. Staatliches Handeln vor der Herausforderung von 'neuen sozialen Bewegungen' und linken Organisationen in den 1970er und 1980er Jahren" organized at the Forschungsstelle für Zeitgeschichte, Hamburg, Germany, in November 2014. We would like to thank Jane Hutton for the kind invitation to participate in this publication and her thoughtful editorial guidance. Special thanks go to our colleagues Anne Kockelkorn, Gregor Harbusch and Stephan Becker for their critical, yet always constructive feedback.

and sensibilities, the history of Görlitzer Park is closely linked to its material culture and urban ecology. The nineteen-eighties park design, in both its materiality and processes, is a key example of the era's confrontation with the ruins of the modern urban economy, in conjunction with a trend towards *Spurensicherung*, i.e. tracking the material traces of history.—2 Berlin's alternative scene, engaged residents, and alternative planners developed new strategies for the reuse of existing structures and the recycling of urban wastelands, fostering a new understanding of urban habitat. At the same time, new approaches to public space emerged from the bodily, habitual relations that residents had with their immediate environment, a relationship politicized during the planning process for the park.

2 For more on this tendency, see: Anke te Heesen, "Spurensicherung und das Jahr 1979. Über Kunst und Wissenschaft," in *Geschichte denken. Perspektiven auf die Geschichtsschreibung heute*, ed. Michael Wildt (Göttingen: V&R unipress, 2014), 244–49.

Görlitzer Bahnhof around 1980

By the end of the nineteen-seventies, Görlitzer Bahnhof in the district of Kreuzberg was an industrial and infrastructural site in transition. While freight trains continued to run, the railway station had not been in use for passenger traffic since 1951.—3 Its main building, damaged during the Second World War, had been partially torn down between 1962 and 1964 and then finally demolished in 1975. In the early nineteen-eighties, when a radical change in urban development happened, traces of the sheds and tracks of the train yards and the brick retaining wall that had once enclosed the station still remained on the plot. Also from a legal perspective, the site was complex. Görlitzer Bahnhof—while located in West Berlin—also carried special political and economic privileges. The property had an exterritorial status within the Federal Republic of Germany and was managed by the administration of former assets of the Deutsche Reichsbahn, which was a GDR institution.

3 Emil Galli, *Görlitzer Bahnhof, Görlitzer Park*, (Berlin: SupportEdition, 1994), 24.

Despite, or perhaps because of this unresolved urbanity and territoriality, different groups of people started to appropriate the grounds. Kreuzberg's district office had leased some parcels from the Reichsbahn to sublet them to small businesses:—[4] several car workshops, a trucking firm, a scaffolding company, a gravel supplier, and in the southeastern corner a scrap press that threatened to pollute the groundwater with hydrochloric acid from old batteries and oil spills. These were dirty and, in part, marginalized economies that one would usually find in industrial parks. Besides, the federal state of Berlin, in need of open space, rented parts of the former rail yards for sports grounds and a traffic school for children, and stored tons of briquettes—the so-called *Senatsreserve*—to secure an energy supply in case of a second Berlin Blockade.

4 Ibid., 24–29. Also see: Dieter Kramer, *Kreuzberg. 1968–2013. Abbruch, Aufbruch, Umbruch* (Berlin: Nicolai Verlag, 2013).

The first local residents to make use of Görlitzer Bahnhof as "green" spaces were members of emergent alternative scenes.—[5] Squatters of vacant houses in Wiener Straße appropriated land for house gardens; simultaneously, some parents installed an adventure playground and others managed to get public funding to establish a children's farm. Soon after, Kreuzberg's parks department committed to building a "Ben Wagin," or wild garden, named after Berlin's artist and tree protector, who was popular in the alternative milieu. Yet, despite first appropriations of a space in transition, the character of the land was still that of a semi-industrialized urban wasteland.

5 For participation procedures and residents' projects from 1980–1982, see: Friedrichshain-Kreuzberg (FHXB) Museum, Berlin: 49/215.

These grassroots landscape initiatives helped to solidify a broader citizens' movement for a full-fledged park in Görlitzer Bahnhof. To better understand citizens' hopes and desires, we have to consider the site's immediate urban context and location in SO 36, the southeastern part of Kreuzberg. The geopolitical effects of the Second World War, the division of Germany, and the Cold War manifested in the 1961 construction of the Berlin Wall, and dislocated the district from a central to a marginal position in the urban fabric that was mostly enclosed by the actual border installation.—[6] Furthermore, Berlin's modernist city planning of the nineteen-sixties and seventies exacerbated the consequences of this

6 In Berlin, the declaration of the "1. Stadterneuerungsprogramm" by the Berlin Senate of 1963 for the first time defined urban renewal areas.

marginalization.—[7] On behalf of the federal state of Berlin, public and private housing corporations developed large-scale, tabula rasa reconstruction projects, hence incentivizing de-investment and speculative vacancy. The streets adjoining Görlitzer Bahnhof were designated as an urban renewal area to be cleared and redeveloped from scratch. Consequently, most of the existing housing stock had not been modernized for decades, and owners—speculating on subventions for the construction of new apartment buildings—awaited its destruction. Moreover, according to a general traffic plan fixed in the zoning plan of 1965, Görlitzer Bahnhof was a designated site for a new city expressway that would have cut Kreuzberg apart. As a result, the largest part of Kreuzberg showed symptoms of a downward spiral of neglect, with single flats and, eventually, whole old residential buildings remaining empty for years and falling into disrepair. Due to material decay and a lack of green spaces, the district became notorious as a *Steinwüste* (stone desert). The mainstream media and architectural journals portrayed Kreuzberg as a "ghetto" or "slum," referring to social segregation and other structural problems.

Kreuzberg's social structure, like its physical fabric, was also shaped by West Berlin's specific housing and urban developments and the Federal Republic of Germany's immigration policies.—[8] The former working-class district had become an immigrant neighborhood as better-off German populations left due to material decay. Indeed, a substantial number of Kreuzberg's residents had only moved there since the nineteen-sixties. Around 1980, 30 percent of the population of SO 36 did not have German citizenship—the majority of non-Germans were Turkish immigrants with "guest worker" status.—[9] At the time, Kreuzberg offered cheap rent and many open and underused spaces. This attracted different cohorts: teenage runaways, young male residents (who according to a special law in Berlin were exempted from military service), and those who wanted to experience alternative forms of living and working.—[10]

7 Harald Bodenschatz, Volker Heise, and Jochen Korfmacher, *Schluss mit der Zerstörung? Stadterneuerung und städtische Opposition in West-Berlin, Amsterdam und London*, vol. 11 of Werkbund-Archiv (Giessen: Anabas, 1983).

8 Esra Akcan has started to historicize the effects of immigration on housing and urban development in Berlin, see her essay: "Immigration, Participation and IBA 84/87," in *25 Jahre Internationale Bauausstellung Berlin 1987. Ein Wendepunkt des europäischen Städtebaus*, ed. Harald Bodenschatz, Vittorio Magnago Lampugnani, and Wolfgang Sonne (Sulgen: Niggli, 2012), 57–74.; and her forthcoming book titled "Open Architecture and the Noncitizen: Urban Renewal of Berlin-Kreuzberg in IBA 1984/87."

9 Internationale Bauausstellung Berlin, ed. "Press Release: Stadterneuerung im Gebiet SO 36," 1980.

10 Barbara Lang, *Mythos Kreuzberg. Ethnographie eines Stadtteils 1961–1995* (Frankfurt/New York: Campus, 1998)

These people initiated self-run and self-organized businesses, projects, stores, as well as district groups and local projects.—11

11 *ARCH+* 55, February 1, 1981: "Kampf um Selbsthilfe."

In the wake of 1968, as in German cities elsewhere, an alternative milieu formed out of the new social and ecological movements.—12 This scene repositioned the left and tested new ways of life beyond the social democratic model. In Kreuzberg, a network of so-called *Mieterläden* (storefronts run by tenants' organizations) addressed poor housing conditions through empowerment, self-help initiatives, and political lobbying.—13 At the same time, several more traditional social and religious institutions—such as the Arbeiterwohlfahrt (the German workers' welfare association) and the local parishes—were also active in the district. In addition, a new generation of engaged architecture and planning students and young professionals identified Kreuzberg as an experimental terrain, an object of research for seminars, papers, and projects.—14 Local initiatives—often with eco-feminist agendas—redeveloped and modernized old housing stock, greened courtyards, façades, and roofs, redesigned the streetscape, and above all created self-run cultural and social centers in abandoned factory and backyard buildings. As identity-creating elements, these projects appreciated the apparent authenticity of the neighborhood's tenement buildings, embracing the patina of the historical, the seemingly unplanned, the crooked and unforeseen, the unique, the unusual, the nonserial, while also positioning themselves as an alternative to modern aesthetics and rationalized planning cultures of the previous decades.—15 More and more squatters and anarchist youth moved into the vacant, run-down buildings, reaching its peak in 1981. They not only acted against its decay, but also actively fought the wholesale redevelopment and upgrading of Kreuzberg. These so-called *Instand(be)setzer*—squatters who quickly and proactively repaired old housing stock, to make it habitable—formed a movement comprising radical and non-radical proponents.[16]

12 Sven Reichardt, *Authentizität und Gemeinschaft. Linksalternatives Leben in den siebziger und frühen achtziger Jahren* (Berlin: Suhrkamp, 2014), 502, 518–71.

13 Rainer Graff, "10 Jahre Instandsetzungsbesetzungsforderung. Dokumentation eines politischen Kampfes," *ARCH+* 55, (February, 1981): 20–24. See also: Dieter Hoffmann-Axthelm, "Instandsetzungsforderung und Hausbesetzung. Notiz zu den gegenwärtigen Konflikten in Kreuzberg," *ARCH+* 55 (February, 1981): 19–20.

14 Harald Bodenschatz, "Zur Instandbesetzerbewegung in Berlin. Stellungnahme aus dem ISR der TU-Berlin," *ARCH+* 55 (February, 1981): 25–26.

15 Uli Hellweg, "Ausweg Selbsthilfe? Zur aktuellen Situation der Selbsthilfe und der Mietermobilisation," *ARCH+* 55 (February, 1981): 14–18.

16 Rolf Lindner, "Von 'Freakland' zu 'Slumland.' Zur Mythologie Berlin-Kreuzbergs," foreword to Lang, 1998, 9–16.

Seven years prior to the 1984 competition, another ideas competition for the park called "Strategien für Kreuzberg" had been primarily directed at residents. Klaus Duntze, a local priest who was engaged in the neighborhood, had initiated this first competition as a call for locally based strategies to improve the district, which started a new kind of participatory practice from below.—[17] The competition objectives were of both material and social character: to improve residents' living conditions, their identification with the district, and their social interaction. Supporting Duntze's good intentions, the Berlin Senate issued the call for ideas as a new experiment of urban policy that would both stop the flight of the German population and encourage remaining homeowners to invest in the building stock—almost without public funds. As a result, a citizens' commission selected eleven projects to be further developed, among them the project for a citizens' park on the grounds of the former Görlitzer Bahnhof. The park had a strong lobby in Kreuzberg's emerging alternative local press, as it was featured recurrently in the monthly newspaper *Südost-Express*.—[18]

17 See *ARCH+* 34, (June 1977): "Strategien für Kreuzberg"; see also: Galli, 1994, 29–30; "Strategien für Kreuzberg," 1979. Source: FHXB Friedrichshain-Kreuzberg Museum, Berlin: 64/370.

18 *Südost-Express* No. 1, 1978 (ed. Bürgerinitiative SO 36).

Ecologists and urban planners, debating the ecological value of former traffic landscapes isolated by the Berlin wall, influenced the neighborhood initiatives. Abandoned or underused spaces were identified and analyzed not as wastelands but as ecosystems. Citizen protests to protect a unique habitat in the former Anhalter Bahnhof in Berlin Schöneberg led to the founding of the Bürgerinitiative Schöneberger Südgelände.—[19] At the Institut für Ökologie at TU Berlin, a research project run by botanist and ecologist Herbert Sukopp mapped the rail yards of the former Görlitzer Bahnhof. Here, pioneer and ruderal vegetation and unique birds and small mammals had thrived since the Second World War due to favorable microclimates, the physical structure of the elongated plot, and the lack of a continuous vegetation cover. The representatives of this

19 Eventually, Park am Gleisdreieck designed by Atelier Loidl opened in 2011/2013 linked to Natur-Park Schöneberger Südgelände, which functioned as ecological compensation sites for developments at Potsdamer Platz, by the Flaschenhalspark (2014).

fairly new field of urban ecology thus ascribed high ecological relevance to the site of Görlitzer Bahnhof and were inclined to preserve its "third nature," since it had become a refuge of threatened or delicate plants and animals. In a coauthored 1979 article, published in the urban design magazine *Stadtbauwelt*, Sukopp called on the professions of architects and planners to support the preservation of the former rail yards as an open space, and campaigned for the reconception of Görlitzer Bahnhof as a new kind of ruderal park that could serve as an ecologically significant space for recreation and playground for children.—[20]

20 Hermann Matthes and Herbert Sukopp, "Anmerkungen zur ökologischen Bedeutung des Geländes am Görlitzer Bahnhof," *Stadtbauwelt* 33 (1979): 1362–63.

The Görlitzer Bahnhof park initiative with the IBA paralleled a major planning event in West Berlin. As a para-institutional organization, the IBA—which was inaugurated in 1979—stood for new, postmodern urban planning, and rallied against Kreuzberg's mega-structural developments from the nineteen-sixties and seventies, as well as the large housing estates in West Berlin's periphery.—[21] In order to regenerate the inner city as space for living and working, the IBA followed the two guiding principles—that of *Kritische Rekonstruktion* (critical reconstruction) and *Behutsame Stadterneuerung* (careful urban renewal). The IBA encompassed both new construction of public housing in different sites (*Neubau*) and—primarily in Kreuzberg—the house-by-house modernization of *Mietskasernen*, the old housing stock of the Wilheminian era, by the inhabitants (*Altbau*). Moreover, having an urban ecological focus, it fostered the greening of Kreuzberg's streets, rear courtyards, façades, and roofs and enforced an ecological turn of architecture and planning both as profession and discipline. Advocating for the reuse and preservation of dilapidated tenement and former factory buildings, and for the construction of new social and cultural centers in Kreuzberg, however, the IBA remained a quasi-institutional actor until the principles for urban renewal were approved in 1982 and confirmed in 1983. As the IBA-Altbau also became active in Kreuzberg SO 36, the conception of a citizens' park then fell within

21 Harald Bodenschatz, Vittorio Magnago Lampugnani, and Wolfgang Sonne, *25 Jahre Internationale Bauausstellung Berlin 1987. Ein Wendepunkt des europäischen Städtebaus* (Sulgen: Niggli, 2012).

the considerations of the building exhibition and the project for Görlitzer Park attracted the interest of IBA planners.—[22]

22 Bauausstellung Berlin GmbH (eds.), *Internationale Bauausstellung Berlin 84/87: Projektübersicht Stadterneuerung und Stadtneubau* (Berlin, 1984).

Görlitzer Park was one of the major infrastructure projects supported by IBA in the district, but without broad popular support it would not have been realized. It was sustained by various local citizens' initiatives and action groups:—[23] for example, the Bürgerinitiative SO 36, which since 1977 supported the maintenance of vacant, squatted buildings; Verein SO 36, founded in 1978 with the financial support of the Berlin Senate to concretize the *Strategien*; Aktionskreis Südost e.V., which primarily fought for the relocation of the scrap press; and Initiativgruppe GRÜN. Although each group had a specific agenda—a fact that led to what local historian Emil Galli called a complex tangle of interests—almost all of their members were part of the alternative scene's less radical wing and the older German population in the district. Moreover, most of them were inclined to engage in a dialogue with public authorities alongside their protest activities. From 1982 onwards, a district-initiated working group, AG Görlitzer Bahnhof, became the leading agent of communication. As disseminator of the park concept, AG Görlitzer Bahnhof took over the control of the participatory planning, communicating central ideas and aiming to represent all of the resident organizations: for example, by producing a newspaper on the planning process; by holding meetings in local nursing homes, daycare centers, and church halls; or by speaking publicly in the district's committee meetings.—[24] Yet, while they claimed to act for the interests of all the district's residents, the AG did not include guest workers or more radical residents.

23 Galli, 1994, 36–37 & 38.

24 In press statements, the AG Görlitzer Bahnhof persistently demanded a speedy lease of the entire plot from the GDR.

Following the advice of AG Görlitzer Bahnhof, the Senate sponsored a competition in 1983, calling upon experts to take on a difficult task: legitimizing the redefinition of the space, the redesign of nature and landscape, while considering and incorporating the intricacies and complexities.—[25] Leading up to the competition, they organized a public symposium followed by several topical seminars.—[26] In this framework, AG representatives presented reports on the state of the terrain, on existing vegetation and future uses, as well as on soil contamination and waste problems. Their avowed opponents were the semilegal commercial users—small businesses whose activities were termed "temporary use" and whose contribution to city production remained unnoticed. The conceptual considerations addressed in the seminars included participatory planning and decision-making. Also for the first time in the park project, a planning group was consulted, which was composed of architects, planners, and other experts who made recommendations, defined immediate measures in special reports, and prepared a planning concept.—[27]

During this series of events, the groups involved in the planning process made the first demands about the actual design and use of the park, and their divergent claims clashed. The district administration intended to use the land for much-needed sports facilities; whereas IBA-Altbau insisted on the establishment of work and training facilities on-site, due to its sociopolitical agenda. The residents and activists opposed the segmentation of the park for the sake of what they considered to be special interests. Under the slogan "Ein Park für alle" (one park for all), they promoted a fence-free, open park with a durable lawn and only sporadic trees, on which various activities should freely develop. This plan also argued against the park's use by sport clubs and schools, integrated the presence of the farm, but protested a building used as a mosque by the Islamic community, and indeed put an end to the small businesses on the site.—[28] One member of the committee, though, opposed this unifying and beautifying solution and declared himself in favor of a piecemeal strategy; architectural and urban historian Dieter Hoffmann-Axthelm was a polemical critic and strong proponent of the special *Kreuzberger Mischung*

25 Galli, 1994, 43–48; see also: Der Senator für Stadtentwicklung und Umweltschutz, ed. *Engerer landschaftsplanerisch-städtebaulicher Ideen- und Bauwettbewerb Görlitzer Park*, 1984. Source: FHXB Museum, Berlin: 11/64.

26 "Beitrag der AG Görlitzer Park des Stadtteilausschusses SO 36 zum Symposium am 22. Oktober 1983." Source: FHXB Museum, Berlin: 50/225; see also: Der Senator für Stadtentwicklung und Umweltschutz, ed. *Wettbewerb Görlitzer Park: Vorbereitungskolloquien*, November/December 1983. Source: FHXB Museum, Berlin: 50/222.

27 The committee included: Eduard Neuenschwander (Switzerland) and Gunnar Martinsson (Sweden); Erhard Mahler, the department head in the Senate's administration for construction and housing; local architectural historian Dieter Hoffmann-Axthelm; and the architect Bruno Schindler.

28 As another temporary use of the site, the fundamentalist Fatih-community occupied a former service building in August 1981 and transformed it into a mosque. See: Rochus Wiedemer, "Fatih Moschee und Pamukkale Brunnen. Migration und bürgerbeteiligte Freiraumplanung am Görlitzer Park" (Studienarbeit, Universität der Künste, 2002.) Wiedemer is working on a doctorate on the architecture of mosques, which also features the mosque conflict at Görlitzer Park.

(Kreuzberg Mix) of living and working in the same block. At the same time, he pleaded for the preservation of historical buildings, the consideration of topography, and a focus on existing structures as both identity markers and guides for the inhabitants of the neighborhood.

When the ideas competition for the park was officially announced by the Senator for Urban Development in the summer of 1984, a forum was created to combine the goals of residents and activists with those of parties, politicians, administration, and offices—a total of eight offices contributed.—[29] The competition brief asked for a master plan and a first step for realization; furthermore, the decision-making process was presented as democratic, since the jury included experts, professional judges, as well as citizens. Still, a major problem continued to be the confrontation of actual uses and the availability of the land, because there were twenty-four leaseholders left and the territorial issue with the GDR was still unresolved.

29 The participants were Schaal, Pfrommer, Lehndorff, Partner (Attenweiler/Stuttgart); Kluska and Schröder (Munich/Berg); Jacoby, Martin, Pächter, Kippschild, Müller, Wehberg (Berlin); the group Ökologie und Planung (Berlin); AG Luz / Luz (Berlin); the group Freiraumplanung (Hannover); Behnisch / Grzimek (Stuttgart) and Freie Planungsgruppe Berlin. See Galli, 1994, 73–81.

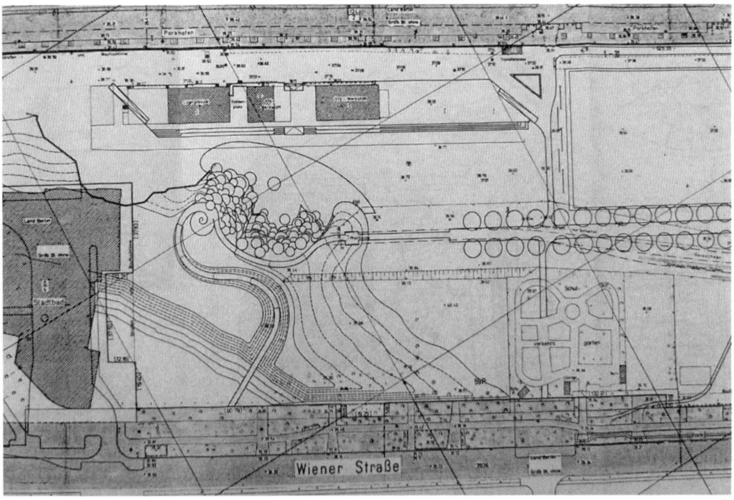

Section of the plan for Görlitzer Park by landscape architects Freie Planungsgruppe Berlin, showing the Pamukkale-Brunnen, 1984.

In November of 1984, the local collaborative office Freie Planungsgruppe Berlin (FPB) emerged as the winner of the competition, likely because the team was already familiar with the tasks and processes of the district's administration, because they had previously been involved in the "Strategien für Kreuzberg."—30 Their winning design seemed to satisfy the contradictory and conflicting claims and ideals previously brought forward by merging them into a promising design of material, social, and symbolic nature. Indeed, the planners proposed the comprehensive design as a solution to the problems that the interest groups involved in the discussions had stated during the planning process.—31 They took up and synthesized these different expectations, and offered answers to at least some of the lofty aspirations.

30 Der Senator für Stadtentwicklung und Umweltschutz, ed. *Görlitzer Bahnhof*, February 1985. Source: ZfB Zentrum für Berlinstudien, Berlin.

31 From a sociological perspective, the problem focus and solution orientation is at the heart of the professional role of the designer, see: Silke Steets, *Der sinnhafte Aufbau der gebauten Welt: Eine Architektursoziologie* (Berlin: Suhrkamp, 2015), 106–14; 148–63.

In so doing, Freie Planungsgruppe drew aesthetically from the strategies explored by the IBA in Kreuzberg and included some of the emerging ecological concerns. Görlitzer Park thus became a precursor of many revitalization projects of derelict industrial and infrastructural sites. Both existing architectural objects and urban structures were kept and integrated in the scheme: the railway sheds and the rail yard's enclosing wall remained standing and were renovated only slightly. The central axis of the design, the so-called Lindenallee, retraced the direction of the railways that had once crossed the site. A former pedestrian underpass underneath the tracks was excavated and burst open—its ruins remained on-site and paralleled the now open pathway. The remains of Görlitzer Bahnhof were thus translated into symbols and interpreted as key markers of identity that stood for Kreuzberg's past as a working-class district.

A similarly symbolical—and for some unsatisfactory—answer was found for the informal mosque that operated on the site. In 1984, during the competition, AG Ausländer (working group of foreigners)—a subgroup of Verein SO36, two-thirds of whom were Turkish immigrants—proposed erecting a cultural center with a place of prayer on the site, which would have given the neighborhood's Turkish community an officially recognized place to assemble. This idea found political support and the group even forwarded a design; however, the advance was discarded during the decision-making process.—[32] In the end, the planners, sensitized through the local conflicts and the intervention of the interest groups, included a symbolical—and highly questionable—homage to Kreuzberg's large immigrant population in their design: the Pamukkale-Brunnen, designed by artist Wigand Wittig, an infrastructure for recreation, play, and bathing that was supposed to be reminiscent in its materiality and topography to the lime terraces of the acclaimed Turkish region of the same name.

32 Previously, Meinhard von Gerkan at the TU Berlin in 1979/80 had made a cultural center for the Turkish community in Kreuzberg the design task for the diploma. Following the initiative of the AG Ausländer, a coalition of the new political party the Alternative Liste and the IBA-Altbau campaigned for a Turkish cultural center; see: Ulrike Harnisch and Ozcan Ayanoglu, *"Mit-Bürger-Beteiligung" am Gülizar Bahnhof* (Berlin: IBA, 1985). Source: FHXB Museum, Berlin: 128/70. In the end, the district administration removed the controversial program from the competition brief.

Although Freie Planungsgruppe only partially opted for preserving the ruderal vegetation on site, the overall approach to the park design was meant to grant residents a unique experience of artificial "nature" in the city. Access to the park was organized through a few openings in the wall, and to enter one first had to pass through an "overgrown" edge zone of native shrubs. Inside, a huge meadow for games, BBQs and picnics, sunbathing, and relaxing allowed for a clear view of the sky, almost free of obstructing trees. The material selection for surfaces, elements, trails, and furniture reflected the park's scenography as pastoral urban landscape; maintaining the concrete ramps and rail yard's brick buildings, the designers chose granite for horizontal surfaces (e.g., flagstones) and similar bricks for vertical structures (e.g., the pergola).

The park design was successful in the competition not least because of the powerful pictorial scheme and the varied scenery it suggested. Görlitzer Park comprised three horizontal strata: two artificial hills at both ends, the green ground layer with leisure uses, and a man-made depression in the middle of the site. The park as a whole—with its juxtaposition of "nature" vs. planning, wilderness vs. orderliness, and its ambiguities of integration vs. exclusion—could be read as a huge postmodern ornament: a postindustrial, yet landscaped, almost baroque garden, that followed a picturesque and playful approach to a central visual axis in southeastern-northwestern direction.

For a moment, the park design had fueled the hopes of the citizens' initiatives, as it elegantly pushed certain claims and sublimated others, transferring them to a new level of symbolical representation. The proposal proved satisfactory to the representatives of the park initiative and to at least some of the experts and city officials, because it produced a convincing image onto which they could project their ideals. Yet new problems sprang up following the competition. First, the realization of Görlitzer Park was delayed by the disinterest of the authorities and the unruliness of the terrain. Moreover, as the first segments of the park materialized, it became clear that the daily practices of some resident groups, as well as their ideas of the site's future, differed from what had been stated during the planning process. In particular, those residents who had thus far not participated in the debates with the planners and city officials—because they had not been interested or integrated previously—proved sensitive to the transformation of their material surroundings and openly opposed the realization of the design.

In 1986, the Berlin Senate had accorded a budget of DM 37 million for the park, which was to be released in tranches to allow for a piecemeal realization of the winning design. In the years to follow, Görlitzer Park Verein (an association that stemmed from AG Görlitzer Park), continuously had to argue for the actual payment of the annual tranche, which was only accorded with considerable delays. In the meantime, the negotiations between the Senate and the GDR proprietors proceeded slowly. Over the years, the park remained a work-in-progress, a visual patchwork realized through acts of protest and appropriation coordinated mainly by the park association. In parallel with a media campaign, citizens employed creative protest strategies that engaged with the site and strived to change and improve its material conditions. According to the pragmatics of the day and the practices of DIY preservation, renovation,

33 "Wie kam die Schiene auf den Lauseplatz?" *SO 36* 3 (June 1986). See also: Rainer Sauter, "Entgleisung," *SO 36* 18 (September 1988).

34 Cay Dobberke,, "Flickwerk mit hohem Nutzwert," *Der Tagesspiegel*, June 22, 1998; "Görlitzer Park wird weiter gebaut," *Berliner Zeitung*, April 29, 1994.

and modernization popular in Kreuzberg, they practiced the system of "self-help with chisel and wrench."—33 German reunification in 1990 also caused a new situation regarding territorial matters, since the former owner of the GDR no longer existed. Yet, it was not until 1994 that the Berlin Senate approved the payment of the last tranches of funding—after a long period of doubt and important cuts to the budget.—34 The last component of the park, the Pamukkale-Brunnen, was only finished in 1998.

Görlitzer Park materialized slowly, with great struggle, over the fourteen years following the original competition. Indeed, although the general outlines were realized, the actual landscape never fully matched the plans the designers had drawn for the site. The most drastic failure was the case of the Pamukkale-Brunnen: projected as a

The last rails of Görlitzer Bahnhof before their removal, 1987.

terraced landscape of waterfalls, it had to close only a few months after its construction due to structural and material damage, because the supporting structure was defective and the sandstone-blocks imported from Portugal could not survive the Berlin winter. The site was fenced off for another decade and left to decay. On a more general level, the envisioned ambiance and experience of the park proved difficult to realize. The parts in the periphery, with their hidden pathways and their playful bridges, did not generate picturesque images as intended, but instead turned into uncanny spaces hidden away from the public eye that took on a swamp-like appearance. Moreover, plans to maintain the site's ruderal ecology were confronted with the fact that, in the southeastern part of the park, the soil was heavily contaminated and the upper layer of

Trash sculptures in Görlitzer Park before the pedestrian underpass was opened, 1989.

two meters depth had to be replaced. In 1993, the Berlin magazine *Zitty* suggested that those who might have dreamed of a romantic quiet and joyful environment had to give up some of their dreams: "Let's not fool ourselves," it quoted Dagmar Elbrandt, the district's park administrator, "nightingales will never breed here in the park."—35

35 "Die Stadt, das Grün und der Zoff," *Zitty* (1993): 16–19; quote p. 17–18 (all translations by the authors).

Despite the failure of some of the more symbolical and utopian ideas of the park initiative, Görlitzer Park became extremely popular. Beginning with a small parcel of grass, the park successively emerged and served a diverse population from the neighborhood, becoming a place where "lovers pick bouquets from the bushes, dog owners cut sticks from trees, teenagers gaily climb on ecological slopes and try out their butterfly knives on the young shrubbery, and trash Coke cans on toad habitats."—36 The park attracted various groups of people, including those who were under-

36 Ibid., 18.

represented in the planning process: "squatters' dogs romp with dogs of Turks, Die Republikaner (a German right-wing party, with extremist tendencies) voters united in small streams, and at night wild punks burn all sorts of wood from the park in sky-high bonfires."—[37]

37 Ibid., 18.

Yet, the use of Görlitzer Park turned out to be more controversial than expected. The design, taking up the rhetoric and working methods of IBA-Altbau, had emphasized Kreuzberg's past as a district of small manufacturers and industries and tried to evoke memories of the train station that had once been the point of arrival for many workers. This clearly appealed to some of the park's strongest supporters, who still remembered the site as a busy, public place.—[38] For them, the derelict and contaminated urban wasteland of Görlitzer Bahnhof was a symbol of the district's general decay, and the idea of reviving the site raised their hopes.

38 See the description by Irmgard and Dieter Klette, who were among the leading figures of the park initiative. Ibid., 19.

Nevertheless, other groups of residents had also formed a distinctive image of the material landscape of their Görlitzer Bahnhof.—[39] In 1987, a group that called itself "Wildwuchs" (a botanical term for grown in the wild) committed an arson attack on an earthmover parked on the construction site of the park to mark their disapproval of the park design.—[40] At the same time, the group circulated a pamphlet that articulated a radical critique against planning in general, the state, and the transformation of the site into a neat and clean park. Here, Wildwuchs voiced the interests of young activists who had recently arrived in Kreuzberg, and who had no personal memory of the former character of the railway station, nor attachments to the local working-class identity—be they invented or real. Instead, they were attracted by the open spaces the district offered, with vacant houses and underused lots. In their eyes, the material structure of Kreuzberg stood not for decay and neglect, but for personal freedom.

39 For alternative and radical perspectives on Görlitzer Park, see documentation "Görlitzer Park" at local archive Papiertiger - Archiv und Bibliothek der sozialen Bewegungen, Berlin-Kreuzberg.

40 Wildwuchs K36, "Für einen Görlitzer Wildpark—so nicht," Berlin, 1987; "Es ist unmöglich, eine Fackel durch ein Gedränge zu tragen, ohne jemandem den Bart zu sengen," Berlin, 1987; Wildwuchs K36, "... und das Gejammer folgt sogleich," Berlin, 1987. Source: Papiertiger, folder "Görlitzer Park."

The park's construction also annihilated spaces that had previously allowed for specific experiences and daily practices. Over the years, residents had interacted with the plot's materiality and had discovered and appropriated certain uses that remained hidden to the planners. For example, the former pedestrian underpass of the train station that cut through the site had served not only as a public toilet for passers-by, but also as a giant amplifier for people gathering there to play instruments. To solve the problem of smells and to produce a picturesque ruin, the planners disassembled a portion of the tunnel. But the transformation also destroyed a specific performative and aural space and prevented certain practices and ambiences that had emerged more recently. In response, a group that identified with "Kreuzberg's tunnel pissers, music makers, sewer rats, swamp flowers, and other figures," spread another leaflet in which the destruction of the structure popularly known as "urethra" (due to its foul odor) was criticized.—[41] While the design proved sensible to the memories of a looming past, it was less sensitive to people's direct material interactions in the present. Thus, the destruction of the urethra in a way transformed an appropriated space into an artifact that was charged with rather abstract meanings.

41 "Hey Kreuzberger Tunnelpisser, Musikmacher, Kanalratten, Sumpfblumen und andere Gestalten," Berlin, circa 1987/88; Source: Papiertiger; folder "Görlitzer Park."

Even if they were partly confrontational and destructive, both cases of local protest against the realization of the park design, utilizing radical actions and rhetoric as a means of expression, proved how deeply members of the immediate neighborhood felt challenged by the supposedly participatory upgrading of their material surroundings. Thus, we consider them within the context of a much broader tendency among residents and park visitors to actively get involved and interfere directly on the grounds. As these interests existed throughout the whole planning and realization process of Görlitzer Park, they ran parallel to the officially recognized discourse and debate and added a tangible, more practice-based commentary on the uses and meanings of the park.

Recently, local initiatives to upgrade the dilapidated space have multiplied. The district of Friedrichshain-Kreuzberg has pushed forward the redesign of some troubled areas of the park. To enhance "safety" and to deter illegal activities, wild vegetation on the edges of the park has been sacrificed, hedges and bushes have been cut back, and new entrances have been opened in the enclosing wall. The professionals redesigning Görlitzer Park in 2015, took similar direction: widen the entrances, integrate the peripheries, and reconceive the lawns.—[42]

42 A project with the suggestive title "Wake up Görli!" was conceived by Atelier Loidl.

While design might be an inadequate tool to prevent drug dealing and social inequalities, there might still be a lesson to be learned from Görlitzer Park's history for its future development. Analyzing the discussions leading up to the original design and its realization helps to identify certain tensions. On the one hand, the competition of 1984 resulted in a particular image that many stakeholders could work towards. This imagined landscape made it possible for Görlitzer Park to materialize at all. On the other hand, by highlighting symbolical and constructed identities the winning design of Görlitzer Park also hid specific conflicts; the participatory process lacked the representation of certain subcultures, dissidents, activists, nonconformists, dropouts, and fringe groups; what is more, chances for the integration of the migrant population beyond mere symbolism were missed.

To conclude, the postmodern landscapes created for Görlitzer Park did not engage enough with the site's materiality. Although some of the relics of Kreuzberg's past became cornerstones of the design, the symbolical narrative of the whole park obliterated those identities that are formed through an interaction with the objects and structures and thus went against some existing interests in the actual landscape. Instead, the design suggested new sites of identification for both the petty bourgeoisie and the alternative German population, as well as the most fragile communities of new migrants. The concentration on picturesque notions of nature not only prevented a critical discussion on what it could have meant to address "third nature," but also prevailed over the question of how the maintenance of Görlitzer Park could be granted over the years.

In the end, Görlitzer Park exemplifies both the promises of a highly symbolic postmodern design and its social and bureaucratic obstacles, which eventually prevented its immediate and full implementation. The result is that the park—in transcending the boundaries between architecture, landscape, sculpture, and nature—stages its contradictions even more poignantly than a conscious and completed postmodern design would have done.

Local residents barbecuing and picknicking in Görlitzer Park's great depression.

What, then, could we learn from this material artifact? Perhaps it teaches us about the pitfalls of a rhetoric that simplifies claims that are too divergent to be harmonized. When today's residents groups consciously or unconsciously take up the slogan once coined by the Görlitzer Park AG—"One park for all"—we should read this as an invitation not to pacify and subsume the right to the city that different cohorts demand, but to unearth and politicize them. In the meantime, despite the controversial debates, Görlitzer Park in all its incompleteness and untidiness remains reminiscent of Kreuzberg's openness and heterogeneity in the nineteen-eighties—a utopian place at Berlin's center, where park visitors and local residents can hang out and relax, but where they might still be confronted with the strange and the uncanny.

Robert Smithson (1938–1973), *Mono Lake Non-Site (Cinders Near Black Point)*, 1968.

Matter Displaced, Organized, Flattened: Recording the Landscape

Martin Hogue

> Just as the right tools facilitate design, a well-considered kit helps us to comfortably move through and work in the landscape. Our rucksacks include clothing for different environmental conditions, water, food, navigational devices (mobile phone, mirror), protection (first-aid kit, sun cream, sunglasses) and professional tools (camera, tripod, sketchbook, pencils, plant press, sample bags, geological hammer, etc.).—[1]

1 Günther Vogt, *Distance and Engagement* (Baden, Switzerland: Lars Müller Publishers, 2010), 372.

Access to varied and powerful sources of geographic data affects the ways in which designers engage sites for speculation. Information that, twenty years ago, would have taken days or even weeks to acquire at great cost, can now be accessed by just about anyone in mere seconds and often for free with the simple click of a mouse. The accessibility of sources like GIS, Google Maps, Google Street View, online USGS state clearing houses, and even crowd-sourced photography act as both a blessing and a curse: while providing important facts about the site, this information is acquired *passively*—that is, without direct input from the designer and without the broad set of tools described by landscape architect and educator Günther Vogt. Christophe Girot, observing that "a designer seldom belongs to the place in which he or she is asked to intervene" and fearing that "the introduction to a site project has all too often been reduced to systematic and quantitative formulas for analyzing this site from a distance," asks, "How can outside designers acquire the understanding of a place that will enable them to act wisely and knowledgeably?"—[2]

2 Christophe Girot, "Four Trace Concepts in Landscape Architecture," in *Reclaiming Landscape*, ed. James Corner (New York: Princeton Architectural Press, 1999), 60–65.

I would like to suggest that the direct experience, collection, organization, and display of site materiality has the potential to connect designers in meaningful and often unexpected ways with their sites that passively acquired data cannot. This is hardly a romantic proposition: I am not suggesting that the designer, simply by wandering about the site barefoot, might suddenly and magically glean new insight into the place of work. Site materiality is subject to a broad range of indexes and descriptors, from the rigorous metrics of scientific analysis—identification of vegetation genus, chemical composition of soils, airborne or ground contaminants—to those fuzzier qualities that Jane Bennett, author of *Vibrant Matter*, characterizes as "impressive, dynamic, incalculable, awesome and awful."—[3] For Bennett, the use of the word "incalculable" does not suggest that these qualities are imprecise, subjective, or even of secondary importance, but that they are subject to a different kind of precision for which fewer tools and recording techniques exist. In landscape architecture, where printed (two-dimensional) forms of representation constitute the standard of exploration and communication, Bennett's call to harness the vibrancy of physical matter is provocative. Can or should these approaches be codified into methodologies applicable to a broad range of sites? What are its implications for design?

3 Klaus K. Loenhart, "Vibrant Matter, Zero Landscape: An Interview with Jane Bennett," *GAM magazine 07: Zero Landscape—Unfolding Active Agencies of Landscape* (Graz: Graz University of Technology, 2011), 17.

Taking cues both from within and outside the discipline, I highlight a range of approaches to recording materiality in landscape fieldwork. These include not only the work of established practitioners like Gilles Clément, Günther Vogt, and SCAPE, but also the work of artists like Robert Smithson, Stan Brakhage, Candy Jernigan, and herman de vries. Three key issues are identified with respect to methodology: the displacement of matter from the site to the studio workspace; the organization of this matter; and, finally, techniques for situating matter within the conventional two-dimensional space of landscape representation. I argue that often the very same standards that drive design exploration—curiosity, experimentation, craft, and rigor—constitute key ingredients for approaching site research and analysis.

The consequences of this type of approach are potentially far-ranging: designers who actively explore the site and construct new frameworks for engaging with the site are less prone to resorting to formulaic responses to passively received data. I am not suggesting that designers do away with that type of information altogether, but that this data needs to be approached critically so that we do not lose unscripted, often meaningful, encounters with the site. By looking both within and outside the field of practice for new references, by considering what on the surface might appear to be simple, pragmatic questions regarding fieldwork methods, I hope to open up new ways of approaching this exciting topic. Collecting, organizing, and displaying site matter are not precursors to landscape design investigations, but an integral part of the process of design speculation itself.

Matter, Displaced

> Perhaps there are always 2 landscapes: one which we physically perceive and one which we mentally construct.—4

4 Robert Smithson, as quoted in Marc Treib, "Traces Upon the Land: The Formalistic Landscape," *Architectural Association Quarterly* 4 (1979): 37.

In design professions, the term "site" denotes a transient condition: the precise interval of time during which a work is first conceived (at which point it is referred to as the *project site*) and later built (the *construction site*). Once completed, the work performed may take on a more permanent designation—a field, a park, a garden—at which point it often ceases being known as a *site* altogether. Before this crucial period, however, the very same location exists merely as a place of unfocused attention because it has yet to command any specific meaning that is the result of design speculation. Christophe Girot's use of the aviation term "landing" describes "the specific moment when a designer still does not know anything about a place and yet is prepared to embark on a lengthy process of discovery" and suggests touching down into a new realm, a new world.—[5] For him, landing marks "the beginning of the odyssey of the project."—[6]

5 Christophe Girot, "Four Trace Concepts," 61.

6 Ibid.

A site is, therefore, less a real place and more of a designation, an intellectual construct. Ever the imaginative craftsman with regard to words and language, the artist Robert Smithson (1938–1973) coined the term "Nonsite" to characterize the limits of the process by which the site emerges as "a landscape which we mentally construct." Although not commonly employed by design professionals, the term "Nonsite" may be useful to characterize the simulacrum of documentary evidence—samples, maps, photos, etc.—present in the studio at the moment of conceptualization of the project.—[7] Smithson points to the gap, familiar to designers, that exists between the unprocessed, found reality of the land and its translation as a project *site*, and so reminds us that this material is, quite literally, *not-the-site*, that place "which we physically perceive" or experience.

7 Elements of this discussion regarding Robert Smithson's *Nonsites* first appeared in my article: "The Site as Project: Lessons from Land Art and Conceptual Art for Architecture," *Journal of Architectural Education* 57, no. 3 (2004): 54–61.

Located in a gallery or museum, each of Smithson's *Nonsites* is an installation intended to represent, through a number of constituent parts—maps, extracted ground samples contained in manufactured steel bins, photographs, written narratives—an actual site located outside the gallery and visited by the artist. The title of each work bears its geographic location: *A Nonsite (The Palisades)*; *A Nonsite, Pine Barrens, New Jersey*; *Non-Site: Line of Wreckage (Bayonne, New Jersey)*; *Mono Lake Non-Site (Cinders Near Black Point)*, among others. For Smithson, the goal of these installations was to point out the gap that exists between the unprocessed, found reality of the land and its appropriation in ways that provide specific interpretations of the site. The artist described this condition as a "Dialectic between Site and Nonsite," a process that directly engages both the empirical and the imagined, the sight and the non-sight.—[8]

8 Robert Smithson, "The Spiral Jetty," in *Arts of the Environment*, ed. György Kepes (New York: G. Braziller, 1972). Reprinted in Holt, *The Writings of Robert Smithson*, 115.

Taken individually, the artifacts that form each *Nonsite* evoke a series of distinct operations that define the site

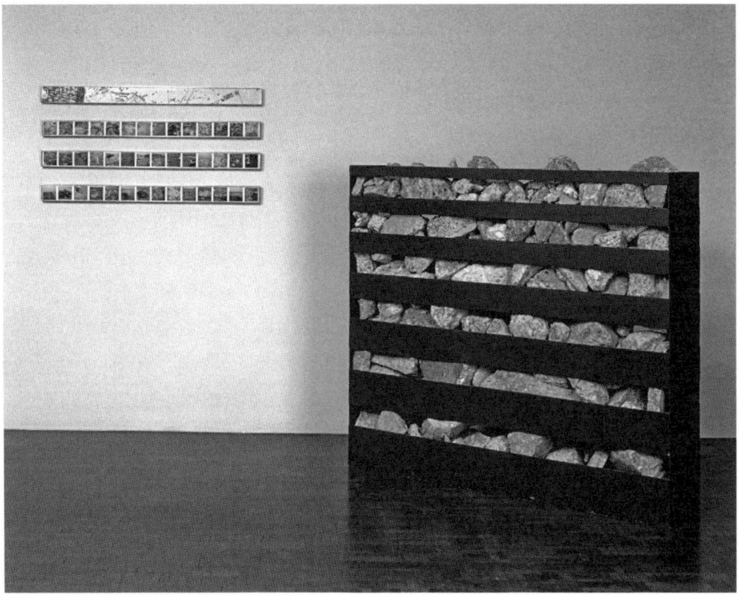

Robert Smithson (1938–1973), *Non-Site: Line of Wreckage (Bayonne, New Jersey)*, 1968.

as actively constructed: the rocks indicate collecting and displacing of matter; the bins frame or establish boundaries; the photographs suggest walking or moving about the site; the maps establish location, and so on. While the sum of these artifacts resists definition as a single, cohesive whole or *site*, the land that has been transposed into the gallery reclaims above all else the status of the *neutral* piece of ground that we come to associate with the traditional open site awaiting intervention:

> The site, in a sense, is the physical, raw reality—the earth or the ground that we are not really aware of when we are in an interior room or studio or something like that—and so I decided that I would set limits in terms of this dialogue … and as a result I went and instead of putting something on the landscape I decided it would be interesting to transfer the land indoors, to the nonsite, which is an abstract container.—9

This displacement of earth from the actual *site* to the (gallery) *nonsite* produces the shift in awareness between found and constructed ideals of site that was desired by Smithson. Like many of his peers during this period, the artist is posing a number of important questions about

9 Robert Smithson, as quoted in Dennis Wheeler, "Four Conversations between Dennis Wheeler and Robert Smithson," in *Robert Smithson Unearthed- Drawings, Collages, Writings*, ed. Eugenie Tsai (New York: Columbia University Press, 1991), 112–113.

the fundamental nature of the art object: is it enough to place a common ground sample in a museum or gallery for it to acquire a new status as an artwork? How can *ground*, a spatially extensive term that knows no boundaries, be turned into an object? For Smithson, answers to these questions are often less than straightforward: in *Mono Lake Non-Site*, for example, samples of earth extracted from the site and a map describing the same site are purposely displayed differently. The samples sit on the floor of the gallery and are presented perspectivally to the viewer while the map, hung on the wall at eye level, appears in orthographic projection as an undistorted image. Thus the same *site* is presented two ways—one (the ground samples) concerned with the experience of sight, the other (map) with an intellectualization or rationalization of the land. A full reconciliation of the actual site is possible only in the mind. The sites of each *nonsite* are firmly rooted in the mind not as a single *picture*, but as a rich set of representations open to the viewer's scrutiny.

Smithson's meticulous installations inside a gallery or museum recall the care with which designers display fieldwork and sketches in their work studio. The arrangement of this information often becomes part of the spatial continuum of the office on a semipermanent basis during the conceptualization and execution of the project. A peek into Günther Vogt's office helps illustrate this idea: the firm is renowned for its immersive fieldwork and site expeditions, which often last several days at a time. During this period, sketches and diagrams, photographs, rubbings, soil and rock samples, plant pressings, bark castings, and the like are produced, collected, and later displayed in the studio. Within the workspace lies a dedicated area of such intricate complexity that it cannot easily be taken down or moved at will. Indeed, what Vogt refers to as the Bremen European Harbour project studio, for example, might as well be known as the *Bremen Harbour Nonsite*: along one wall of the space, a multilevel shelving system helps the design team organize collected field materials, samples (pavers, grouts, etc.), while in the background a vertical wall display is set up to help organize photos, maps, and historical documentation. At the center of the room sit large design models of the project—another hallmark of the firm's work. While Smithson purposely left the dialectic of *site* and *nonsite* open to personal interpretation, Vogt's studio setup deliberately connects the site analysis with a concrete design response.

Vogt shares Smithson's deep interest in the ground as both physical and conceptual matter: in the case of Basel's Novartis Campus Park, the vertically eroded edges lining the depressed walkways suggest the alluvial sedimentation caused by the movement of the Rhine River and its tributaries around the city. Also of note is the great care dedicated by the design team to the representation of the ground in study models, as shown by the carefully cast plaster elements that form the ground plane of the model for the Novartis Campus Green, which emulate limestone pavement formations observed in the Glattalp, near Silberen.—10 Similarly, a model for London's Parliament Square proposal depicted the World Heritage Site "on top of 300 million years' worth of sedimentation."—11 As such, the iconic buildings that form the upper crust of the thick study model seem to dissolve within the geological history of the site. This extraordinary model echoes architect Carol Burns's call to rethink the conventional assumption that sites exist "solely at or above the surface of the earth."—12 This, in turn, greatly opens up inquiry of the site in both its depth and expanse.

10 Günther Vogt, *Distance and Engagement*, 102.

11 Ibid., 414.

12 Carol J. Burns, "On Site: Architectural Preoccupations," in *Drawing, Building, Text: Essays in Architectural Theory*, ed. Andrea Kahn (New York: Princeton Architectural Press, 1991), 165.

Matter, Organized

> To reconstruct the diversity of the site in its totality would require not only an exhaustive inventory of the elements that can be equated with the site's specific biodiversity, the number of plants and animal species that occupy the place, but also a census, a kind of ecological index to evidence human presence on the site, objects that speak of certain behaviors and practices.—13

13 Gilles Clément, "The Chandelier," in *Gilles Clément Philippe Rahm: Environment—Approaches for Tomorrow*, ed. Giovanna Borasi (Milan: Skira / Canadian Center for Architecture, 2006), 104.

Realized in 1968, Smithson's *Nonsites* are grounded (literally) in the realm of minimalist art of the late nineteen-sixties. The gray steel containers that contain the rock matter evoke the work of Donald Judd and other contemporaries; the rocks, the accompanying black-and-white photographs, and the maps that complete each work's monochromatic palette do little to elucidate the diversity of matter present on any site. Smithson's written descriptions often prove enigmatic, as in the following description of the *Spiral Jetty*:

> North by east—Mud, salt crystals, rocks, water…
> Northeast by North—Mud, salt crystals, rocks, water…
> Northeast by East—Mud, salt crystals, rocks, water…
> East by North—Mud, salt crystals, rocks, water…—[14]

14 Robert Smithson, "The Spiral Jetty," in *The Writings of Robert Smithson,* ed. Nancy Holt (New York: New York University Press, 1979), 113.

Smithson's work resonates strongly with French landscape architect Gilles Clément's concept of *Third Landscape*. Clément coined the expression to characterize places—often-disaffected urban areas—that act as a "refuge for the earth's biodiversity."—[15] Like Smithson—who remarked of the *Nonsites*: "the site is where a piece should be but isn't"—Clément asserts that the role of the landscape architect in such situations is not to transform or alter, but to stay out of the way, to observe, bear witness, to monitor and assess over an extended period of time the emergent richness within existing sites.—[16]

15 Gilles Clément, "Working With (and never against) Nature," in *Gilles Clément Philippe Rahm: Environment—Approaches for Tomorrow*, 92.

16 Liza Bear and Willoughby Sharp, "Discussions with Heizer, Oppenheim, Smithson," *Avalanche* 1, no. 1 (1970). Reprinted in *The Writings of Robert Smithson*, 177.

Illicit photographs of Smithson defiantly trespassing fenced areas on his way to remote areas of the New Jersey landscape suggest that performance—gaining access to / visiting sites, acquiring matter, hauling it back to the city—was an integral part of these works. These are, after all, nonsites: places not meant to be experienced by casual passers-by. Clément's methods are far more transparent: *Le Champ* (1977) and *La Vallée* (1993) are tracts of land privately purchased by the designer to function as laboratories for testing and experimentation into the concept of third landscape.—[17] Clément continued this line of exploration with a series of awarded commissions,

17 Ibid., 94.

first around Lake Vassivière (2002), and later with *Le Lustre*, an installation at the Canadian Center for Architecture in Montreal (2006). It is here, around the museum's formal grounds, sculpture garden, and adjacent expressway and onramps, that the landscape architect set about trying to constitute a rigorous material inventory, a "reservoir" or "time capsule" that testifies to the ecological diversity found within the site.—[18] Clément described the collection of found materials as "organic specimens and inorganic objects," ranging from grasses, leaves, and insects, to found detritus like a tube of toothpaste, a cell phone cover, rusty nails, an empty coffee cup, etc.—[19] These last few discarded artifacts recall artist Candy Jernigan's (1952–1991) single-minded inventory of drug paraphernalia collected around her lower Manhattan neighborhood during the mid nineteen-eighties. Her materials take on a strange power from being aggregated into a single artwork: how many different junkies unwittingly contributed to this project? Jernigan's careful notations for *Found Dope II* (1986) establish the place and moment of collection of each item, suggesting a limited system of local users. Similarly, Clément's broad physical array of natural and manufactured matter is part of the same ecosystem: "Each plant and animal—even just its trace in leaves, roots, pods, shells, carapaces, or skeletons—is connected to all the others, and thus to a behavioral system that has evolved over time. In the same way, each found object produced by human industry is connected with a habit of use, an ancient practice preceding its presence on the site, a use in fact connected with the site's very existence."—[20] And while this inventory could not express the true richness and diversity of the site, "it could represent the idea of it."—[21] Clément's title for the piece was deliberately chosen to embody irony and contradiction. The term *lustre* (chandelier) evokes the elaborate light fixtures adorning the ceilings of the most elegant dining rooms. Although it provides no illumination, *Le Lustre* does look like a chandelier to be sure, but a

18 Clément, "Working With (and never against) Nature," 92.

19 Clément, "The Chandelier," 105.

20 Ibid., 104.

21 Ibid.

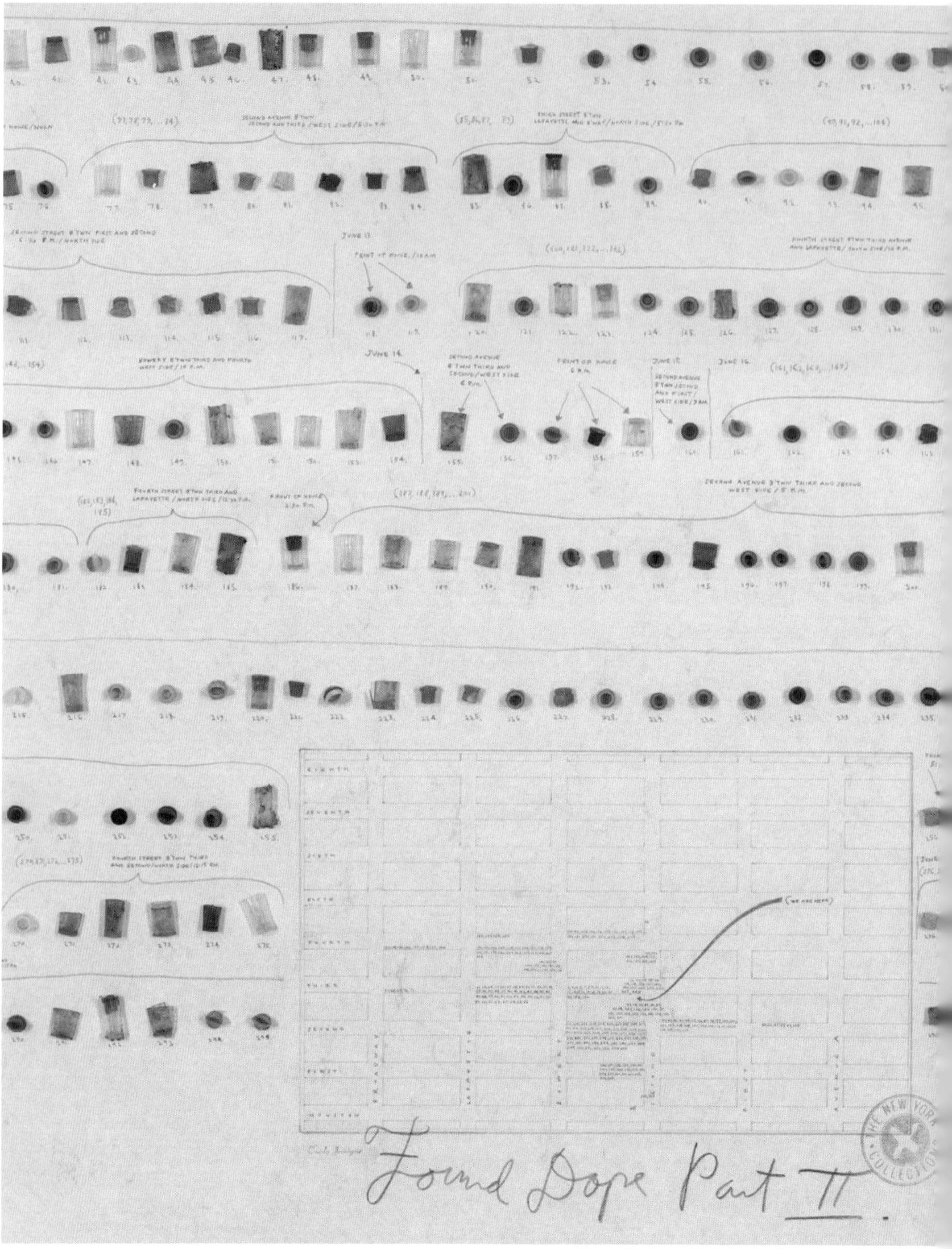

Candy Jernigan (1952–1991), THE NEW YORK COLLECTIONS, *Found Dope: Part II*, 1986. Detail.

Gilles Clément, *Le Lustre*. Displayed in the *Environment: Approaches for Tomorrow, Gilles Clément/Philippe Rahm* exhibition held at the Canadian Center for Architecture, 2006.

chandelier made from site debris. Furthermore, this matter may have seemed an ill fit within the rarefied, institutional confines of an important museum like the Canadian Center for Architecture. Clément cast over one hundred site samples into individual, teardrop-shaped vessels made of translucent acrylic, recalling a chandelier's arrangement of carefully faceted glass drops. In so doing, the artifacts become permanently frozen, further removed from the deteriorative effects of time and atmospheric site conditions—*museified*, so to speak. Floating above the ground, their status is elevated both spatially and symbolically; matter once encountered underfoot is now experienced at eye level. Whereas the original collection could fit inside a medium size garbage bag, the samples now swell to become the center of attention of an entire room. For Clément, the internal arrangement of individual artifacts do not reflect any particular kind of hierarchy: all these samples are part of the same ecosystem. Showing little interest in prescribing the viewer's experience and insights, Clément challenged those "who visit the site and the museum

Specimens gathered for Gilles Clément's *Le Lustre* installation at the Canadian Center for Architecture, 2006.

22 Ibid.

23 Robert Smithson, *A Nonsite (The Palisades)*, 1968. Underline by Smithson.

installation in the galleries to imagine possible scenarios for [the artifacts]."—22 Smithson had similarly stated, "Between the site and the Nonsite one may lapse into places of little organization and no direction."—23 For Clément and Smithson, the role of the imagination is to bridge the gap between site and nonsite, between the museum and neglected spaces outside of it.

As he did with *Le Lustre*, Clément deploys meticulously high standards of craft and design for the *Vassivière Box*. These two works are fascinating and highly unusual in the field of landscape architecture, because site analysis rarely leads to such highly polished, three-dimensional end products. The box Clément fashioned for Lake Vassivière is highly interactive: like the artworks of the American Joseph Cornell (1903–1972), it features an assortment of niches, drawers, and compartments designed to hold annotated maps, aerial photographs, slides, and organic matter. Roughly fifteen by fifteen inches in size when closed, the box hinges open and is as intimate as the *Lustre* is public. In both cases, Clément proposes a new framework through

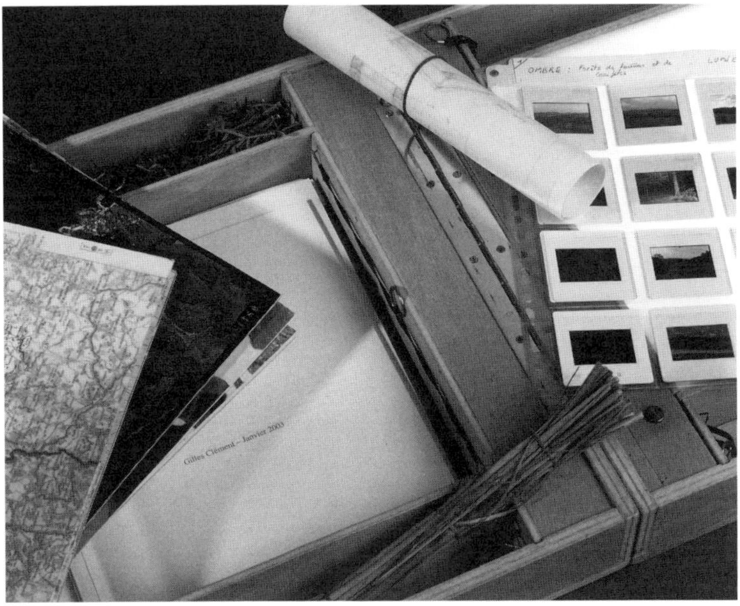

Gilles Clément, *Étude pour le CIAP sur l'île de Vassivière*, Vassivière en Limousin, 2003.

which site matter can be stored, organized, displayed—*found* anew. These installations challenge conventional wisdom by illustrating that creativity and craft are skills that can be deployed at any stage of development of the design process, including fieldwork, analysis, and research.

Matter, Flattened

> That is what I do when I collect—I like the original. I don't want a photo. —24

24 "herman de vries interview in the dutch pavilion at the venice art biennale," designboom, http://www.designboom.com/art/herman-de-vries-dutch-pavilion-venice-art-biennale-05-13-2015/ (accessed June 22, 2015).

The works and practices discussed so far retain field matter's original physical bulk. There also exist important historical precedents integrating physical site matter directly into conventional (flat, two-dimensional) systems of landscape representation. Perhaps the most popular among these is the practice of pressing botanical specimens—plants, leaves, flowers—between the pages of large albums, a practice that gained broad popularity during the Victorian era and remains a honored field technique today.

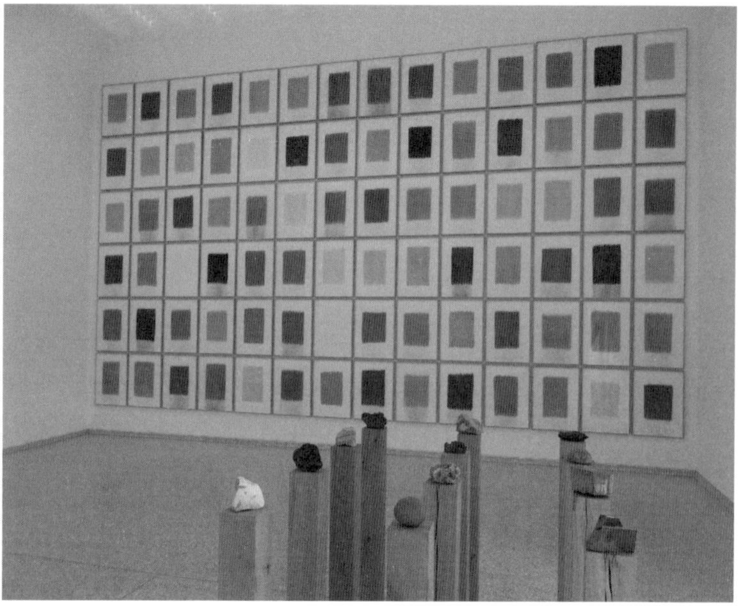

herman de vries, *from earth: everywhere*, 2014–2015. Dutch Pavilion, Venice Biennale.

Rubbing is another powerful analog technique that references the direct experience prized in fieldwork. Executed with charcoal or lead sticks, rubbings derive their name from the very act of rubbing a soft sketching medium on a thick sheet of paper laid directly over the surface to be documented. The result is a full-scale impression that highlights the relief present in the surface. Because it employs the observer's own hands, the technique makes plain the labor of having personally visited the site, conveying a direct, sensory experience that more sophisticated field instruments and tools often cannot approximate. Practitioners like Vogt use the method to produce studies of tree bark and other textural impressions; similarly, the architect Ben Nicholson created large rubbings of the terra cotta pavement patterns hidden beneath the floorboards of Michelangelo's Laurentian Library reading room. However, the technique enjoys far broader popular use outside the visual and design arts, as witnessed, for example, in the hundreds of rubbings performed each day at the Vietnam Veterans Memorial in Washington, D.C.

herman de vries, *from earth, the earth museum*. Musée Gassendi. Digne-les-Bains, France.

Dutch artist herman de vries—[25] and American experimental filmmaker Stan Brakhage bring unique perspectives to these fieldwork methods. Less interested in the technique than in collecting the medium used to perform the rubbing itself, de vries conveys the immediacy of place by gently rubbing site soil samples directly onto paper. The color pigment of earthen matter is slowly worn down against the tooth of the paper to reveal subtle hues unique to each new site. In other words, de vries' *rubbings* are drawings made of soil. On recent display at the Dutch pavilion for the 2015 Venice Art Biennale was an installation of eighty-four of these rubbings, executed on sheets of paper equal in size and laid out in a six by fourteen grid. The contrast between the almost white earth found on the island of La Gomera, Spain, and the greenish hues of North Cyprus is indicative of the range of colors found in the installation. These rubbings and de vries' ongoing collection of 8,000 earth samples from around the world are stored in the remarkable Musée des Terres (Earth Museum). Held at Musée Gassendi, in Digne-les-Bains, France, this collection is a wonderful example of fieldwork and truly unique in its scope.

25 Note that de vries insists on spelling of his name in lowercase.

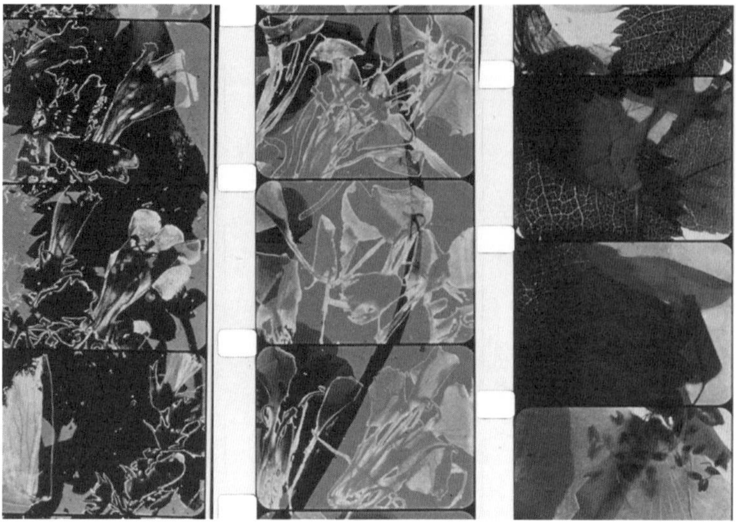

Stan Brakhage (1933–2003), *The Garden of Earthly Delights*, 1981. Detail.

Like de vries, the American filmmaker Stan Brakhage (1933–2003) was interested in using low-tech methods to convey an intuitive, primary experience of matter that transcends conventional identification. Brakhage's restless sense of invention suggests a willingness to completely upend cinematic conventions of image, perspective and compositional logic, while at the same time working with the tools of the craft (projector, film strips, etc.).—26 For *The Garden of Earthly Delights* (1981), Brakhage sandwiched ground matter collected around his Lump Gulch cabin near Boulder, Colorado, between two protective layers of 35mm film. He then printed the assemblage of leaves, blades of grass, seeds, and dead flowers so that the results—a single, flattened strip of film—could be shown through a movie projector. For Brakhage, film acts not only as a compositional and structural substrate, much like paper does in botanical albums of pressed specimens, but it also retains its properties as a time-based medium. Film scholar Scott McDonald writes that when projected at a rate of twenty-four frames per second, the 2,496 frames that make up the 156-foot long montage "seem to pile onto the retinas, creating evanescent collages."—27 Interestingly, the hours, weeks, and months that Brakhage

26 Scott McDonald, *The Garden in the Machine: A Field Guide to Independent Films About Place* (Berkeley and Los Angeles: University of California Press, 2001), 68.

27 Ibid., 71.

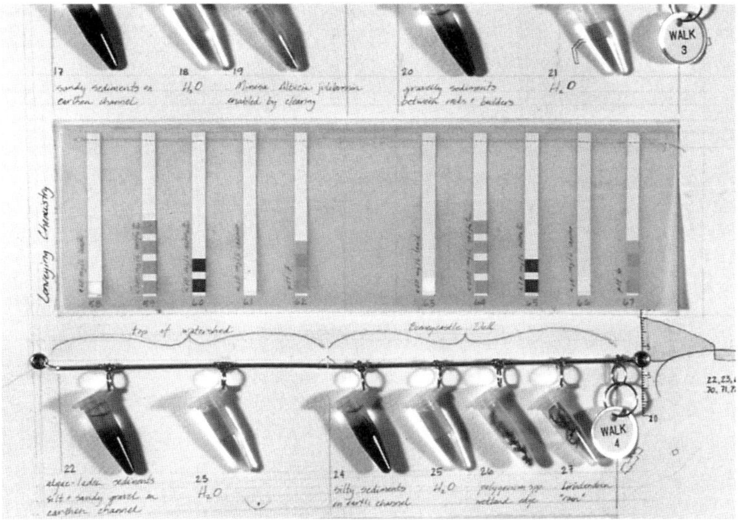

Kathy Poole, *The Life of Water*, circa 2000. Detail.

spent carefully composing the site matter onto this one-inch wide surface are experienced cinematically in less than two minutes. This visceral encounter with the site is further magnified by the scale and orientation of the projection: though the film is silent, one can almost hear the cracking of the leaf matter underfoot, now floating on a vertical screen and at a radically enlarged scale. For McDonald, the viewer experiences "a flickering kaleidoscope" made from bits of seed, flowers, leaf matter in a broad range of colors.—[28] Though short in length, the film conveys the daily cycle of natural illumination, beginning in near darkness in the dawn of early morning, to the full light of the midday, and ending in the darkness that comes with dusk.

28 Ibid., 69–71.

de vries' and Brakhage's approaches to fieldwork are remarkable for their rigor, their sense of craft, their sheer ambition (8,000 soil samples, nearly 2,500 film frames), and willingness to approach conventional media in new ways. Outside the sketchbook, such analog methods have few contemporary equivalents in the increasingly sophisticated digital graphics of contemporary landscape representation. The period of the mid nineteen-nineties—before digital software like AutoCAD, Adobe Illustrator, and Photoshop became the professional standard—offers insight into the flattening of field matter in landscape representation. During this period, practitioners like James Corner fashioned new hybrid methods by combining traditional drafting with collage elements enhanced by carefully typeset annotations. For Corner and his contemporaries, the layering of such elements—USGS maps, photographs, etc.—produced a thick, "2.5-dimensional" construction. This is to say that these representations occupy a space between flat, two-dimensional representations and the fully three-dimensional space of analog models. In other words, they are not quite flat, but not quite thick either.—29 In *The Life of Water* (circa 2001), landscape architect Kathy Poole explores the tectonic qualities of such layered arrangements; like Candy Jernigan, she thickens this 2.5-dimensional space of representation by adding layers of site materiality. Placed under protective covers of translucent vellum, delicate pH strips are fastened to single sheet of Strathmore, on which a reference map of the site is drawn. Annotations correlate the strips with the location of field tests. The thick arrangement of these three paper layers is sewn in place. Finally, a linear sequence of small vials containing water samples is hung in front of the paper elements. Like the *Vassivière Box*, the piece invites physical interaction. For Poole, the shadows cast by the vials—onto the vellum, the pH strips, and the map—and the subtle lines and words traced by thread and drafting pencil, elegantly fuse into a thick, tectonic montage of site information.

29 Such juxtapositions remain in great use today by proponents like Anuradha Mathur and Dillip da Cunha, but the very real, material thickness of these early montages is now largely virtual.

Conclusion

When combined with traditional streams of documentation, the role of direct observation is to inject the site with the kind of curiosity and insight that are the hallmark of design exploration, combining into what Christophe Girot describes as the process of *founding* the site.—30 Indeed, the designer should approach the exploration of the site not merely as a set of objective, *passively received*

30 Christophe Girot, "Four Trace Concepts," 61–64.

features—legal boundaries, dimensions, topography, vegetation, building locations, etc.—but also as an area shaped by ideas and perceptions that should be an integral part of the design process. Girot himself has championed time-based techniques of site exploration like short films, suggesting new ways for the designer / student to engage with the site as a place of work by integrating "into complex representations such volatile factors as immersion, the perception of atmospheres, the role of the sound, and our own activity in space that all together form the experience of large scale environments."—[31]

The current work performed by SCAPE on the *Living Breakwaters* project in Staten Island, NY stands as another strong illustrative argument for this kind of hybrid methodology. For principal Kate Orff, the project is unique in that it is "equal parts design strategy and community conversation."—[32] *Living Breakwaters* brings together design professionals with nearby stakeholders by engaging them directly in the work. To be sure, the project employs cutting-edge technology—like the ADCIRC/SWAN storm surge and wave modeling system—but perhaps the most important insight comes from the direct encounter with oysters as a concrete form of site matter: shore tours, charrettes, and community events create opportunities for local residents to take on active roles in growing spat into the millions of oysters that will form the protective reefs along the southern shore of the island.—[33] These activities bring this diverse group of actors into direct contact with the work and frame their place within it as eventual stewards of the project.

The methods described in this article call into service a unique set of design skills: a deep curiosity, the capacity to design and conduct rigorous field experiments and organize its results, the ability to work synthetically, and a highly tuned sense of craft, to name only a few. The result is that the site, with its potential for transformation and change, is allowed to emerge in provocative and unexpected ways.

31 "Landscape Video: video analysis and design tool," Swiss Federal Institute of Technology Zurich, http://girot.arch.ethz.ch/research/digital-media-perception/landscape-video-research (accessed May 24, 2016).

32 Kate Orff/SCAPE, *Towards an Urban Ecology* (New York: Monacelli Press, 2016), 258.

33 Ibid., 242.

Tangle of red, brown, and green algae on the surface of a canal, Venice, 2012.

Feminist Hydro-logics in Joan Slonczewski's *A Door Into Ocean*

Katie Lloyd Thomas

In the early nineteen-nineties, while looking for imagined future environments in science fiction that might yield visions of what a feminist architecture could be, I came across an extraordinary novel by the American microbiologist Joan Slonczewski. *A Door into Ocean* (1986) is set on Shora, a moon of the future that is entirely covered in ocean and inhabited only by women.—[1] "Sharers" dwell in small communities on porous living rafts and practice a highly developed science of "life-shaping" through which they modify plant and animal life, enabling them to adapt their own bodies and ways of living to the marine environment and to reproduce without men! Once a year when the life-threatening seaswallowers migrate across the ocean, the rafts move too, propelled by large squid-like creatures called starworms harnessed beneath the rafts. Sharer women live according to a principle of exchange as a reciprocal process that pervades every aspect of their lives. Boundaries and rigid classifications are an anathema to them. They abhor "dead" stone and metal. They refuse to recognize distinctions between subjects and objects in their language, and when forces from their neighboring stone-loving planet Valedon invade Shora—the central plot line of the novel—Sharers' strategies of nonviolence render the incursion impossible.

1 Joan Slonczewski, *A Door into Ocean* (London: The Women's Press, 1987, first published, New York: Arbor House, 1986).

Slonczewski's holistic vision of Shora was acclaimed as soon as it was published in the United States (U.S.) and the following year it won the John W. Campbell Memorial Award for the Best Science Fiction Novel. Although Slonczewski attributes Sharer principles to Quaker philosophies of nonviolence,—[2] not to feminism, the London-based The Women's Press made it readily available to a feminist readership when they published the novel in their science fiction series in 1987. By the early nineteen-nineties, *A Door into Ocean* was featured in a number of studies of feminist science fiction and utopian writing. Informed by concerns of identity and language common to feminist theory at the time, these interpretations tended to highlight themes such as Sharer subjectivity and interrelations, and the dissolution of boundaries in their language and approach to the world. Surprisingly little was said about the science practiced on Shora, despite the contemporaneous work in feminist science studies of writers such as Evelyn Fox Keller, Sandra Harding, and Donna Haraway.—[3] Moreover, hardly any attention was paid to the shift from a land-based to water environment that distinguished *A Door into Ocean* from other women-centered science fiction. For example, both Marge Piercy's *Woman on the Edge of Time* (1979),—[4] and Sally Miller Gearheart's *The Wanderground* (1985)—[5] had imagined women-only communities of small agrarian settlements, in contrast to the dystopia of the patriarchal city. That *A Door into Ocean* needs to envisage life lived on and with another element to build its fluid, relational, women-only utopia is perhaps the novel's most remarkable feature.

A return to Shora is timely for a number of reasons. First, with the emergence of new materialism and the burgeoning field of ocean studies, we have new tools—more adequate than the psychoanalytic and deconstructive feminism of the early nineteen-nineties—to appreciate the degree to which *A Door into Ocean*'s account of relational ocean dwelling is holistic; integrating both a changed worldview with altered material practices and ways of living.

2 See Joan Slonczewski, "Study Guide to A Door Into Ocean" under the sections "Quakers" and "Non-violent Traditions," http://biology.kenyon.edu/slonc/books/adoor_art/adoor_study.htm (accessed January 21, 2016).

3 For an excellent recent study of this issue, including reference to *A Door into Ocean*, see: Christy Tidwell's "No Longer Estranged: Women, science, science fiction" (unpublished PhD, The University of Texas at Arlington, 2011).

4 Marge Piercy, *Woman on the Edge of Time* (London: The Women's Press, 2001).

5 Sally Miller Gearheart, *The Wanderground* (London: The Women's Press, 1985).

Second, *A Door into Ocean* is anticipatory insofar as it provides what Peg Rawes has called a "relational ecology." Sharers exist as part of an interconnected ocean environment that they share with all forms of life. They reject "dead" inert materials and instead partly "engineer" and grow their rafts and dwellings through their plant-based science. Their elaborate techniques resonate with the experiments and speculations of a small group of designers, researchers, and fine artists now working with living systems or systems building materials—such as Rachel Armstrong's "Vibrant Venice," which proposes introducing programmable chemistries to the foundations of Venice in order to grow a limestone reef to support the city. In these projects, as on Shora, design is no longer an imposition of a predetermined order by humans, rather a collaboration where, as Rachel Armstrong puts it, "non-human actants work alongside humans as co-designers of their environment."—[6]

6 See Rachel Armstrong, *Vibrant Architecture: Matter as a Codesigner of Living Structures* (Warsaw: De Gruyter Open, 2015).

Third, I am interested in revisiting the altered conceptual framework and material practices of Slonczewski's women-only, ocean-dwelling community in the light of feminist critical materialism. The French feminist Luce Irigiray made figurations of fluidity central to her project to introduce sexed difference to a Western discourse that recognizes only one (male) subjectivity, in a number of books that appeared around the same time as *A Door into Ocean* was published (and in the early nineteen-nineties in English translation). Indeed, Elizabeth Williams positions Irigiray's work as "foundational" work in this area,—[7] and since the nineteen-eighties water has been important for many feminist imaginaries, ranging from queer theory to more empirical studies in feminist new materialism. For example, in 2013 *Feminist Review* published a special issue on water, where the editors' aim was "to build a bridge between the strand of research that focuses on water management and governance and which highlights the emergence of and formation of subjectivities, either individual or collective, via water."—[8]

7 Elizabeth Williams, "Feminism and New Materialism: The Matter of Fluidity," *Pismo Poświęcone Studiom Queer: A Journal of Queer Studies* no. 9, Special Issue on Bodily Fluids (2014): 186.

8 Rutvica Andrijasevic and Laleh Khalili, "Water," *Feminist Review* 103 (2013): 1.

To what extent might Sharers' techniques and the work of the many women designers and artists working today with living systems—[9] be understood in terms of what, following Edna Keah Garrison, we might call "Feminist Oceanography"?—[10] Rather than illustrate these projects directly, a series of watery photographs taken in and around Venice by Rachel Armstrong accompany the text, evoking the shared themes and relations between Slonczewski's imaginary ocean world and contemporary design practices, ocean studies, and feminist theory.—[11]

9 To name a few: Rachel Armstrong, Neri Oxman, Kate Orff, Špela Petrič, and Carolina Ramirez Figureroa.

10 Edna Keah Garrison coins the term "Feminist Oceanography" in "Are We On a Wavelength Yet? On Feminist Oceanography, Radios, and Third Wave Feminism" in *Different Wavelengths: Studies of the Contemporary Women's Movement*, ed. Jo Reger (New York: Routledge, 2005), 237–56.

11 I am grateful to Rachel Armstrong for her generosity sharing her writing and references with me and agreeing to provide the illustrations to this article.

Oceanographies: Empirical and Speculative

In rejecting the terrestrial as a site of occupation, and turning to the fluid, mobile, waters of the ocean as an alternative space, Slonczewski's novel can be considered alongside the growing corpus of work in geography, anthropology, social, and cultural studies that examines water and the ocean. Particularly when it is read alongside its more economically explicit sequel, *The Daughter of Elysium* (1993)—[12]—in which Shora's oceans also host twelve vast cities encapsulated in vast glass spheres, housing a wealthy race of tech-savvy immortals who provide banking services to the rest of the planets in the intergalactic "Fold"—*A Door into Ocean* provides a fascinating "empirical" case study (albeit fictional) for ocean studies' incisive and often hard-hitting critiques of power, capitalism, inequity, and injustice. In fact, geographer Philip Steinberg includes a short description of the novel in his seminal book *The Social Construction of the Ocean*. There, he argues not only that the ocean is no more "natural" than the land it is so often opposed to, but as "a marginal space, apparently on the fringe of social structures and institutions," and subject to different laws and forms of ownership, it has the potential as "a space for imagining and actualizing social change."—[13]

12 Joan Slonczewski, *The Daughter of Elysium* (Rockville, MD: Phoenix Pick, 1993)

13 Philip Steinberg, *The Social Construction of the Ocean* (Cambridge: Cambridge University Press, 2001), 189, 205.

In common with many other researchers working on the ocean, Steinberg's study is both empirical and

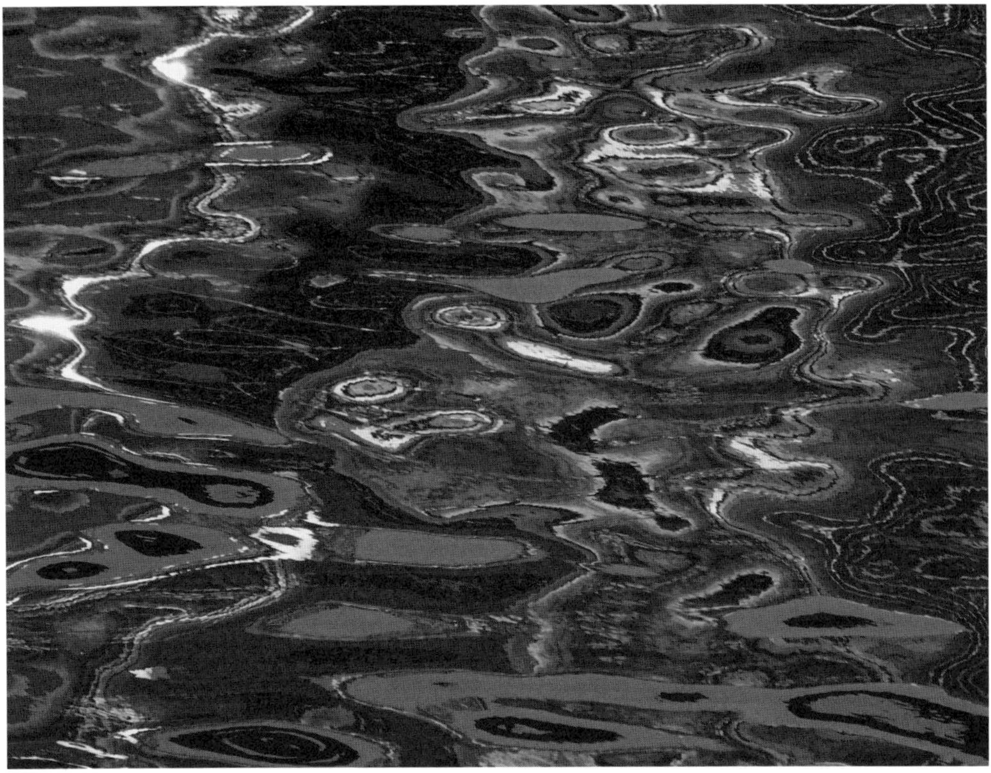

Reflection of Madonna dell' Orto in a canal. Cannaregio, Venice, 2016.

speculative. The ocean is a site or "object" to be analyzed and understood, and an alternative figure to think with. His more recent article with Kimberley Peters is yet more explicit in exploring the "wet ontologies" engendered by the ocean. Ocean space lends itself, they suggest, to understanding through volume and depth more than through surface, and bodily experience is reoriented, necessarily incorporating time and motion.—[14] In Matt Lee's "Oceanic Ontology and Problematic Thought," the ocean with its "fluidity of changing states, continuous movements and the flows of various and variable currents," lends an image to a Deleuzian philosophy that is not "too weighted down by earth."—[15] Such studies mobilize the ocean as what the anthropologist Stefan Helmreich names a "theory machine" (a term coined Peter Galison) to describe "an object in the world that stimulates a

14 Philip Steinberg and Kimberley Peters, "Wet ontologies, fluid spaces: giving depth to volume through oceanic thinking," *Environment and Planning D: Society and Space* 33 (2015): 247–64.

15 Matt Lee, "Oceanic Ontology and Problematic Thought" (unpublished PhD, University of Greenwich, 2007), http://www.lulu.com/gb/en/shop/matt-lee/oceanic-ontology-and-problematic-thought/ebook/product-17438095.html (accessed 21 January, 2016).

theoretical formulation."—[16] Not all oceanic formulations are as affirmative as these. For others, it is the paradigmatic figure for the boundless mobility of global capitalism; it must be regulated, protected, and kept open for free trade and the transportation of goods. Zygmunt Baumann begins his critique of contemporary society in advanced capitalism, *Liquid Modernity*, with an account of the properties of fluids. According to Baumann, the dissolution of the solid is no more than the removal of resistance to the flow of capital and we should beware of celebrating mobility and flux.—[17] Peter Sloterdijk argues in his brief and fascinating history of globalization in *Globes*, that it was not so much the domination of territory that marine circumnavigation achieved, but rather the introduction of risk-taking, insurance, and speculation.—[18] As an all-encompassing element, "only the sea," he writes (in a passage on Herman Melville), "offered a foundation for universal thoughts; the ocean alone could bestow the graduation caps of the true Modern Age."—[19] Within these varied and contradictory interpretations, water reflects its own properties. It is itself a fluid and indeterminate concept with which to think.

A Door into Ocean is a pertinent case for the exploration of these issues, not just because of the richness of the ways of living imagined by Slonczewski. While this is a fictional world, it is at the same time highly specific and located. As I hope to show, the novel hovers between the empirical and historical cases investigated in contemporary oceanic studies and Irigaray's "impossible" feminist figurations—imaginaries in which sexed difference is acknowledged beyond the limitations of phallogocentric logics.—[20] Feminist science fiction is a form of feminist critique that reaches, as Patricia Duncker has put it, "a broader audience than feminist theory. Women who might not broach Mary Daly's *Gyn/Ecology* might well read *The Wanderground*."—[21] It also offers positive visions of alternative futures and ways of being. Debra Benita Shaw acknowledges this double potential of the genre:

16 Stefan Helmreich, "Nature/Culture/Seawater," *American Anthropologist* 113, no. 1 (2011): 132.

17 Zygmunt Bauman, *Liquid Modernity* (London: Polity Press, 2000).

18 Peter Sloterdijk, *Spheres: Volume 2: Globes*, trans. Wieland Hoban (South Pasadena, CA: Semiotext(e)), 824–25.

19 Ibid., 811.

20 The term "impossible" is used both by Tom Moylan and by Linda Daley to distinguish "impossible" future imaginaries from utopias, in so far as they are not intended to describe societies to aspire toward, but rather to invent altered imaginaries for thought. See: Tom Moylan, *Demand the Impossible: Science Fiction and the Utopian Imagination* (London: Methuen, 1986); and Linda Daley, "Luce Irigaray's Sexuate Economy," *Feminist Theory* 13, no. 1 (2012): 59–79.

21 Patricia Duncker, *Sisters & Strangers: An Introduction to Contemporary Feminist Fiction* (Oxford: Blackwell, 1992), 105. Cited in Christy Tidwell, *No Longer Estranged*, 16.

> The appeal of science fiction for women has always been that it allows opportunities both to express and explore alienation as well as to offer a fictional description of the kind of world that a gender-free or differently gendered science might produce.—[22]

22 Debra Benita Shaw, *Women, Science and Fiction: The Frankenstein Inheritance* (New York, Palgrave: 2000), 5–6. Cited in Tidwell, *No Longer Estranged*, 12.

Works of feminist science fiction such as *A Door into Ocean* can therefore offer an opportunity to consider together, as Elizabeth Grosz put it, "the relation between bodies, social structures and built living and work environments and their ideal interactions."—[23] Unlike the designer's future projection, so often imagined in isolation from other forms of change, the alternative material environment of science fiction is imagined as part of and integral to social and corporeal relations.

23 Elizabeth Grosz, *Architecture from the Outside: Essays on Virtual and Real Space* (Cambridge, MA: The MIT Press, 2001), 150.

The oceanic material practices described in *A Door into Ocean* are yet more compelling when seen today alongside contemporary design and fine art practices, which also experiment with the potential of lifelike and living systems to generate new co-designed forms. To an architecture student in the early nineteen-nineties, the thought of growing an architecture anything like Sharer rafts went about as far as a green roof, and the idea of Sharer "life-shaping" and their manipulation of living organisms seemed pure science fiction. Now I teach in an architecture school at Newcastle University where it is not just colleagues in Experimental Architecture—Rachel Armstrong, Martyn Dade-Robertson—who work in the lab with techniques of synthetic biology and "ecological living technologies," but also PhD, BA, and MArch students who bring their petri dishes of protocells, slime molds, and bacteria into the studio and speculate on their potentials to co-design new architectures. At the MIT Media Lab, Neri Oxman's team co-designed with silkworms. While their CNC router-produced scaffold dome only mimicked the silk worm's capacity to extrude a silk thread structure, the team then let loose live 6,500 silkworms to make the translucent skin of *Silk Pavilion* (2013) in response to both steel web and light levels.—[24] Artist Špela Petrič's project, *Ectogenesis: Plant-human monsters*, explored

24 "Spinning up a Silk Pavilion," Wyss Institute, May 21, 2013, https://wyss.harvard.edu/spinning-up-a-silk-pavilion/ (accessed January 13, 2017).

Biofouling along a canal wall with oysters and green algae. Arsenale, Venice, 2016.

phylo-centered co-production, and recalls Sharer life-shaping. She extracted sex hormones from her own urine to help "mother" the embryo development of weedy thale cress, and in response, the plantlets altered their epigenetic patterns and constructed a specific human-plant body morphology (2016).—[25]

Moving to the scale and waters of the oceanscape, Armstrong's speculative project, "Vibrant Venice," works with the "unruly garden of Venice's marine biology which uses the technology of life to persist in the face of perpetually changing environments."—[26] Armstrong proposed the introduction of a new species of programmed droplets into the waterways to develop artificial limestone reefs that could shore up the sinking piles of the city (2009). SCAPE studio, the New York-based landscape and urban design practice headed by Kate Orff, who aim to incorporate

25 Ewen Chardonnet, "Špela Petrič and her plant-human embryos," October 31, 2016, http://www.makery.info/en/2016/10/31/spela-petric-et-ses-embryons-humains-plantes/ (accessed January 4, 2017).

26 Rachel Armstrong, *Vibrant Architecture*, 206.

natural cycles and systems into their projects, developed "Oyster-tecture" for New York's polluted harbor.—[27] A matrix of "fuzzy rope" (frayed polyethylene rope) supports a "living reef" of oysters, mussels, and eel grass whose biotic filtration processes clean the water (2010). A pilot project tested the scheme in a portion of the pier at SIMS municipal recycling center at the South Brooklyn Marine Terminal (2013),—[28] and following Hurricane Sandy, a larger version of this project is being realized at Tottenville, Staten Island as part of the New York State Storm Recovery Program (2014).—[29] As in Oxman's *Silk Pavilion*, "Oyster-tecture" builds an artificial matrix to (in Orff's words) "recruit" living organisms; but whereas Oxman's silkworms are redundant as soon as their silk has been harvested, each layer of oyster-growth provides the detritus for the next in an ongoing living process

With the exception of "Oyster-tecture," these experiments in co-designing with living systems remain innovative prototypes, which resonate with the inhabited/"built" environments imagined in *A Door into Ocean* and in Irigaray's work. In so far as they remain separate from the wider, social environment, they are, to use Carolina Ramirez Figureroa's term, "material probes" that both exemplify and test out material ideas in a gallery or lab condition, without needing to intersect with the world beyond.—[30] In contrast, the living systems in *A Door into Ocean* are integrated into an altered social, economic, ethical, and conceptual framework. "Dwelling" and "building" are inseparable from the conceptual frameworks—or "hydro-logics," to use Astrida Neimanis' term—[31]—and from the economic systems in which they emerge. *A Door into Ocean*'s holistic vision reminds us to ask what kinds of social and conceptual environments beyond the lab or studio are implied by these new living architectures? This essay attends to each of these issues, beginning with the material implications of ocean-living on Shora, then exploring its hydro-logics, and finally turning to its economies. The argument presented here is

27 "Oyster-tecture," http://www.scapestudio.com/projects/oyster-tecture/ (accessed January 4, 2017); also see: Kate Orff's TED talk at https://www.ted.com/talks/kate_orff_oysters_as_architecture (accessed 4 Jan 2017).

28 Michelle Cohen, "Living Breakwaters: An award-winning project brings oyster-tecture to the shores of Staten Island," January 28, 2015, https://www.6sqft.com/living-breakwaters-an-award-winning-project-brings-oyster-tecture-to-the-shores-of-staten-island/ (accessed January 13, 2017).

29 "Living Breakwaters, Tottenville," https://stormrecovery.ny.gov/living-breakwaters-tottenville (accessed January 13, 2017).

30 I am grateful to Carolina Ramirez Figureroa for her incisive and helpful comments on this piece and suggestions of experimental practices in this field. The term "material probe" is from her research work.

31 Astrida Neimanis, "Feminist subjectivity, watered," *Feminist Review* 103 (2013): 30.

that in a "sexuate environment"—one that incorporates sexed difference—conceptual, linguistic, and ethical frameworks; economies; and material, spatial arrangements are inextricably linked. If the ocean is to be a theory machine for feminist theory and practice—in philosophy, science, architecture, geography, landscape, art, and so on—each of these spheres and their interrelations should be taken into account.

Everything Flowing

> Once we have left the waters of the womb, we have to construct a space for ourselves in the air for the rest of our time on earth—air in which we can breathe and sing freely, in which we can perform and move at will. Once we were fishes.
> Luce Irigaray—[32]

32 Luce Irigaray, "Divine Women," in *Sexes and Genealogies*, trans. Gillian C. Gill (New York: Columbia University Press, 1993), 66.

When I asked Slonczewski directly whether she had come across Irigaray's philosophy while writing *A Door into Ocean* or indeed if she regarded it a feminist novel, she replied that sexual differences seemed to her "rather small" given the full range of beings—"from viruses on up"—that she deals with in her work.—[33] Instead, she had been influenced by "the hypothesis that humans evolved in water, with an emphasis on women" and by Sarah Blaffer Hrdy's alternative evolutionary account *The Woman Who Never Evolved*.—[34] Her comment recalls Irigaray's reminder (presented above) that our originary element—in both the extended temporality of our evolution from sea creatures and our more recent (though just as deeply unconscious) coming into life in the womb—is water. According to Irigaray: just as sexual difference is overlooked in patriarchal culture, so too is materiality, and with it then corporeality—the prerequisite for any possibility of sexed difference. She devoted a number of works to the four elements which, outside poetry, were "misunderstood in our culture, which has tended to refuse to think about the material conditions of existence."—[35] For Irigiray, water is one of these neglected elements.

33 Joan Slonczewski, in correspondence with author on January 7, 2016: "Given that I deal with the full range of creatures/beings, from viruses on up, sexual differences seem to me rather small."

34 See Sarah Blaffer Hrdy, *The Woman Who Never Evolved* (Cambridge Massachusetts: Harvard University Press, 1999).

35 Luce Irigaray, "Divine Women," 58.

Oyster biofouling produces rich niches for fish fry. Accademia, Venice, 2016.

In science, its behaviors and logics exceed the limits of rationality. Water is traditionally associated with the feminine: excessive, threatening, disruptive, as well as life-giving. Irigaray seeks to recuperate water's fluidity as a figuration for ways of being and thinking that provide an alternative to "the framework of the ruling symbolics" and "the solid walls of principle"—[36] built by a patriarchy that excludes the possibility of sexed difference. At the same time, Irigaray recognizes that our notion of the fluid is also already defined from within the same regime of solids we seek to displace.

36 Luce Irigaray, "Mechanics of Fluids," in *This Sex Which Is Not One*, trans. Catherine Porter and Carolyn Burke (Ithaca, NY: Cornell University Press, 1985), 106.

According to Irigaray, we learn to dwell in air, just as the Sharers are not fishes but humans who have developed ways to live on the ocean. They exhibit only minor evolutionary adaptations to water and have self-modified through their techniques of life-shaping—webbed hands and feet, lack of body hair, and a purplish sheen due to an all-over layer of oxygen-storing microbes enabling them to stay longer underwater. The microbes are temporary residents on their bodies. When Spinel, the male visitor from their neighboring stone-loving planet Valedon, decides finally to stay on Shora, he has to come to terms with the fact that he too has turned purple, and it has taken only a matter of weeks. The Sharers transform the ocean into a habitable environment by harnessing and manipulating existing plant and animal life forms, as well as their own bodies. As one of the Valan invaders, a leading geneticist, exclaims, "In a sense one might say … the whole planet is their laboratory."—[37]

37 Slonczewski, *A Door into Ocean*, 215.

The Sharers' ability to dwell in water is achieved then, through both their deep knowledge of the patterns of the ocean and their fellow life forms, and through their ongoing relational practices. Moreover, living within and as the "body of water" entails structures that are alive, porous, oozing, even abject. Spinel is repeatedly unsettled by the spaces he encounters. First there are the rafts themselves: thickets of living branches and tendrils, overgrown with a slimy green matting, permeated by networks of channels, stretching as wide as fifteen miles, and continuing to grow and extend at the feathery raft-edges:

> The soil became moist, and long weeds straggled across it. Then the soil gave out altogether where branches immense as fallen sequoias extended out to sea, covered with barnacles and other scaly things. At Merwen's footfall, half the scaly things slithered down the side. Spinel recoiled, but Merwen unconcernedly went out onto the branch, so he followed, more slowly.—[38]

38 Slonczewski, *A Door into Ocean*, 51. Her study guide to the book includes an inverted image of forest to show her inspiration for the raft constructions, and attributes her inspiration to mangroves. See http://biology.kenyon.edu/slonc/books/adoor_art/adoor_study.htm (accessed January 21, 2016).

The rafts and dwellings are tended in an ongoing process. Silkweed is an important crop for Sharers, but the raft undercroft also provides food for many other ocean creatures, and this habitat must also be maintained.—[39] Spinel spends his days collecting food, harvesting sea silk, and learning to weave it into panels.—[40] The walls and

39 Slonczewski, *A Door into Ocean*, 60.

40 Ibid., 92–93.

ceilings of the Sharer houses, with no clear demarcations between them, are also tangles of growing branches and vines, covered in slimy fungus for decoration:

> Spinel stepped through the door hole, feeling lost in the confusion. The air he breathed was thick with foreign odors; light-headed, he leaned against a wall. His arm sank into a furry paste that covered the dipping walls and ceilings, glowing in flares of green and amber that created a dizzying illusion of motion. The feel of the squished material added to his queasiness.—[41]

41 Ibid., 54.

Plants perform more functions than simply enclosure. In the house, Sharers feed the leaves of the "pudding plant" with anything they can find—Spinel's sandwich, squid entrails—and in a few days, it has been transformed into their food.—[42] In the life-shaping labs—which occupy a maze of spaces below the rafts—there are no benches, test tubes, phials, instruments, or tools. Instead, vines "form galls whose cavities can be inoculated with pure cultures of microorganisms, other vines are specialized secretors for enzymes, organic reagents, acids."—[43] Others still can wrap around a patient and deliver an injection.

42 Ibid., 55.

43 Ibid., 210.

Figures of the fluid—mucus, milk, the ocean, and so on—play an important, prolific role in Irigaray's work, permeating much of her writing and sometimes forming the central focus of essays such as "Volume-Fluidity,"—[44] "The Mechanics of Fluids," and the book *Marine Lover of Friedrich Nietzsche*. For her, their importance is their capacity to both connect and separate entities, thus preserving the difference between them while maintaining a (material) relation. She often associates them with the lips, with sex organs, and particularly with the womb where the intensely corporeal relation between infant and mother leaves them neither separate nor the same. As Irigaray explains in "Place, Interval":

44 Luce Irigaray, "Volume-Fluidity," in *Speculum of the Other Woman*, trans. Gillian C. Gill (Ithaca, NY: Cornell University Press, 1985, first published in French 1974).

> In gestation, there will always be a gap, an interval between the body that is in the envelope and the envelope itself which will more or less fit that body, and the amniotic fluid which separates the two.—[45]

45 Luce Irigaray, "Place, Interval," in *An Ethics of Sexual Difference*, trans. Catherine Porter and Carolyn Burke (Ithaca: Cornell University Press, 1985), 42.

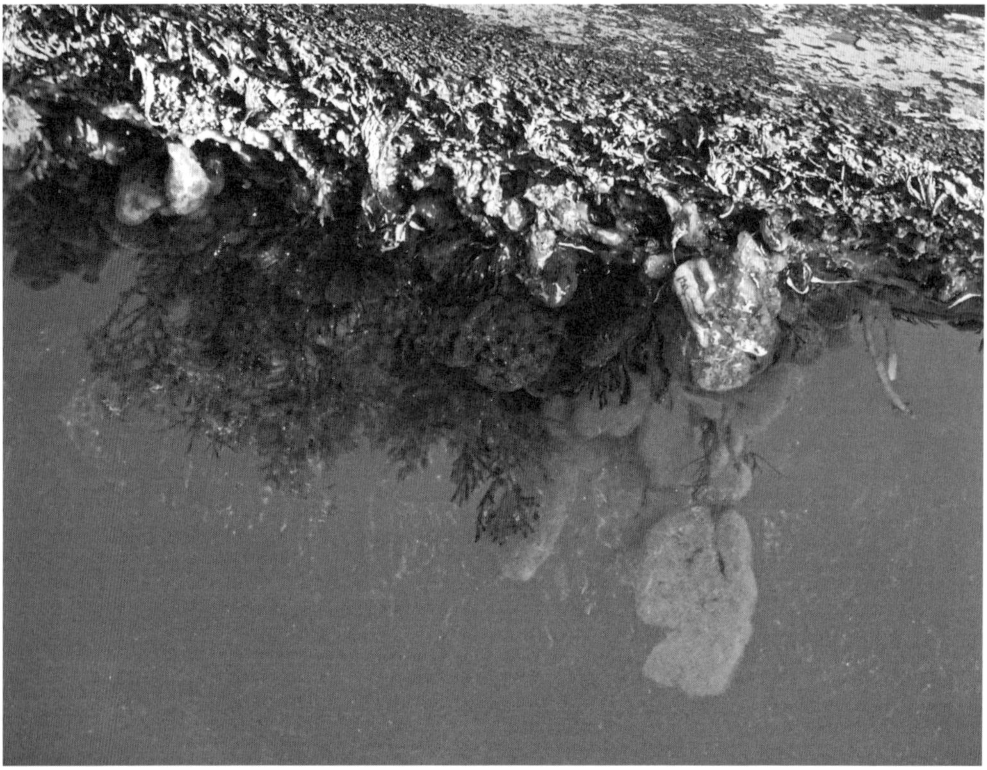

Thick biofilm mat on a canal wall. San Marco, Venice, 2016.

In a passage from *Speculum of the Other Woman* (published in English in 1985), such positive figurations are replaced by the abhorrence the male subject experiences at "everything flowing":

> And there almost nothing happens except the (re)production of the child. And the flow of some shameful liquid. Horrible to see: bloody. Fluid has to remain that secret remainder, of the one. Blood, but also milk, sperm, lymph, saliva, spit, tears, humors, gas, waves, airs, fire … light. All threaten to deform, propagate, evaporate, consume him, to flow out of him and into another who cannot be easily held on to. The "subject" identifies himself with/in an almost material consistency that finds everything flowing abhorrent. And even in the mother, it is the cohesion of a "body" (subject) that he seeks, solid ground, firm foundation. Not those things in the mother that recall the woman—the flowing things. He cathects these only in a desire to turn into the self (as the same). Every body of water becomes a mirror, every sea, ice.—[46]

46 Irigaray, "Volume-Fluidity," 237.

The "subject"—within a society that only has a logic "of the one" (male) sex—seeks the clear, distinct identities of solid things and the remainder or outside of that logic must be repressed. Here, that remainder is the fluid, the body of water, the sea (and "the flowing things" of the mother). When it appears and threatens his very sense of self—then it is repulsive, just as it was for Spinel when he recoils at the furry scum on dwelling walls or the slithery creatures at his feet on the Sharer raft. The Sharer dwellings do not concede to the same solid-seeking, outline-loving desires that he grew up with on Valedon. They do not attempt to cast out that which is fluid and indeterminate. For mucus and fluids are not remainders; they are part of a world in which there is no threat from difference and relation.

A Door into Ocean is an intensely architectural exploration into the possibilities of a world built on other principles than our own. Alongside the work of designers like Armstrong or Oxman, *A Door into Ocean* reminds us that we could inhabit other kinds of material environments, different from the pristine surfaces of most modern architecture. Indeed, Sarah Wigglesworth and Jeremy Till have argued in their essay, "The Future is Hairy," that the multiplication of "the hard surfaces and precision of most modern architecture … during the 20th century" should not be understood as a necessarily rational phenomenon, but rather as a repression or devaluing of the feminine in architecture, at least in so far as it is constructed along binary lines.—[47] Their design for the "straw-bale" house at Stock Orchard Street celebrated "hairy" materialities of imprecision, mess, and inconsistency.—[48] Reading the structures of *A Door into Ocean* with Irigaray suggests a yet richer range of images—or figurations—with which to imagine an alternative material world that acknowledges sexual difference and provides insights into the material ramifications of the logics with which we build our own environments.

47 Jeremy Till and Sarah Wigglesworth, "The Future is Hairy" in *Architecture: The Subject is Matter*, ed. Jonathan Hill (London: Routledge, 2001), 11–28.

48 See Sarah Wigglesworth, ed., *Around & About Stock Orchard Street* (London: Routledge, 2011) including my own essay "The Excessive Materiality of Stock Orchard Street: Towards a feminist material practice," 118–31.

> "Each force has an equal and opposite force," Merwen said. "So who rules without being ruled?"—49

49 Slonczewski, *A Door Into Ocean*, 36.

In her essay, "Feminist Subjectivity, Watered," Astrida Neimanis proposes the "body of water" as a feminist figuration that can provide a positive aspiration for the formation of subjectivities and, at the same time, reinforce the connectedness of humans to other nonhuman bodies whether aqueous (oceans, rivers) or living. While fluidity is an abstract concept, she argues, water has specific, material qualities that build up "ways of being" and also inform how we live together and relate to our world. She calls these "hydro-logics."—50

50 Neimanis, "Feminist subjectivity, watered," 29–30.

Neimanis lists six such hydro-logics: gestation, dissolution, communication, differentiation, archive, and unknowability. Her selection is contingent, but based in part on the hydro-logics she identifies in earlier feminist theory and scholarship. She mentions, for example, Irigaray's development of water's gestational qualities, both in her discussions of the watery environment of the womb and of the ocean in *Marine Lover of Friedrich Nietzsche* that gives Nietzsche life, enables his lofty thoughts, but is neglected by him. We might add the communicative and distancing qualities of the bodily fluids that Irigaray employs: saliva, mucus, blood, and the fluid differentials, which she notes in "The Mechanics of Fluids," tended to escape a science of solids, among many others.

The notion of a hydro-logic suggests that our understandings and uses of materials don't structure only our physical worlds. They also inform our social and conceptual worlds. In giving water such a central role in shaping Shora's alternative society and ways of living, *A Door into Ocean* can itself be considered a hydro-logical fiction.

We've seen some of the more material ramifications of following a watery logic in the Sharers' "built" environment, but, as many of the novel's commentators note, the principles of Sharer living also structure their language.—[51] In the following extract, Merwen, a Sharer, responds to Spinel when he is confounded by the Sharer word "wordsharing" that makes no distinction between listening and speaking:

51 For example, Robin Roberts, *A New Species: Gender and Science in Science Fiction* (Champaign: University of Illinois Press, 1993), 13.

> "What the devil is 'wordsharing'? Does the word for 'speak' mean 'listen' just as well? If I said, 'Listen to me!' you might talk instead."
> "What use is one without the other? It took me a long time to see this distinction in Valan speech."
> Spinel thought over the list of "share-forms": learnsharing, worksharing, lovesharing. "Do you say 'hitsharing too? If I hit a rock with a chisel, does the rock hit me?"
> "I would think so. Don't you feel it in your arm?"
> He frowned and sought a better example; it was so obvious, it was impossible to explain. "I've got it: if Beryl bears a child, does the child bear Beryl? That's ridiculous."
> "A mother is born when her child comes."—[52]

52 Slonczewski, *A Door into Ocean*, 36–37. This passage is also cited by Judith Still in support of her case for a feminine economy organized around abundance, rather than scarcity: Judith Still, *Feminine Economies: Thinking Against the Market in the Enlightenment and the Late Twentieth Century* (Manchester: Manchester University Press, 1997), 158, 186. Still's discussion is one of the few to see parallels between Irigaray's work and *A Door into Ocean*.

Here, the communicative hydro-logic of water informs language, and is expressed by it. If we are to take seriously the dissolution of the nature/culture boundary and resist abstractions in favor of material and embodied concepts, then we need to ask how our conceptualizations emerge in and of the material, and could be otherwise.

The dissolution of subject and object is reflected in Sharer verbs and also informs their ethics and the nonviolent strategies with which they counter the Valan invasion. When Spinel discusses the High Protector who rules Valedon, Merwen points out that if he rules everyone, "Then everyone rules him." In this view, "ruling over" is a response to power and thus it restores a notion of their own power to those who are ruled; or what Lucy Sargisson describes as "power-to" rather than "power-over" in her discussion of *A Door into Ocean*.—[53] Sharers debate key issues and seek consensus at large gatherings. Their strategies of resistance include "whitetrance," where they intentionally freeze into a kind of defiant catatonic state that unsettles any oppressors, as well as turning up in great numbers to protest the imprisonment of their fellow

53 Lucy Sargisson, *Contemporary Feminist Utopianism* (London: Routledge, 1996), 205–7.

Sharers. They resist occupation and invasion by the Valan troops by dwelling on rafts that are in constant motion and not fixed to any territory:

> What was there to invade? On the globe, red points of light marked the inhabited raft systems, two hundred and seven in all. Hardly a jungle for guerillas to hide.

Where or against what should they mount their campaign?

> Usually Headquarters lay well behind the front lines, but here there was no "front line." Or rather the front line was everywhere. Or had the real front line yet to appear?—[54]

54 Slonczewski, *A Door into Ocean*, 207.

As "smooth space par excellence," the ocean's ceaseless movement and lack of fixed points or boundaries offers no territory to breach and defies the Valans' usual military tactics. Hydro-logics permeate every sphere of Sharer living and defy "power-over": from the immaterial realms of language and philosophy, to the large-scale materiality of mobile ocean-based dwelling that make possible an ethics of nonviolence and fends off interplanetary invasion.

Economies

> You forgot, left out of your economy, whatever moves across boundaries from one to the other. —[55]

55 Luce Irigaray, *Elemental Passions*, trans. Joanne Collie and Judith Still (London: The Athlone Press, 1992), 16.

In 1993, Slonczewski published a sequel to *A Door into Ocean*, *The Daughter of Elysium* (the second of the four books of her "Elysium Cycle"—[56]), which fast-forwards at least 1,000 years into Shora's future. Sharers still inhabit their rafts, and the events in *A Door into Ocean* are remembered in "The Web," their book of spiritual wisdom, but twelve great cities now float in hermetic globes on the Ocean Moon, occupied by the immortal Elysians who import all their materials and food from other planets. Production has colonized and ravaged far-flung planets across the galaxy and Elysium is the banking center.

56 The other two novels are *The Children Star* (1998) and *Brain Plague* (2000). See: Bruce Clark, "Some Observations on Joan Slonczewski's Elysium Cycle" (unpublished paper introducing Joan Slonczewski roundtable at SLSA conference, Rice University, Houston, November 12–15, 2015), shared with author on January 12, 2016.

Light notation on the mooring steps of a canal. San Marco, Venice, 2016.

Their loans support vast projects to populate inhospitable planets with ever-increasing numbers of humans and other manufactured beings. Since the immortals are also infertile, Elysium conducts sophisticated scientific research into artificial reproduction in its vast lab complexes (developed from Sharer techniques) to produce children who are raised in nurseries or “shons,” each of which is an independent corporation in competition with the other. Everything comes at a price and is monetized in Elysium. Elysians are under constant surveillance and any breach of the barrage of rules and regulations is subject to a fine.

While Slonczewski is rather less explicit about Sharer economy in *A Door into Ocean*, it is brought into sharp relief in the contrast with Elysium in this second novel.

There is no property ownership or monetary exchange between Sharers, no consumption (although some occasionally barter sea silk with Valan trading posts for wires and fixings, a practice discouraged by many Sharers), and no paid labor. It appears Sharer hydro-logics do not include the concept of exchange value, and this too makes possible their material relations with the living and nonliving environment. Interestingly, for an architectural reader of *The Daughter of Elysium*, this entirely commoditized city society is both serviced by and built out of legions of robots or "servos" produced on neighboring Valedon. The servos operate at every scale from the molecular to the human, and cater to the Elysians' every need and desire. They carry out all the society's mundane tasks—from the cockroach-like servos that scuttle about clearing up every last spillage or trace of dirt,—[57] to the "trainsweeps" that follow behind the Elysians, holding up the long trains of their rich and highly decorated sea silk robes,—[58] and the "nanas" who are responsible for rearing children in the shons.—[59]

Food is micro-engineered and appears from openings in the wall when inhabitants request it. Even "nanoplast"—the material from which their dwellings and cities are built—is "a sort of modeling clay inhabited by billions of molecular servos."[60] Nanoplast constantly reshapes itself in response to the needs of inhabitants. From the seamless surface of the nanoplast walls, doors and windows open whenever needed, making an interplanetary visitor's toes curl just as Spinel recoiled at the Sharer dwellings. When a visitor sat down in a chair and it "oozed to fit his shape …" he asked, "Was there anything in Elysium not 'alive', responsive and motile?"—[61] The servos lend the environment an endlessly animate, responsive quality that, in contrast to the organic fluidity of the ocean world, is entirely engineered and technological (in fact, the plot of this novel centers on a servo uprising, demanding their right to be recognized as sentient beings).

57 Slonczewski, *A Door into Ocean*, 42.

58 Ibid., 15.

59 Ibid., 42–43.

60 Ibid., 20.

61 Ibid., 15.

While matter is rendered lively and endlessly metamorphic in *The Daughter of Elysium*—in a way that recalls current architectural enthusiasm for smart materials and responsive buildings—it has been entirely commandeered, programmed, and engineered to support the Elysians' luxurious lifestyles. The dry, capsular cities of Elysium described in *The Daughter of Elysium* merely instrumentalize and contain water, using Shora's ocean "ground" for their floating city spheres, piping it to power the fountains and water features of their interiorized public spaces, and installing it in "nanoplast" tunnels as propulsion fluid for their transportation network. Elysian attitudes to water recall the shift Ivan Illich identified in *H2O and the Waters of Forgetfulness*. When water is mobilized by cities to transport sewage and waste, water's traditional qualities as a life-giving element, its beauty, and its signification as a carrier of memory are erased. At the same time, a new regime of cleanliness and hygiene is produced whose value and necessity we rarely question.—62

62 Ivan Illich, *H_2O and the Waters of Forgetfulness* (London: Marion Boyars, 1986),

The image of a commoditized environment built by the plundering and exhaustion of other planetary resources brings to mind Irigaray's *Elemental Passions*. Irigaray reads earth as feminine, only to be forgotten when it is transformed into the building material of the patriarchal, commoditized world. The book is full of architectural images that render the earth as woman or mother, used up by man to construct his home, transforming her into property.—63 Again and again, the images emphasize man's need for solid, clearly defined structures and boundaries that exclude or repress fluidity, porosity, and excess. For example, man is described as, "Fencing in our natures, turning our bodies into private properties or readymade homes. With doors or windows open or closed."—64 Such images are in stark contrast to the relational placental economy of the first resting place—the womb—and to the ocean dwellings on Shora with their slippery, undefined boundaries and lack of solidity, hardness, and permanence.

63 Irigaray, *Elemental Passions*, 17.

64 Ibid., 16

Sea anenome and mussel biofouling on a canal wall. Accademia, Venice, 2016.

In words that could just as well be spoken by Sharers to the stone-loving Valan invaders, Irigaray asks, "How can we continue to live if we cling to that hardness … How can I abandon my love of the vegetal? … What does it signify, this attraction of yours for the mineral?"—65

65 Ibid., 33.

Elemental Passions is the most lyrical and enigmatic of Irigiray's elements quartet,—66 but it is peppered throughout with terms such as "value," "consumption," and "price." Linda Daley argues persuasively that the book is concerned with political economy, and is in "critically amorous dialogue" with Marx.—67 Irigaray has argued that the pursuit of univocal universal truth in Western philosophy and science masked the erasure of sexual difference, and she has sought to trace both where

66 Linda Daley, "Luce Irigaray's Sexuate Economy," *Feminist Theory* 13, no. 1 (2012): 59–79, 70.

67 Ibid., 72.

and how these eradications occurred in the philosophies of Plato, Aristotle, Freud, and Marx. By finding the moments where issues of sexed difference almost surfaced in their work, Irigiray proposes alternative sexuate modes of thought and ways of being beyond the univocal terms of masculinist patriarchal discourse. Interestingly, Michele Boulous Walker locates a specific passage in Marx that might have led Irigaray to her characterization of the earth as feminine.—[68] There he sets out the two components—matter and labor—that combine to make use values or "the bodies of commodities." At the same time, he ascribes gender to these two elements, writing that "labour is not the only source of material wealth," rather "labour is its father and the earth its mother."—[69] It is a moment when sexed difference (almost) enters Marx's account of the commodity.

68 Michele Boulous Walker, *Philosophy and the Maternal Body: Reading Silence* (London: Routledge, 2002).

69 Karl Marx, *Capital* Volume I, trans. Ben Fowkes (Harmondsworth: Penguin, 1990) p.134.

Irigiray's economic texts are concerned with the erasure of difference that occurs under capitalism when entities are abstracted or reduced to nothing more than their exchange value, just as in a masculine economy where there can be no acknowledgement of sexed difference. Under patriarchal capitalism then, the erasure of radical difference is doubled in terms of sex, and in terms of economy. So too, when "mother earth" is used up, it is a double transformation. She becomes a commodity and is ushered into a logic of solid and void that leaves no place for (sexed) difference. Boulous Walker's suggestion is persuasive; at the moment sexed difference almost enters Marx's discussion, it cannot be retained, because according to his own argument there can be no place for corporeality. If commodification entails abstraction in order that things can be rendered equivalent in exchange, it also involves the erasure of corporeality, which must also entail, for Irigaray, the erasure of sexual difference. A sexuate economy therefore would require an alternative form of exchange, in which difference (sexual and otherwise) is retained; one that Irigaray describes enigmatically in *Elemental Passions*, and that—like the mucus and fluid so common in Sharer hydro-logics—could move "across boundaries from one to the other."

Irigaray's work makes a sustained case against the abstractions that underlie political economy under capitalism, and also opposes the conceptual models in which form is in binary relation to matter, or ideal to sensible, and so on. It shows, too, that these logics leave no place for sexual difference. In Elysium—a grotesque (or "magnificent"!—[70]) vision of the beneficiaries of advanced financial capitalism—everything has a price and is subject to the logic of exchange. At the same time, the physical environment reflects Irigaray's rendering of a world of solid walls and separations. Elysian life-shaping—which enables the immortality and ontogenesis of this super-wealthy elite who live off the labor of the Fold's other planets—is simulated and carried out in the highly controlled, segregated, clinical environment of the lab. On Shora, where there is no money, commodification, or waged labor, Sharers have invented a way of living on and with the ocean. Sharer life-shaping—which enables adaption to the marine environment and reproduction without men for its self-sufficient society—happens in the oozing, organic, domestic spaces of their living rafts. Plants, marine creatures, humans, raft communities, the elements, and strong mother-daughter relations all retain their identities, and the fluid, connective substances between them both distinguish and "move across boundaries from one to the other."

70 Clark, "Some Observations on Joan Slonczewski's Elysium Cycle."

At the level of what is currently produced, contemporary design practices demonstrate similar sensibilities to the making of the environment on Shora. Oxman's silkworm-spun dome shares characteristics with the sea silk canopies of Sharer homes. Like the Sharers' living rafts, SCAPE Studio's "Oyster-tecture" seeds the growth of natural systems and puts them to work to support the shaping of their own environment. They pursue an altered physical and conceptual paradigm without challenging

Dustbin-lid jellyfish (*Rhizostoma Octupus*) bloom in a canal. Arsenale, Venice, 2016.

the social and economic status quo. In contrast, Shora provides an example of the material implications of a shift away from exchange value that (read alongside Irigaray) preserves potential for sexual difference. Although (or because) it is fictitious, it provides an impossible hydrological imaginary where the material, the conceptual, and the social are inextricably bound up with each other, and at the same time are tied to a specific historicity with its own economy.

Feminist Hydro-logics

A Door into Ocean offers numerous scenarios that resonate with pioneering design practices of living systems, with new materialism's principles of "vibrant matter" and human/nonhuman relations, and with feminist appropriations of the watery and the fluid. Its significance in relation to them, however, lies in the holistic scope of its account. *A Door into Ocean* provides an ocean-based vision in which ontology, ethics, language, physical environment, material practices, and economy are interrelated. In this sense, it allows us to see our own new material practices and modes of thought embedded in a socioeconomic context where fuller transformations in ways of living have already taken place. Through an imaginary vision like *A Door into Ocean*, we can extrapolate the possible wider implications of our experiments and test them against our broader social, political, and economic aspirations for them. We are reminded that these discrete, bounded propositions require wider change if they are to be meaningfully transformational, and that we need to consider how easily they are co-opted into existing logics of capital and accumulation. Reading *A Door into Ocean* alongside Irigiray's feminist philosophy highlights Slonczewski's choice to make her raft-based, wordsharing biologists female. It also makes a claim for Irigiray's foundational contribution to hydro-logics, which is at worst overlooked, and at best sidelined or discredited in recent scholarship on water. Nevertheless, the refusal to separate the material from the conceptual is at the heart of Irigiray's project, as is reinforced by the numerous similarities between her own propositional and lightly sketched material visions and Slonczewski's more fully detailed imaginaries.

Moreover, Irigiray resists abstraction because of its necessary role in exchange value and because it denies the corporeality grounding any possibility of sexed difference. Sexuate difference—the possibility of feminine logics, not just the logic of one—is at the center of Irigiray's imaginary of alternative ways of living, being, thinking, and making. Given their commonalities with Irigiray's figurations, Sharers' ocean-based ways of living might also be understood in terms of the flourishing of sexed difference. Keeping in mind Sharers' techniques for shaping their environment and working with living systems, to what extent might we also examine the practices of designers such as Orff, Oxman, or Armstrong in terms of their latent feminist hydro-logics? To propose that we consider their work in terms of feminism is not to essentialize the practices of women designers, artists, scientists, or writers, but to recover the feminist legacy in ecological and hydrological approaches and to remember that issues of subjectivity, politics, and economics are always implicated in our material practices. Now that we are becoming able to realize some of *A Door into Ocean*'s figurations—to engineer living systems to stabilize structures and harness their capacity to filter our polluted seas—reading the novel today reveals even more clearly that it is not enough for material innovations to take place in isolation. Meaningful material innovation must take place alongside other social, economic, and conceptual transformations.

Merapi seen from the air, circa 1945.

We All Live in the Wrong Place: Thinking Beyond Resilience in Volatile Environments

Adam Bobbette

Elisabeth told me about the dinner in 2010 when her friend, a French volcano scientist, excused himself from the table at the Indian restaurant to take a call. When he returned, he didn't sit down, but put his hands on the table and gently said he had to leave immediately for the observatory. The seismograph machines had broken, and the scientists working in the observatory felt that the volcano was about to explode. They didn't know when, but they suspected it would be massive. Later, when Elisabeth was driving home after dinner, the shoulders of the streets were lined with people milling around, holding sleeping babies, or crouching in the grass, texting. It was dark out and as usual, poorly lit. They'd run from their houses because of the earthquakes caused by the volcano. It was safer outdoors. When magma moves through the network of subterranean fissures, it liquefies rock, shifting and jolting the mass around it. That's what triggered the earthquakes that had traveled up to fifty kilometers away. Because it was night, no one could see the volcano. During the day, it was normally like the backdrop of a theater set—its perfect, pointed cone always smoking just a little as the action of daily life went on in front of it. However, that night it could only be felt; people said the ground "buzzed." The explosions that followed later started inside the mouth, then echoed like the crack of a whip through the valley below.

The volcano continued to explode for a little over two months. A hundred thousand people were evacuated into emergency camps thrown together in haste. The people forced to flee into the camps changed identities—they became refugees. A day or week before, they had been farmers, schoolteachers, moms, or dads. The newspapers and television channels reported on them and aired pleas for help. People from across the country sent in food and clothes, or got on their motorbikes and descended into to the valley to help. Elisabeth's large house, about twenty-five kilometers away from the volcano, was opened to refugees, as were schools, hospitals, and sports grounds. The evacuation was so vast and the eruption so intense that the hospitals were at capacity; the airport shut down, schools closed, neighborhoods were quarantined by the police. Entire towns evacuated, bridges were broken by rolling boulders, roads split down the centre. Fourteen square kilometers of forest were in cinders. Everything else paused and was covered in gray ash.

But this was six years ago. Elisabeth was telling me her version of the story in a grungy café a few kilometers from the caldera. We were in a small town that had been badly burned and parts of it turned to rubble after weeks of being beaten by what scientists call "pyroclastic density currents" (PDC): massive, dusty clouds of super-hot gasses that, during the eruption, rolled down the flanks of the volcano almost daily, reaching as far as sixteen kilometers away.

Over a dozen people refused the government's evacuation orders and died. Their resistance had become famous in Indonesian popular media. The house in which they had assembled before they died had been rebuilt as a memorial. There were other signs of the eruption, too; overgrown foundations and empty lots with young banana trees. In a few fields, gray deposits from the PDC could still be seen, but much of it had disappeared behind thick green brush and young trees. Otherwise, the small town had transformed into a thriving disaster tourism site. Families had bought jeeps with their government reconstruction funds and began carting tourists around the ruins, reminiscent of European aristocrats visiting the ruins of Vesuvius. The final stop on the tour was a vista of the perfectly shaped, gently smoking caldera to see where it had all started and take a few rounds of selfies. The lookout point was situated in a vast, gray and black, dust-filled river valley with a buried observation bunker. A guard working during the eruption had been unable to close the door before a mudslide drowned him inside. They carved him out but left a narrow column of hardened mud from floor to ceiling. Stepping inside and touching the cold, damp column was the tour's finale.

In the small town, shops were rebuilt and new restaurants sprung up to feed the tourist market. Kitsch was abundant: volcano T-shirts and mugs, calendars with photos of the disaster, teas with special powers from the ash mixed-in. From Elisabeth's point of view, these were all signs of resilience: turning tragedy into opportunity, moving on, starting fresh. After all, the volcano tended to erupt every five or six years. Sometimes massively, sometimes it was just a little wheeze, pop, and landslide. Yet people always came back, rebuilt, shifted from being refugees back to being farmers, mothers, fathers, school-teachers, and disaster tour guides.

People have many different ideas about why anyone would live in a dangerous place like this, including the people who actually live there. Some say it is because the tropical soils are productive—even though farming has become less profitable than disaster tourism, or mining the sand and rocks after eruptions. Others say it is tradition, this is just the way things are. Others say that the volcano is god, the source of all existence, so when it erupts it is not dangerous but simply doing what it does, and it's up to us to get out of the way. As a friend who lives there told me, when the volcano erupts it is "going to work," just like you or I "go to work" in the morning.

Geophysical expidition on Merapi recording subsurface geothermal movement.

This is confusing: why people seem to *choose* to live in dangerous places. It is a question that applies not only to the volcano but also Tornado Alley, New Orleans, Chernobyl, but also Los Angeles, San Francisco, Lisbon, Naples, Tokyo, Santiago, or Christchurch. Or, as climate change begins to bring about planetary-scaled effects, why do people seem to *choose* to live in any delta, coastline, or low-lying island?

It's an absurd question, of course, one usually asked by people who assume they live in a place perfectly well suited to them. There is another common answer: people *don't* choose it; the decision is made for them by their socioeconomic position. This seems especially self-evident for poor people, who we (usually not poor) sometimes like to think don't make decisions for themselves, but are subjected to big forces beyond their control. Impoverished Americans in the environmentally volatile American South, and peasants living on the slopes of Indonesian volcanoes—all are subjected to the volatility of their environments because they have been put there by forces outside themselves; they didn't choose it. However, this minimizes the more daunting and complex ways that people make decisions and how big and small forces intersect. It is also difficult to quantify the web of personal commitments, dues, debts, loves, and the many kinds of relations that give value to a certain environment and encourage people to stay in the "wrong place." What if instead we thought that choosing to be in the wrong place was the norm of the human condition?

Some of us maintain the illusion that we live in the right place. Like people who live in places that get so cold during the winter that they can die outdoors without adequate protection. Or, if they tried to survive without the vast heating infrastructures, energy sources, and buildings that keep them warm. The work of infrastructure makes it appear as if people live in the right place.

If living in the wrong place is more common than we assume, then sharing stories of people's cohabitation strategies with vulnerable and volatile natures can help us rethink our condition. Architects—including you, dear reader—have much to contribute to this, particularly because making buildings and landscapes has always been about grappling with how to stay put, settle in, and make relationships with what is around us. The point is not to achieve some moment in the future when we would be free of the encumbrances of volatile nature. This is where we are often mistaken in how we think, for instance, about climate change: it is not about the future; it is about the way we live today. It is about how we build, arrange, and conceptualize our relationships to nature; how and where we draw and redraw the line that separates the human from the natural. This is why climate change is contentious; its battle front is the distinction between nature and culture, a line that is inherently controversial because it runs so deep and has been drawn so differently by different traditions and histories. Architecture matters because it works on this line, crafting spaces that reinforce traditions and histories or that cut holes in it, building new kinds of arrangements between us and nature.

When Elisabeth invoked the idea of "resilience" in the village, she was using a key word that has by now been exhausted in academic circles. It suggests ideas of technological flexibility, and a kind of permanent innovation. It also suggests a neoliberal, chin-up, dust off your jacket, gung-ho optimism. It is no accident that the term finds its way into the vocabulary of contemporary economists just as often as it features in those of architects, planners, development NGOs, and heads of state, for whom the world is a risky place full of surprises. Sometimes they can be calculated, we can try our best to predict them, but the concept of resilience suggests that culture negotiates an uncertain nature best by surfing the uncertainty. Not being an academic, but rather a seasoned journalist and novelist, I suspected that Elisabeth's invocation of resilience had come from its diffusion through other channels. But in the past few years, like many keywords that gain circulation, resilience has lost its potency in allowing us to see things in fresh ways. Hence, I want to put forward a few other terms that have helped me to think through what it means to live in the wrong place. I want to do this while getting a little closer to this volcano.

Mount Merapi is in central Java, Indonesia. It is one of the most active volcanoes in the world and its surrounding areas have roughly one million inhabitants. The population density is about the same as New York City. Two urban centers, which are nineteenth-century sultanates formed in the Dutch colonial period, Yogyakarta and Surakarta, are in the plains at the foot of the volcano. The flanks are filled with a kind of rural-urban hybrid of high-density agriculture and small towns and has been continuously inhabited for over a thousand years.

Mount Merapi has a dedicated *juru kunci* appointed by the Sultan in Yogyakarta, which is often translated as "gatekeeper." The term "juru" carries the sense of "laborer" and "craftsperson," while "kunci" is simply "key." Thus, juru kunci is a kind of "key worker" or "key expert." The English "gatekeeper" suggests "warden," "police," even Kafka's gatekeeper in "Before the Law," with his "… long, thin, black Tartar's beard," who never lets you through the gate and even causes you to doubt that anything exists on the other side. The role of the juru kunci is to negotiate the inheritance of the nature-culture divide. Like all monarchies, Sultanates have a cosmological dimension. His power is founded in both the earthly, corporeal realm and the transcendent domain, and he is tasked with maintaining their order. A volcanic eruption, or any

Scientific observatory outpost on Merapi, circa 1980s.

kind of natural disaster, can indicate a disorderly cosmos. Because the Sultan is unable to continuously keep watch over the volcano, he outsources this responsibility to the juru kunci. When something goes amiss in the volcano, the gatekeeper translates the meaning of the material event in relation to the social and political spheres and is then responsible for communicating between the spirit world inside the volcano (which governs its action) and the socio-political realm. As such, he draws society into the depths of nature by suturing human and natural agency. This is not so dissimilar from climate scientists arguing that the transformation of the Earth's climate is a result of the history of human made industrialization. In other words, in nature, we see society. For the juru kunci and the Sultan, this argument has long been made: the volcano responds to the arrangements of the social order. The gatekeeper has to successfully translate between dissimilar events (eruptions, earthquakes, PDCs, rainstorms) and human, social forms. The line that distinguishes humans from nature is plastic enough that it can be reshaped to speak to current controversies, to make sense of the present. Natural law is therefore not nature's puppetmaster, operating it from the shadows. Instead, it is a fundamental, ontological plasticity. The gatekeeper doesn't so much guard gates, but opens them to allow the disparate realms of society and nature to make hybrids and mixtures between the things we so often separate.

We have Western Enlightenment to thank for amplifying the idea that humans are exceptional. Matter has been placed into hierarchies that range from the lowest (the inorganic, non-life) to the highest (the organism, consciousness, reflection). Humans think and act in the world but the inorganic is subject to it. Life animates matter. In this mortal coil coursing through dead matter version of things, humans have an exceptional form of agency and intention. Both climate scientists and the juru kunci have a common ground in jettisoning this story of the nature-culture distinction. Instead, agents like carbon and volcanoes are lively animated beings making decisions, having responsibility, causing political controversies and conflicts. Nature is not projected upon or exposed by knowledge, but participates in its production by prefiguring us to know it. This means that the conventional distinction between the animate and inanimate begins to break down. Rocks, wood, tephra, gneiss, minerals—all the *stuff* we once separated from the "organic," the living—are no longer passive (without agency) in the production of ourselves and what we know about the world.

Scientists created conditions for the volcano to speak in new ways. When they first used seismographs to monitor it in the early twentieth century, their instruments transformed the volcano into a drawing machine. The seismographs were set in motion when a tremor was emitted and the stylus hovering above a roll of paper would inscribe the shaking of the machine onto the paper. They would then be read as pictures of the movement of seismic waves in time. Scientists compared drawings made at different locations to create a three-dimensional image of how waves propagated through the interior. Mount Merapi was coaxed into representing itself in a completely new way through networks of machines and representations. Accessing its distant, hidden interior took the accumulation of action at a distance; these two movements in opposite directions—surrounding the exterior with machines to get closer to the inside—coproduced each other. They added layers of mediation and representation on top of each other in order to get closer to the source. Each layer increased the dimensions in which the volcano was animated, its capacities to act spread through the machines onto paper and into the decisions of scientists. This was not the discovery of truth hidden behind the veil of nature, so much as the redistribution of animation. If nature is full of animate beings, our social and technical systems bring these them to life in new ways. We find ourselves back at the idea of nature according to the juru kunci: it is because it is mediated.

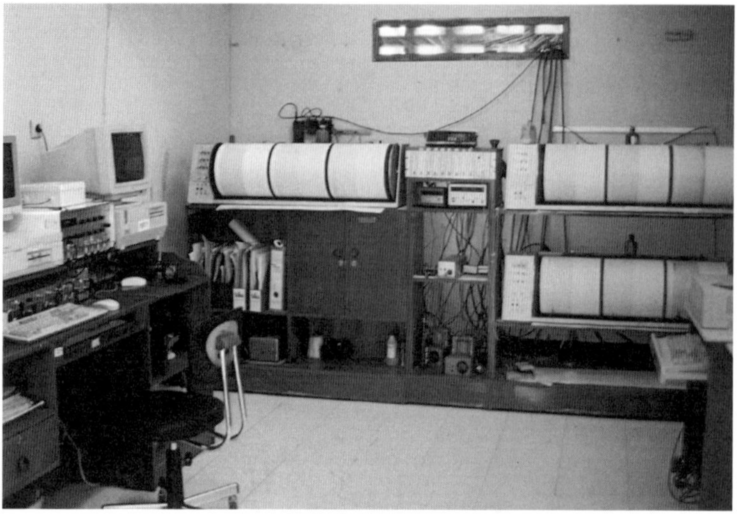

Seismographs in the Merapi observatory Yogyakarta, circa 1980.

Secular modernists often dismiss as charlatans people who call themselves mediums. Gone is the world where the dead speak through mediums, photographs take pictures of spirits, and telephones connect with ancestors. John Durham Peters has asked that we reconsider our attitudes to mediums because they help us deal with the basic human problem of communication: how to connect.—[1] There is, for him, a subterranean line that links spirit mediums to cell phones; they are both technologies of connecting with the distant, whether spatial or temporal. Communication is making contact, touching, and getting access to something. Juru kunci, volcano scientists, even architects, are all in this sense, also mediums. They translate and connect between human communities and nonhumans. Even the earth itself is a medium. It emits broadcasts that we receive and try to decode. Seismologists think this way when they describe the crust as a medium for seismic waves and volcanoes as mediums of distant tectonic action. Mediums are everywhere.

1 John Durham Peters, *Speaking into the Air: A History of the Idea of Communication* (Chicago: University of Chicago Press, 1999), 304.

At the heart of the Western idea of mediation is an anxiety about the medium distorting the message. We have long since tried to build machines that transmit without noise or interference and find methods of understanding nature without obstructed messages. We want communion through a medium that brings us into direct contact with each other and nature. This is why it is important to consider spirit mediums and shamans, because they are struggling with the same problem. The question then is what do different forms of mediation do? What do they allow us to touch, how do they make contact?

In a small town on the west side of Mount Merapi, Elizabeth and I met a mayor and his wife in an unadorned room with a concrete floor. There was an old bookcase in the corner with shelves bowing under the weight of books. He called it the town's public library. His wife sat on the floor, he across from us in a wicker chair. As is customary, they offered coffee and cakes. We started talking about eruptions and dreams. They explained that in addition to the usual communication systems—cell phones, televisions, and radios—that were used to alert people about on-coming eruptions, there were also dreams. They came to anyone in the village, cutting through the conventional gender and age hierarchies that usually give older men authority. The figure in the dream was always the same: a woman, in

A Shaman's laboratory, Merapi, January 2016.

green clothes and beautiful. She was perhaps originally from the sea but now lives in the volcano and tends to her ghost animals along its slopes. Like the people in the village, she too is a farmer. They are like each other except that she can circulate from one body's interior to another and remain herself; unlike us, who only circulate between each other via words and pictures. One of the requirements for her to enter someone's dream in the town was that the sleeper can not be in distress about everyday life, because their dreams will be too self-referential—about work, love, fights in the family. The dreamer needs to be clearheaded for their dreams to come from outside and overtake them. In a way this isn't so hard to understand, we already think that our dreams are alien to ourselves, a kind of internal otherness that we give ourselves over to at night. The people in this town think this too, but argue that this otherness is the farmer in green, telling them what the volcano is going to do. According to the mayor and his wife, our internal otherness is her, and she is the volcano.

What does all of this tell us about living in the wrong place? So much hangs on how we draw the line that separates nature from society. One way that I like to think of the act of drawing that line is in terms of intimacy. Our concepts of what separates "us" from "nature," where those separations are, and how we make them, is in part about establishing proximity and distance. The act of being possessed by a dream establishes an intimacy with something as formidable as a volcano—it enters us. In doing so, it also changes the kinds of gratitude and obligations we have to the things that enter us, the things we become intimate with. Our most private sense of self is inhabited and woven through the other. This is an idea about surrender, intimacy as surrender, to be overtaken. We can begin to see vulnerable nature as an opening for us to rethink not only ourselves, but also how we are intimate with each other and the world. The way in which we draw lines of connection, continuity, and distinction is a way of creating forms of togetherness.

Offerings to Merapi.

EDITOR

JANE HUTTON is a landscape architect and Assistant Professor at the University of Waterloo. Her research focuses on the expanded consequences of material practice in design and examines links between the landscapes of production and consumption of common construction materials. She is currently completing a book manuscript that traces five seminal landscape materials that have ended up in New York City over the past century. Hutton is a co-founding editor of the journal *Scapegoat: Architecture, Landscape, Political Economy* and is co-editor of issues 01 *Service*, 02 *Materialism*, and 06 *Mexico D.F./NAFTA*, all of which look at the political dimensions of material practice in design.

AUTHORS

GARTH ANDERSON is the University of Virginia's Facility Historian in the Office of Facilities Management. His office sits on the site of the original stone quarry on the east slope of Observatory Mountain. His interests span the architecture, history, archaeology, and landscape of the university, covering its 200-year history.

ADAM BOBBETTE is a PhD candidate in the Department of Geography, Cambridge.

JANA CEPHAS is a designer and historian who studies the interactions between people, places, and technologies. She is the founding director of Studio Plat, a research and development lab that collects, interprets, and visualizes spatial information to help solve urban problems. She is especially interested in how spatial history can contribute to contemporary urban research, community engagement processes, and the management of cultural and physical landscapes. She holds a PhD in the History of Architecture and Urban Planning from Harvard University and an MArch from University of Detroit Mercy.

SONJA DÜMPELMANN is a landscape historian and Associate Professor of Landscape Architecture at the Harvard Graduate School of Design. Her publications include *Flights of Imagination: Aviation, Landscape, Design* (University of Virginia Press, 2014), *A Cultural History of Gardens in the Age of Empire* (Bloomsbury Publishers, 2013), *Women, Modernity, and Landscape Architecture* (with John Beardsley; Routledge, 2015), and a book on the pioneering Italian landscape architect Maria Teresa Parpagliolo Shephard and landscape architecture in twentieth-century Italy (VDG Weimar, 2004). She is currently writing a book on the history of street tree planting and urban forestry.

CORNELIA ESCHER is an architectural historian and a junior professor at Kunstakademie Düsseldorf. Her research and publications focus on the architectural theory of the twentieth century with a special interest in transnational networks of knowledge transfer and the history of architecture's exchanges with the neighboring disciplines. From 2011 to 2013, she was a researcher at the Institute for the History and Theory of Architecture, ETH Zurich; from 2009 to 2011 a member of the editorial team of *ARCH+*. She was part of the curatorial teams of exhibitions such as *Atelier Bow-Wow* (ETH Zurich, 2013) and *Megastructure Reloaded* (Former State Mint, Berlin, 2008). Her most recent book, *Zukunft entwerfen. Architektonische Konzepte des GEAM 1958–1963*, was published in 2017.

KIM FÖRSTER is an architectural historian and works as Associate Director for Research at the Canadian Centre for Architecture, Montréal. Having studied English and American Studies, Geography, and Pedagogy, he holds a PhD in Architecture from ETH Zurich, where from 2013 to 2015 he taught in the doctoral program at the Institute for History and Theory of Architecture. He has published in architectural magazines and journals such as *Arch+*, *Architectural Histories*, *Archithese*, *Bauwelt*, *Clog*, *Places*, *Project*, *werk, bauen + wohnen*, and was co-editor of *An Architektur*. He has collaborated on several publications with common room and is currently guest editor of *Candide*. His monograph on the Institute for Architecture and Urban Studies (New York, 1967–1985) is forthcoming.

JENNIFER FOSTER is an Associate Professor in the Faculty of Environmental Studies at York University. Her research focuses on postindustrial urban green spaces, environmental justice, ecological aesthetics, and habitat creation in sites in Toronto, Paris, Milwaukee, and New York City, where she examines the socioecological evolution of former industrial spaces. She is the Coordinator of the York University graduate Planning Program, as well as the undergraduate Urban Ecologies Certificate. Dr. Foster is a Registered Professional Planner and an active member of the Toronto organization Promoting Education and Community Health.

MARTIN HOGUE teaches landscape architecture in the College of Environmental Science and Forestry at the State University of New York in Syracuse. Trained as an architect and landscape architect, and working primarily with analytical drawings as a mode of inquiry, his research explores the notion of *site* as a cultural construction—specifically, the mechanisms by which locations become invested with the unique potential to acquire the designation of "site." His work has been displayed in solo exhibits at over twenty-five venues across the United States, and his book *Thirtyfour Campgrounds* was published by The MIT Press in November 2016.

After completing a Master of Architecture at the Southern California Institute of Architecture in Los Angeles and practicing architecture in California, STEPHAN KOWAL has been teaching courses on architectural representation and design at the École d'architecture, Université de Montréal since 2003. Recipient of the J. Armand Bombardier Scholarship Award (SSHRC) for his PhD, Kowal has recently completed a doctoral dissertation titled "Architecture and Cartography in the Age of the Digital: The Birth of the Canada Geographic Information System."

KATIE LLOYD THOMAS is Professor of Theory and History of Architecture and Co-director of the Architectural Research Collaborative at Newcastle University. With Tilo Amhoff and Nick Beech, she recently edited *Industries of Architecture* (Routledge *Critiques*, 2015) and her monograph *Preliminary Operations: Material Theory and the Architectural Specification* is in preparation. A founder member of the feminist collective taking place, www.takingplace.org.uk, Katie's research often explores the intersections between gender and technology. She recently contributed to Dr. Nathalie Bredella's "Fluid Geometries" seminar at Univeristät der Kunst, Berlin and was visiting scholar at the CCA, Montreal for her project "The Architect as Shopper" (2017).

ALESSANDRA PONTE is Full Professor at the École d'architecture, Université de Montréal. She has also taught at Princeton University, Cornell University, Pratt Institute New York, the ETH Zurich, and at the Università Iuav di Venezia. She curated the exhibition *Total Environment: Montreal 1965–1975* (Canadian Center for Architecture, Montreal, 2009) and collaborated on the exhibition and catalogue *God & Co: François Dallegret Beyond the Bubble* (with L. Stalder and T. Weaver, London: A. A. Publications, 2011). She has published extensively including the collection of essays *The House of Light and Entropy* (London: AA Publications, 2014).

HEIDY SCHOPF, who holds a Master of Environmental Studies, is a Cultural Heritage Specialist at Stantec Consulting Ltd. She has six years of experience in the field of cultural heritage resource management, has worked as both a research archaeologist and a heritage specialist, and is a professional member of the Canadian Association of Heritage Professionals. Heidy has worked on a wide variety of projects throughout Ontario, including: archaeological assessments; cultural heritage resource assessments; heritage impact assessments and documentation reports; cultural heritage evaluations; and heritage conservation district studies and plans.

NANCY TAKAHASHI's interest in Observatory Mountain at the University of Virginia (UVA) developed after many hikes on the hill with her dog, during her term as the Principal of Hereford Residential College, which sits on the hill purchased by Thomas Jefferson. She is a Distinguished Lecturer and former Chair of the Department of Landscape Architecture at UVA. Takahashi's interest in cultural landscapes extends to the city of Winneba (Ghana), where she is working with the community and students to envision a new economic and environmental future for this coastal community in the face of rising sea levels.

JANE WOLFF is an Associate Professor at the University of Toronto's Daniels Faculty of Architecture, Landscape, and Design. Her design research investigates the complicated landscapes that emerge from interactions between natural processes and cultural interventions; her goal is to articulate terms that make these difficult (and often contested) places legible to the wide range of audiences with a stake in the future. She grew up in Saint Louis.

SARA ZEWDE is a landscape designer, urbanist, and public artist. Concurrent to independent creative work and research, Sara is a designer at Gustafson Guthrie Nichol, where she contributes to the development of large-scale and civic landscapes around the world. Sara holds a Master of Landscape Architecture from the Harvard Graduate School of Design, a Master of City Planning from MIT, and a BA in Sociology and Statistics from Boston University. Sara was named the 2014 National Olmsted Scholar by the Landscape Architecture Foundation and a 2016 Artist-in-Residence at the Robert Rauschenberg Foundation. Her design work in Rio de Janeiro, Brazil was featured at the 2016 Venice Architecture Biennale.

PICTURE CREDITS

pages 22, 24, 28: Albert and Shirley Small Special Collections Library, University of Virginia
page 29: Betts Collection #38, Albert and Shirley Small Special Collections Library, University of Virginia
pages 31: Albert and Shirley Small Special Collections Library, University of Virginia
page 34/35: Illustration by Peter Russell
pages 36, 40: Photographs by Nancy Takahashi
page 38: Paul Benneche, School of Engineering and Applied Science collection
page 46: Former City of Toronto Fonds, 1980–1998, *Leslie Street Spit under construction*, Fonds 200, Series 1465, File 148. Item 2
page 49: Former City of Toronto Fonds, 1980–1998, *Leslie Street Spit looking north-west*, Fonds 200, Series 1465, File 148. Item 4
page 55: James Salmon Collection, 1917, *Logan's Brick Yards looking north, Greenwood Avenue widening*, Fonds 1231, Item 786
page 56: James Salmon Collection, 1928, *Toronto Brickyards Quarry below Felstead Avenue*, City of Toronto Archives, Fonds 1231, Item 728
page 58: Former City of Toronto Fonds, 1922, *Concrete Mixing Plant*. City of Toronto Archives, Fonds 200, Series 372, Subseries 27, Item 68
page 66/67: Photograph by Kassandra Bonneville
pages 72, 76: Drawing and photograph by Stephan Kowal
page 78: Drawing by Kassandra Bonneville, David Gilbert, and Emmanuelle Lauzier
page 79: John Bland Canadian Architecture Collection, Rare Books and Special Collections, McGill University Library
page 80: Photograph by Sebastien Carzunel
page 82: *Cahiers de géographie du Québec*, vol. 14, no. 33, 1970, p. 310
page 82: *Cahiers de géographie du Québec*, vol. 14, no. 33, 1970, p. 320
page 88: Photograph by Stephan Kowal
page 90: Chicago History Museum, DN-0054469; *Chicago Daily News*
page 92: From J. H. Prost, *Trees and Lawns for the Streets* (City of Chicago, Special Park Commission: Chicago, 1914)
page 94: From A. Des Cars, *A Treatise on Pruning Forest and Ornamental Trees*, translated from the seventh French edition. 3rd ed. (Boston: Massachusetts Society for the Promotion of Agriculture, 1894)
page 96: From William Solotaroff, *Shade-Trees in Towns and Cities* (New York: John Wiley and Sons, 1911), plate 43
page 97: From J. H. Prost, *Trees and Lawns for the Streets* (City of Chicago, Special Park Commission: Chicago, 1914)
page 100: Chicago History Museum. i74134.
page 108: From Charles A. Stewart, "Forestry Considerations in Land Use Planning: The Role of the Urban Forester," (1972)
page 110: From Karl Kasthofer, *Der Lehrer im Walde* (Chr. Alb. Jenni: Bern, 1828)
pages 115, 116, 117, 118, 119, 120, 121, 122: Illustrations by Jane Wolff
page 124: Joseph John Kirkbride, " The chain gang, Thomasville, Georgia," Photographic print. circa 1884–1891 Library of Congress Prints and Photographs Division Washington, D.C. 20540 USA. LC-USZ62-127557
page 142, 144, 147, 149, 150, 151, 152, 153: Images by Sara Zewde
page 154: Hermann Matthes / Herbert Sukopp: "Anmerkungen zur ökologischen Bedeutung des Geländes am Görlitzer Bahnhof in Berlin," Stadtbauwelt (1979), 33, 1363
page 164: Papiertieger. Archiv und Bibliothek der sozialen Bewegungen. Photograph by Cornelia Escher
page 168: Wikipedia. Photograph by Roehrensee
page 169: Wikipedia. Photograph by Burkhard Kehl
page 173: Photograph by Cornelia Escher
page 174: Collection Museum of Contemporary Art San Diego. Museum purchase, 1981.10.1-2. Photograph: Philipp Scholz Ritterman. © Estate of Robert Smithson / Licensed by VAGA, New York NY
page 179: Milwaukee Art Museum, Purchase, National Endowment for the Arts Matching Funds, M1969.65. Photograph: Efraim Lev-er. © Estate of Robert Smithson / Licensed by VAGA, New York NY
page 184: Whitney Museum of American Art, New York; purchase, with funds from the Drawing Committee and partial gift of The Philip Glass Family and the Greene Naftali Gallery 2015.57. © Estate of Candy Jernigan, New York. Courtesy of Greene Naftali, New York
page 185: Photograph © CCA, Montréal
page 186: Photograph © CCA, Montréal
page 187: Centre national des arts plastiques, FNAC 02-1494. © All rights reserved, CNAP. Photograph by Yves Chenot
page 188: Photograph by Cees de Boer
page 189: Photograph by Peter Foolen, 2012
page 190: Courtesy of the Estate of Stan Brakhage and Fred Camper (www.fredcamper.com)
page 191: Courtesy of Kathy Poole
page 194, 199, 202, 205, 208, 213, 216, 219: All photographs by Rachel Amstrong
page 222: *Visual Images of Merapi Volcano* (Bandung: Geological Agency of Indonesia, 2012), 195
page 226: Photograph by Adam Bobbette
page 229, 232: Balai Penyelidikan dan Pengembangan Teknologi Kebencanaan archives, Yogyakarta. Consulted in February, 2016
page 233, 235: Photographs by Adam Bobbette

IMPRINT

Editing: Jane Hutton
Proofreading: Inez Templeton
Graphic design: Willi Schmid & Radim Peško
Layout and setting: Eveline Lam
Lithography: Bild1Druck, Berlin
Typefaces: Landscript Condensed (radimpesko.com), DeVinne
Paper: Fedrigoni constellation snow, 350 g/m^2 (cover) and Amber Graphic, 115 g/m^2
Printed in the European Union

Bibliographic information published by the Deutsche Nationalbibliothek
The Deutsche Nationalbibliothek lists this publication in the Deutsche Nationalbibliografie; detailed bibliographic data are available on the Internet at http://dnb.d-nb.de

jovis Verlag GmbH
Kurfürstenstrasse 15/16
10785 Berlin

www.jovis.de

ISBN 978-3-86859-214-6